Threshing Floors in Ancient Israel

Threshing Floors in Ancient Israel

Their Ritual and Symbolic Significance

Jaime L. Waters

Fortress Press
Minneapolis

THRESHING FLOORS IN ANCIENT ISRAEL

Their Ritual and Symbolic Significance

Copyright © 2015 Fortress Press. All rights reserved. Except for brief quotations in critical articles or reviews, no part of this book may be reproduced in any manner without prior written permission from the publisher. Visit http://www.augsburgfortress.org/copyrights/ or write to Permissions, Augsburg Fortress, Box 1209, Minneapolis, MN 55440.

Cover design: Alisha Lofgren

Library of Congress Cataloging-in-Publication Data is available

Paperback ISBN: 978-1-4514-8523-3

Hardcover ISBN: 978-1-4514-9972-8

eBook ISBN: 978-1-4514-9660-4

The paper used in this publication meets the minimum requirements of American National Standard for Information Sciences — Permanence of Paper for Printed Library Materials, ANSI Z329.48-1984.

Manufactured in the U.S.A.

This book was produced using PressBooks.com, and PDF rendering was done by PrinceXML.

Contents

	Preface	vii
	Abbreviations	xi
1.	Introduction	*1*
2.	Divine Control and Use of Threshing Floors	*29*
3.	Threshing Floors in Legal Contexts	*59*
4.	Threshing Floors as Sacred Spaces	*77*
5.	Temple Construction upon a Threshing Floor	*125*
	Conclusion	*145*
	Addendum: Threshing Floors as Sacred Spaces in Ugarit	*151*
	Bibliography	*165*
	Index of Names	*199*
	Index of Bible and Ancient Literature	*201*

Preface

Threshing Floors in Ancient Israel: Their Ritual and Symbolic Significance explores the depiction of threshing floors in the Hebrew Bible. As locations used for threshing and winnowing crops, these areas were essential for food processing in ancient Israel, and yet the Hebrew Bible seldom highlights this fact. Instead, several significant cultic events are situated on threshing floors, a phenomenon that is intriguing and worthy of exploration. This book unpacks the multiple dimensions of threshing floors, with a particular interest in how they are viewed as both agricultural and sacred spaces.

This book is written as a revision of my dissertation, *Threshing Floors as Sacred Spaces in the Hebrew Bible*, completed at The Johns Hopkins University in 2013. Many people contributed to this work. In particular, my dissertation advisor Theodore J. Lewis provided immense guidance, thought-provoking questions, and heartfelt support, and my second reader P. Kyle McCarter Jr. provided invaluable conversations and ideas. Dissertation committee members—Sara Berry, Jane Guyer, and Michael Harrower—offered stimulating questions and suggestions. Each of these professors has shaped this revised work. My writing group members, Drs. Erin Fleming and Heather Dana Davis Parker, have read many drafts of this work through the dissertation and book phases. To say that their feedback and support are appreciated is an understatement. Our group has sustained me throughout the years. In various ways, my teachers, colleagues, and friends at Johns Hopkins, Yale Divinity School, and Boston College have encouraged my scholarly endeavors. For all of their support, I am grateful.

Since completing my Ph.D. at Johns Hopkins, I have found a new scholarly home in the Catholic Studies department at DePaul University. My colleagues and students have been very encouraging and supportive, and I look forward to many more years at DePaul.

Special thanks also to Fortress Press for publishing this book. I had hoped to find a publisher to take interest in what I call "oft-overlooked yet very important agricultural spaces," and I am happy that Fortress Press has greatly supported me in this endeavor and provided me the opportunity to share my work.

Just like threshing floors, there are multiple facets to me. I am fortunate to have scholarly and professional support, but the support of family and friends is even stronger. When it comes to thanking family, my grandmom, Delores B. Waters, will always be at the top of the list. She has been my foundation, inspiration, and greatest supporter. My parents, Delores and John, continue to give their love and encouragement without which this work would not be possible. I am very thankful to have Dr. Uncle Tony available to provide many laughs and "creative suggestions" for this publication. Thanks also to Fr. Uncle Sam, Aunt Mia, Cousin Nita, and Godmom Cherie for their prayers and support. Many thanks to my life partner and best friend, Joe, whose love has endured for many years and whose stimulating conversations have influenced this work. Several other family members and friends have been supportive throughout the process, and they all have my sincere gratitude.

PREFACE

My first book is dedicated to my mom, Delores B. Waters, for her years of love, guidance, sacrifice, and support. Thanks for helping me to be where I am today.

Abbreviations

AASF   Annales Academiae Scientiarum Fennicae

AB   Anchor Bible

ABD   *Anchor Bible Dictionary*. Edited by D. N. Freedman. 6 vols. New York, 1992

ANET   *Ancient Near Eastern Texts Relating to the Old Testament*. Edited by J. A. Pritchard. Princeton, 1969

AOTC   Abingdon Old Testament Commentaries

BA   *Biblical Archaeologist*

BAR   *Biblical Archaeology Review*

BASOR   *Bulletin of the American Schools of Oriental Research*

BBB   Bonner biblische Beiträge

BDB   Brown, F., S. R. Driver, and C. A. Briggs. *A Hebrew and English Lexicon of the Old Testament*. Oxford, 1907

BSac   *Bibliotheca sacra*

BN   *Biblische Notizen*

BR   *Biblical Research*

BZ   *Biblische Zeitschrift*

BZAW   Beihefte zur Zeitschrift für die alttestamentliche Wissenschaft

CAD   *The Assyrian Dictionary of the Oriental Institute of the University of Chicago*. Chicago, 1956–2011

CBET	Contributions to Biblical Exegesis and Theology
CBQ	*Catholic Biblical Quarterly*
CBR	*Currents in Biblical Research*
CC	Continental Commentaries
CDA	Black, Jeremy, Andrew George, and Nicholas Postgate. *A Concise Dictionary of Akkadian*. Harrassowitz Verlag, 2000.
COS	*The Context of Scripture*. Edited by W. W. Hallo and W. Younger. 3 vols. Leiden, 1997–2003
CRBS	*Currents in Research: Biblical Studies*
DUL	Del Olmo Lete, Gregorio, and Joaquín Sanmartín. *A Dictionary of the Ugaritic Language in the Alphabetic Tradition*. Translated by Wilfred G. E. Watson. 2 vols. Leiden, 2003
ESV	English Standard Version
FAT	Forschungen zum Alten Testament
FRLANT	Forschungen zur Religion und Literatur des Alten und Neuen Testaments
HALOT	Koehler, L., W. Baumgartner, and J. J. Stamm. *The Hebrew and Aramaic Lexicon of the Old Testament*. Translated and edited under the supervision of M. E. J. Richardson. 5 vols. Leiden, 1994–2000
HR	*History of Religions*
HSM	Harvard Semitic Monographs
HTR	*Harvard Theological Review*
HTS	Harvard Theological Studies
HUC	Hebrew Union College
IDB	*The Interpreter's Dictionary of the Bible*. Edited by G. A. Buttrick. 4 vols. Nashville, 1962
IEJ	*Israel Exploration Journal*
JAOS	*Journal of the American Oriental Society*
JBL	*Journal of Biblical Literature*
JBQ	*Jewish Bible Quarterly*
JETS	*Journal of the Evangelical Theological Society*

JIR	Jewish Institute of Religion
JNES	*Journal of Near Eastern Studies*
JNSL	*Journal of Northwest Semitic Languages*
JPS	Jewish Publication Society
JQR	*Jewish Quarterly Review*
JSOT	Journal for the Study of the Old Testament
JSOTSup	Journal for the Study of the Old Testament: Supplement Series
JTS	*Journal of Theological Studies*
KAI	*Kanaanäische und Aramäische Inschriften*. H. Donner and W. Röllig. 2nd ed. Wiesbaden, 1966–1969
KTU	*Die Keilalphabetischen Texte aus Ugarit*. Edited by M. Dietrich, O. Loretz, and J. Sanmartín. AOAT 24/1. Neukirchen-Vluyn, 1976. 2nd enlarged ed. of *KTU: The Cuneiform Alphabetic Texts from Ugarit, Ras Ibn Hani, and Other Places*. Edited by M. Dietrich, O. Loretz, and J. Sanmartín. Münster, 1995
LXX	Septuagint
MT	Masoretic Text
NEB	New English Bible
NICOT	New International Commentary on the Old Testament
NIV	New International Version
NKJV	New King James Version
NJPS	New Jewish Publication Society of America Tanakh
NRSV	New Revised Standard Version
OBO	Orbis biblicus et orientalis
OBT	Overtures to Biblical Theology
OJB	Orthodox Jewish Bible
OTE	*Old Testament Essays*
OTL	Old Testament Library
PEQ	*Palestine Exploration Quarterly*
RB	*Revue biblique*

RES	*Répertoire d'épigraphie sémitiques*
RS	Ras Shamra
RSV	Revised Standard Version
SBL	Society of Biblical Literature
SBLWAW	Society of Biblical Literature Writings from the Ancient World
ScrHier	Scripta hierosolymitana
SR	*Studies in Religion*
TDOT	*Theological Dictionary of the Old Testament*. Edited by G. J. Botterweck and H. Ringgren. Translated by J. T. Willis, G. W. Bromiley, and D. E. Green. 8 vols. Grand Rapids, 1974–2006
ThSt	*Theologische Studien*
TZ	*Theologische Zeitschrift*
UF	*Ugarit-Forschungen*
UNP	*Ugaritic Narrative Poetry*. Edited by Simon B. Parker. SBLWAW 9. Atlanta, 1997
VT	*Vetus Testamentum*
VTSup	Supplements to Vetus Testamentum
WBC	Word Biblical Commentary
ZAW	*Zeitschrift für die alttestamentliche Wissenschaft*

1

Introduction

As the title of this work openly indicates, the focus of this study is on threshing floors in ancient Israel. This work examines these oft-overlooked yet very important agricultural spaces where crops are threshed and winnowed to release grain. At the outset, one might suppose that there will be a discussion of how threshing floors were created, where they were located, and the types of agricultural activities that occurred on them in antiquity. One might also expect a discussion of the ancient Israelite threshing floors that have been uncovered in the archaeological record. While that information will be considered in this introductory chapter, the larger trajectory of this book is more complicated and perhaps unexpected. What will be revealed with a careful look at the major textual source of the region, the Hebrew Bible, is that, in the minds of biblical writers, threshing floors served purposes beyond their agricultural functionality. The bulk of this study focuses on the literary depictions of these spaces and asserts that in ancient Israel threshing floors were not only agricultural spaces but were regarded as sacred spaces. In the Hebrew

Bible, these essential food-processing sites are highlighted as locations under divine control and locations for human-divine contact. The passages that will be examined in the forthcoming chapters will elucidate how and why threshing floors exhibit qualities of sacred space. First, however, some introductory remarks about threshing floors and sacred space are provided in this chapter.

Threshing Floors: An Overview

At their most basic level, threshing floors are locations where people perform the agricultural activities of threshing and winnowing. In ancient Israel, these floors were located on hard substrates such as bare rocks or were created by beating down the earth until a flat floor was formed. For the convenience of transporting crops to and fro, threshing floors were often situated in close proximity to fields on rock shelves or on infertile soil.[1] Conversely, threshing floors could also be located outside of the perimeter of a village or on high ground in order to take advantage of the open air and wind that are necessary for winnowing.[2]

Threshing and Winnowing

Threshing is the process of releasing grain from crops by crushing stalks. In ancient Israel, wheat and barley were two common crops that required threshing in order to harvest grain. Based on modern agricultural practices, interpretations of the Gezer Calendar,[3] and the

---

1. Ruth Shahack-Gross, Mor Gafri, and Israel Finkelstein, "Identifying Threshing Floors in the Archaeological Record: A Test Case at Iron Age Tel Megiddo, Israel," *Journal of Field Archaeology* 34 (2009): 171–84.
2. John C. Whittaker, "The Ethnoarchaeology of Threshing in Cyprus," *Near Eastern Archaeology* 63 (2000): 62–69.
3. The Gezer Calendar has been dated paleographically and orthographically to the tenth century BCE. The small calendar helps to establish and clarify the sequence of agricultural seasons in ancient Israel. The calendar suggests that an agricultural season might be as follows: two months of ingathering, two months of sowing, one month each for hoeing, harvesting, measuring, two

Hebrew Bible, Oded Borowski has suggested that in ancient Israel wheat and barley were sown in November and December. Barley was gathered and harvested in April and wheat in May. Borowski also notes that these agricultural seasons might vary from city to city based on natural conditions.[4] Following the harvest, crops were brought to a threshing floor, laid flat, and threshed by crushing in order to separate the grain from the stalks. The crushing could be done using a stick, an animal, or a threshing sledge. After threshing is completed, the refuse is removed, and the stalks are winnowed. Winnowing is the process of tossing or waving stalks in the wind so that the inedible protective cover over grain, the chaff, is blown away, and the grain falls to the ground. Done by hand or with the aid of a winnowing fork, winnowing is typically performed after threshing so that the loosened grains can be separated from the stalks and chaff more easily. After the grains are released, they are gathered together and put through a sieve to remove any lingering debris.

Ethnographic studies are helpful in understanding how threshing and winnowing may have been used in antiquity. Although caution must be used when employing modern threshing-floor examples, many ancient principles and techniques are still in use and shed light on this discussion. In 1980, Linda Cheetham completed an ethnographic study in Greece and Cyprus regarding threshing and winnowing practices.[5] Cheetham observed the use of flails, animals, and sleds/sledges for threshing. Flails are agricultural tools used to beat stalks on the ground. Before flails, sticks were probably used to thresh. Animals, usually donkeys or oxen, are also effective resources

---

months of harvesting grapes, and one month of gathering summer fruit. For more on the Gezer Calendar, see Seth Sanders, *The Invention of Hebrew* (Urbana: University of Illinois Press, 2009), 109–11; and F. W. Dobbs-Allsopp et al., "Gezer," in *Hebrew Inscriptions: Texts from the Biblical Period of the Monarchy with Concordance* (New Haven: Yale University Press, 2005), 156–65.

4. Oded Borowski, *Agriculture in Iron Age Israel* (Winona Lake: Eisenbrauns, 1987), 32–38.
5. Linda Cheetham, "Threshing and Winnowing—an Ethnographic Study," *Antiquity* 56 (1982): 127–30.

for threshing. Animals walk over stalks, and their hooves and weight separate and crush the grain. Animals are also employed to pull threshing sledges around the threshing floor with a person standing or sitting on the sledge for added weight. Threshing sledges are large boards that have teeth or flints on the underside in order to cut stalks and separate grain faster.[6]

Threshing and Winnowing in the Hebrew Bible

The Hebrew Bible provides some evidence of threshing and winnowing, including the practice of threshing wheat (1 Chron. 21:20) and winnowing barley (Ruth 3:7). Likewise, threshing sledges and boards are attested in the Hebrew Bible as tools used for these agricultural activities. In biblical Hebrew, the lexemes *môrag* and *ḥārûṣ* are attested as meaning "threshing sledge" or "threshing board." For instance, 2 Sam. 24:22 // 1 Chron. 21:23 describe a wooden threshing sledge (*môrag*) that is used to build a fire for a sacrifice offered by King David. Isaiah 41:15 describes a threshing sledge (*môrag*) having sharp edges, which fits well with Cheetham's description of sledges having teeth or flints on the bottoms to slice and separate grain from stalks. Amos 1:3 describes threshing boards (*ḥārûṣ*) made of iron, although the context is metaphorical and probably does not reflect actual threshing boards. While the Hebrew Bible does mention these threshing instruments, there are very few references with only minimal information.

The Hebrew Bible also makes mention of animals assisting in threshing. A law in Deut. 25:4 stipulates that an ox that is treading (*šôr bědîšô*) should not be muzzled. The law requires the humane treatment of animals that perform the work of trampling stalks to loosen grain. The book of Job includes a dialogue between Job and

---

6. Ibid., 128–29.

Yahweh where Yahweh poses a whirlwind of rhetorical questions, one of which asks if a wild ox (*rêm*) can bring grain to a threshing floor (Job 39:12). The purpose of the reference is figurative, but the question presumes the answer to be *no* because it is a wild, undomesticated ox. While it is not attempting to describe a concrete practice, the passage does imply that domesticated animals were used for transporting grain to and from threshing floors in addition to their use for trampling.

The book of Daniel includes the only reference to a threshing floor in biblical Aramaic. In Daniel 2, King Nebuchadnezzar[7] has had a dream and requests various dream interpreters and diviners to tell him his dream (Dan. 2:1–3). As the Judean exile Daniel reveals Nebuchadnezzar's dream, he describes a statue being struck with a stone and the pieces flying away in the wind like chaff on summer threshing floors (*'iddĕrê-qayiṭ*) (Dan. 2:35). This reference suggests that threshing and winnowing were done during the summertime on threshing floors situated in windy areas.

Beyond these passages about threshing and winnowing practices, the Hebrew Bible also provides examples of metaphorical uses of threshing imagery, particularly to describe destruction. First Isaiah describes Yahweh's careful manner of destruction as analogous to a farmer's care in threshing crops (Isa. 28:27–28). Likewise, Second Isaiah describes Israel as a threshing sledge who will thresh and winnow enemies (Isa. 41:15–16). Amos uses similar language when he describes Damascus defeating Gilead with iron threshing sledges (Amos 1:3). Additional passages will be explored in the following

---

7. The Hebrew Bible attests the Babylonian king's name as Nebuchadnezzar in Daniel and Nebuchadrezzar in Ezekiel and Jeremiah. The spelling with *n* may reflect an Aramaic translation of the Babylonian name *Nabû-kudurri-uṣur* or a dissimilation of the *r*'s in the transcription of the name. See John Joseph Collins, *Daniel: A Commentary on the Book of Daniel*, ed. F. M. Cross, Hermeneia (Minneapolis: Fortress Press, 1993), 133.

chapter which assert Yahwistic control and judgment over enemies using threshing-floor imagery.

While it is clear that the activities of threshing and winnowing were performed in order to obtain grain, specific details about these processes are not overly abundant in the Hebrew Bible. This should not suggest that these actions were unimportant; on the contrary, in the schema of food production, threshing and winnowing are important processes. As an agrarian society, agriculture structured life and provided food needed for survival. From plowing and planting to gathering and harvesting, agricultural activities served as critical seasonal work that structured society and allowed for a sustainable lifestyle. Within this agricultural framework, threshing and winnowing are actions on which society hinged. After crops have grown and are gathered, they require processing to remove materials that hinder access to grains. At this juncture, threshing and winnowing are the actions that strip away stalks and reveal the edible food. After these tasks have been completed, grains may be stored for future use or further processed into other foodstuffs such as flour or bread.

Since threshing and winnowing are life-sustaining activities that happen on threshing floors, threshing floors were fundamental locations for human nourishment and survival. At threshing floors, inedible crops were beaten, trodden, and shaken to free the edible food held within. Threshing floors played a significant role as the locations of sustainability and survival. Because of the sustenance so deeply rooted in the agricultural work on threshing floors, these spaces were thought to be controlled and blessed by Yahweh, the ultimate supporter of life. This intrinsic notion of a divine participation in subsistence will be explored in this work.

Archaeology, Ethnography, and Threshing Floors

Though threshing floors were essential to survival in ancient Israel, there have been minimal publications on both ancient and modern threshing floors, which is probably because they are difficult to detect in the archaeological record. Archaeologist Shimon Dar notes, "Many ancient threshing floors have vanished with the expansion of those Arab villages which are located on ancient sites, and with the introduction of heavy mechanical implements into areas of ancient cereal growing."[8] These issues raised by Dar are noteworthy. Indeed, modern sites atop ancient ones make it difficult to access ancient threshing floors. Similarly, the mechanization of threshing and winnowing practices changes how these traditional threshing sites are utilized. Even when ancient sites are excavated, threshing floors are still difficult to detect. When done effectively, threshing does not leave macroscopic or microscopic evidence because the floors are cleaned of grains and threshing by-products.[9] If organic components remain on threshing floors, they likely blow away since these spaces are often located in windy areas. Anthropologist John Whittaker aptly notes:

> More ethnoarchaeological studies of threshing, and more detailed archaeological examination of ancient *alonia* [threshing floors], are both necessary because threshing floors have been important features in village life all around the Mediterranean for thousands of years. Although few archaeologists have attempted to interpret them or even to describe them, the recognition and study of threshing floors could help understand a number of issues.[10]

---

8. Shimon Dar, *Landscape and Pattern: An Archaeological Survey of Samaria 800 B.C.E.–636 C.E.*, Part i, BAR International Series 308[i] (Oxford: B.A.R., 1986), 191.
9. Georgia Tsartsidou et al., "Ethnoarchaeological Study of Phytolith Assemblages from an Agro-Pastoral Village in Northern Greece (Sarakini): Development and Application of a Phytolith Difference Index," *Journal of Archaeological Science* 35 (2008), 600–13; and Shahack-Gross, Gafri, and Finkelstein, "Identifying Threshing Floors in the Archaeological Record," 173.
10. Whittaker, "The Ethnoarchaeology of Threshing in Cyprus," 68.

7

In 1995 Whittaker researched threshing floors and threshing practices in Cyprus, and his work is informative for this discussion. Whittaker interviewed elderly villagers in Cyprus regarding threshing floors and threshing practices. His findings suggest that threshing floors are often clustered together in an ideal part of a village with wind accessibility. The reason for threshing floors to be close together is so that people can socialize and assist one another in the laborious threshing process. According to the villagers interviewed, ideally every family would have its own threshing floor near to the village so that transporting grain to and from would be as easy as possible. When looking for a threshing floor, Whittaker observed that the earth was often packed down, chalky, and would sometimes be plastered. Some threshing floors are marked with walls to delineate one threshing floor from another.[11]

Ethnoarchaeological studies in northern Greece done by Georgia Tsartsidou, Simcha Lev-Yadun, Nikos Efstratiou, and Steve Weiner also provide helpful insights into threshing floors. For example, one study has suggested that threshing floors were dismantled and remade every year. Because of the shortage of viable, fertile land, threshing floors were also used as cultivation plots. After crops were grown and harvested, a plot of land was turned into a threshing floor, and after the harvest, the threshing floor was turned back into cultivated land.[12]

While there have not been many threshing floors uncovered in the archaeological record, there are sites of note. An early Roman period threshing floor has been uncovered at Khirbet Manṣur el-'Aqab, 6 km northeast of Caesarea, Israel. The excavators, Y. Hirschfeld and R. Birger-Calderon, date the site between the first century BCE and the first century CE.[13] The estate includes a residential area and a

---

11. Ibid., 67–69.
12. Tsartsidou et al., "Ethnoarchaeological Study of Phytolith Assemblages," 610.
13. Y. Hirschfeld and R. Birger-Calderon, "Early Roman and Byzantine Estates near Caesarea," *IEJ* 41 (1991): 81–111.

courtyard with various agricultural features, including a threshing floor, a wine press, and an olive-oil press. The excavators describe the threshing floor as a rock-hewn semicircular area, 7.6 m in length and a maximum of 1.8 m in width. Based on the size and shape, they speculate that threshing was performed manually using a flail.[14] They also report that two rectangular basalt millstones used for grinding wheat and barley into flour were found within the residential complex. The outdoor agricultural installations and the millstones support the interpretation of this area as a threshing floor.

Similarly, during excavations at Samaria, Dar uncovered several agricultural installations, including multiple threshing floors, wine presses, and olive-oil presses dating roughly from the Hellenistic period to the Roman period. The threshing floors were typically level areas cut into rock, some with stone fences around them and some without fences, almost always on the outskirts of a settlement. Two threshing floors were found on top of a hill, a traditional location to have access to wind for winnowing. Dar describes one threshing floor with rainwater cisterns near it, which he speculates may have been so that animals had access to water as they assisted in threshing.[15] Dar also notes that several threshing floors were clustered together, which is in line with Whittaker's ethnographic study that suggests people threshed and winnowed together, perhaps to help one another or to socialize.[16]

Other excavators have suggested that threshing floors have been unearthed at their archaeological sites, including Gezer (W. Dever),[17] Khirbet Abu Musarraḥ (Y. Peleg and I. Yezerski),[18] Khirbet ʻAlmit (U. Dinur and G. Lipovitz),[19] and Qibbutz Sasa (H. Bron).[20] While

---

14. Ibid., 99.
15. Dar, *Landscape and Pattern*, 191–93.
16. Whittaker, "The Ethnoarchaeology of Threshing in Cyprus," 68.
17. William G. Dever, ed., *Gezer IV: The 1969–1971 Seasons in Field VI, the "Acropolis," Part I, Text* (Jerusalem: Nelson Glueck School of Biblical Archaeology, 1986).

hard, flat surfaces are sometimes deemed threshing floors because they meet the physical expectations of these spaces, some of these locations have been labeled as threshing floors without in-depth macroscropic and microscopic analysis of the locations. In order to prevent and/or correct this problem, Ruth Shahack-Gross, Mor Gafri, and Israel Finkelstein have published an important article on how to classify threshing floors based on archaeological and ethnographic studies.

At the beginning of their work, they rightly note the difficulty in identifying threshing floors in the archaeological record, and their research at an Iron Age layer of Tel Megiddo can serve as a useful case study of the questions that should be asked for flat surfaces uncovered on an excavation. In their study of a hard, flat surface uncovered at Megiddo, Shahack-Gross, Gafri, and Finkelstein performed geoarchaeological studies of the remnants on the floor and found evidence of wood ash and inorganic remains of livestock dung, neither of which are typically found on threshing floors. Based on these remnants, along with the texture of the soil, they concluded that the area of analysis is a single-family trash heap, not a threshing floor, as previously thought. Based on their archaeological and ethnographic research, they expect threshing floors to be found in open areas outside of a settlement with a single hard surface, signs of trampling, and no artifacts since the floor would have been cleared of produce after threshing.[21] This study is valuable and calls for a

---

18. Y. Peleg and I. Yezerski, "A Dwelling and Burial Cave at Kh. Abu-Musarraḥ in the Land of Benjamin," in *Burial Caves and Sites in Judea and Samaria from the Bronze and Iron Ages*, ed. H. Hizmi and A. De-Groot (Jerusalem: Israeli Antiquities Authority, 2004), 107–56.
19. U. Dinur and G. Lipovitz, "A Burial Cave from the 6th Century B.C.E. in Hurvat Almit," *Niqrot Zurim* 14 (1988): 44–51. (Hebrew)
20. Hendrik (Enno) Bron, *Sasa Hadashot Arkheologiyot: Excavations and Surveys in Israel* 125 (2013), http://www.hadashot-esi.org.il/report_detail_eng.aspx?id=2225.
21. Shahack-Gross, Gafri, and Finkelstein, "Identifying Threshing Floors in the Archaeological Record," 173.

reinterpretation of hard floors discovered on excavations, yet some flexibility in their criteria is needed. As demonstrated at Khirbet Manṣur el-ʿAqab, threshing floors can also be found within domestic contexts, and they may not exhibit signs of trampling if they are rock-hewn floors as at Samaria.

Both archaeology and ethnography provide insights into the location of threshing floors and why they are so difficult to study. These flat floors are often situated in areas with wind accessibility. They are not likely to leave organic material because these materials would be collected, or the wind would blow them away. The floors are likely to contain earth that is pressed down, hard, and chalky, or they can be rock-hewn floors. Threshing floors may have been communal spaces, although owning a threshing floor near to one's property was probably ideal and convenient. Likewise, other agricultural features often accompany threshing floors, such as oil and wine presses. In areas where all of the land was fertile, threshing floors might be temporary so that the land could be used for cultivating crops.

Threshing Floors in the Hebrew Bible

As sites where crops are processed, threshing floors are spaces essential for survival in agrarian societies, and as such, inhabitants of ancient Israel surely used threshing floors for these vital operations. Because threshing and winnowing were ubiquitous practices in ancient Israel, it is likely that everyone had access to a threshing floor, whether privately owned or shared. The Hebrew Bible attests both privately owned (2 Sam. 6:6 // 1 Chron. 13:9; 2 Sam. 24:16 // 1 Chron. 21:15) and communal (1 Sam. 23:1; 1 Kgs. 22:10 // 2 Chron. 18:9) threshing floors.

Gōren

In biblical Hebrew, *gōren* is the lexeme for "threshing floor." Ugaritic, Old South Arabian, and Ethiopic also attest √*grn* as a direct etymological equivalent, while biblical Aramaic has the lexeme *'iddar*. There is only one occurrence of *'iddar* in biblical Aramaic (Dan. 2:35), which was mentioned above. Cognate evidence from Old, Middle, and Neo-Assyrian Akkadian also attests √*'dr* meaning "threshing floor." Septuagint Greek typically translates *gōren* with *halōn*, its usual word for "threshing floor." There are two occasions in which the Septuagint does not translate *gōren* as *halōn* (LXX 1 Kgs. 22:10 // 2 Chron. 18:9) which will be discussed in chapter 4. Though there is a minor debate about the precise connotations, following the scholarly and lexical consensus, *gōren* will be translated as "threshing floor" throughout this work.[22]

While threshing floors were surely used for agricultural activities, their occurrences in the Hebrew Bible are multifaceted, with a variety of nonagricultural activities taking place on these spaces. Mourning rites, divination rituals, cultic processions, and sacrifices all happen on threshing floors, and Solomon's temple is built on a threshing floor. It is possible that these nonagricultural activities are

---

22. A minority of scholars suggests translating *gōren* as a generic "open space" in certain contexts, particularly in 1 Kgs. 22:10 // 2 Chron. 18:9 (see chapter 4, n. xv). Sidney Smith suggests understanding *gōren* as "open space" based on his interpretation of the Arabic cognate word *jurunān*. He also suggests that the Aramaic *'iddar* and Akkadian *adru* should be understood as "plots of land" instead of "threshing floors." See Sidney Smith, "On the Meaning of *Goren*," *PEQ* 85 (1953): 42–45. John Gray notes some problems with Smith's interpretation of the Arabic evidence. He also notes the rabbinic interpretation of the *gōren* in 1 Kgs. 22:10 as a semicircular area. Gray suggests that the *gōren* could be an open area based on the Septuagint. See John Gray, "The *Goren* at the City Gate," *PEQ* 85 (1953): 118–23. Victor Matthews has suggested that *gōren* became equated with *rĕḥôb*, "public square," based on 1 Kgs. 22:10. See Victor H. Matthews, "Entrance Ways and Threshing Floors: Legally Significant Sites in the Ancient Near East," *Fides et Historia* 19 (1987): 25–40. These suggestions do not take into account that the threshing floor is used for divine confirmation of war and instead are likely influenced by the Septuagint translation of *bĕgōren*, "on a threshing floor," as *en tō euruchōrō*, "on a wide space" (LXX 2 Chron. 18:9).

depicted on threshing floors because these are open-access spaces used seasonally for agricultural functions. For several months of the year, threshing floors are idle, so they were available for various activities. Because these areas were cleared after use and were often open-access locations, they may have been ideal and logical choices for other/nonagricultural activities throughout the year. However, close investigation of biblical accounts reveals that many of these nonagricultural activities are sacred and/or ritualistic in nature. Below is a chart which gives a brief synopsis of the passages that most clearly depict sacredness associated with threshing floors:

Passage	Synopsis	Function of the Threshing Floor
Judg. 6:37–40	Gideon performs a divination ritual involving dew and fleece on a threshing floor in order to know if his military battle will be successful.	The threshing floor serves as the location for human-divine contact. On two occasions, a divine answer is provided on this threshing floor.
1 Kgs. 22:10 // 2 Chron. 18:9	Kings of Israel and Judah gather prophets on the threshing floor of Samaria to determine if their war against Aram will be successful.	The threshing floor serves as a location for consulting Yahweh before going to war. A prophetic vision occurs on this space.
Gen. 50:10–11	Joseph and a large group of mourners travel to a threshing floor to perform mourning rites for Jacob.	The threshing floor is the location for a group to gather, pray, and lament.
2 Sam. 6:6–7 // 1 Chron. 13:10–11	David and a large group embark on a sacred procession involving the ark and stop at a threshing floor.	The threshing floor is the location where the ark is brought and is where a divine manifestation occurs.
2 Sam. 24:15–25 // 1 Chron. 21:14–27	David and the prophet Gad witness an angel at a threshing floor. David purchases the threshing floor, builds an altar, and offers sacrifices there.	The threshing floor is a location of divine manifestation and ritual activity.
2 Chron. 3:1	The Solomonic temple is built on the threshing floor purchased by David.	The threshing floor no longer functions as an agricultural space, but now becomes foundational space for the house of Yahweh.

Nearly all of the narratives that occur on threshing floors in the Hebrew Bible include an overt connection to the divine. From rituals to temple construction, the Hebrew Bible provides clear evidence that these spaces were regarded as more than agricultural spaces; they were considered sacred spaces. In addition to narratives on threshing floors, there are also prophetic and legal texts which provide clear examples of divine control over threshing floors and divine blessing of these spaces. By examining the biblical references to threshing floors, this book will assert that Yahweh was considered intimately connected to threshing floors because of the essential life-sustaining activities that happen at these locations.

The following section discusses the theoretical framework that will aid this treatment on threshing floors. Because it will be argued that threshing floors were considered sacred spaces, an overview of sacred space and spatial theorists will enhance this discussion. There will also be some comments on how to embark on studying a variety of literary texts from different time periods and contexts.

Theoretical Framework

Unpacking the literary depiction of threshing floors as sacred spaces will provide an important dimension to understanding the significance of these locations in ancient Israel. Studying the sacrality of threshing floors does not negate the pragmatic use of threshing floors for agricultural purposes; rather, it allows for a more complete and thorough understanding of these vital locations.

Sacred Space and Biblical Study

Definitions abound on how to describe and classify sacred space. Since this work is focused on the Hebrew Bible, in this context a sacred space is a location that exhibits a connection to the deity

Yahweh. This connection may be visible with a theophany, an outward sign of divine presence, a cultic activity, or a perception of divine control or accessibility. Sacred spaces are locations where the connection between Yahweh and humans is actualized.

As seen in the above chart, in the Hebrew Bible there are some passages where the connection between threshing floors and Yahweh is made explicit with a theophany (2 Sam. 6:6–7 // 1 Chron. 13:10–11; 2 Sam. 24:15–26 // 1 Chron. 21:16–27). Other passages are more implicit, showing that threshing floors were thought to be connected to the divine due to their selection for cultic activities (Gen. 50:10–11; Judg. 6:37–40; 2 Sam. 6:6–7 // 1 Chron. 13:10–11; 1 Kgs. 22:10 // 2 Chron. 18:9). In addition to theophany and cultic activity, Yahweh is also considered in control of threshing floors (Hosea 9:1–2; Joel 2:23–24; 1 Sam. 23:1–5; 2 Kgs. 6:27; Judg. 6:1–16), which adds yet another degree of sacrality to these spaces.

Numerous scholars have been influential in studies of sacred space and spatiality.[23] Below is an admittedly selective treatment of these

---

23. For discussions of sacred space from archaeological perspectives, see Michael D. Coogan, "Of Cult and Cultures: Reflections on the Interpretation of Archaeological Evidence," *PEQ* 119 (1987): 1–8; William G. Dever, *Did God Have a Wife? Archaeology and Folk Religion in Ancient Israel* (Grand Rapids: Wm. B. Eerdmans, 2005), 110–75; Israel Finkelstein and Neil A. Silberman, *The Bible Unearthed: Archaeology's New Vision of Ancient Israel and the Origin of Its Sacred Texts* (New York: Touchstone, 2002), 4–25; Garth Gilmour, "The Archaeology of Cult in the Period of the Judges: Theory and Practice," *OTE* 13 (2000): 283–92; Colin Renfrew and Paul Bahn, *Archaeology: Theories, Methods, and Practice*, 2nd ed. (London: Thames and Hudson Ltd, 1996), 390–94; Ziony Zevit, *The Religions of Ancient Israel: A Synthesis of Parallactic Approaches* (New York: Continuum, 2001), 81–266. For discussions of sacred space from anthropological perspectives, see Benjamin Ray, "Sacred Space and Royal Shrines in Buganda," *HR* 16 (1977): 363–73; Harold W. Turner, *From Temple to Meeting House: The Phenomenology and Theology of Places of Worship* (The Hague: Mouton Publishers, 1979), 3–33; Paul Wheatley, *The Pivot of the Four Quarters: A Preliminary Enquiry into the Origins and Character of the Ancient Chinese City* (Chicago: Aldine Publishing Company, 1971), 411–76; and Catherine Bell, *Ritual Theory, Ritual Practice* (New York: Oxford University Press, 1992), 3–54. For discussions of sacred space from literary perspectives, see Nathanael B. Hearson, "'Go Now to Shiloh': God's Changing Relationship with Sacred Places in the Hebrew Bible and Early Rabbinic Literature" (PhD diss., HUC-JIR, 2005), 77–287; Don M. Hudson, "From Chaos to Cosmos: Sacred Space in Genesis," *ZAW* 108 (1996): 87–97; Seung Il Kang, "Creation, Eden, Temple and Mountain: Textual Presentations of Sacred Space in the Hebrew Bible" (PhD diss.,

topics with the goal of seeing how certain theorists (Mircea Eliade, Jonathan Z. Smith, Sara Japhet, Henri Lefebvre, Edward Soja) can assist in understanding how threshing floors could be perceived as sacred.

Mircea Eliade

Mircea Eliade's work has been very influential to discussions of sacred space. In *The Sacred and the Profane: The Nature of Religion*, Eliade juxtaposes the concepts of *the sacred* and *the profane*. He asserts that humans recognize something as sacred because it manifests itself and its otherness and is completely separate from the profane. This manifestation may be through a theophany or some other outward sign. Whatever is sacred is by definition different, as its reality does not belong to the profane world.[24] Eliade uses the example of a sacred stone. On the surface, a stone is just a stone, and it looks identical to any other stone. However, if it reveals itself as sacred, its reality is transformed into a supernatural reality for those who are able or privileged to witness this phenomenon.[25] Accordingly, anything in the profane world has the ability to become sacred, and it can reveal itself as such, in what Eliade calls a *hierophany*, a revelation of the sacred. Eliade's *hierophany* designates the "*act of manifestation* of the sacred ... It is a fitting term, because it does not imply anything further; it expresses no more than is implicit in its etymological content, *i.e.*, that *something sacred shows itself to us*."[26] To Eliade, sacred space appears to be self-revelatory but also completely controlled by

---

The Johns Hopkins University, 2008); Jon D. Levenson, *Sinai and Zion: An Entry into the Jewish Bible* (San Francisco: Harper & Row, 1985), 137–45.

24. Eliade, *The Sacred and the Profane: The Nature of Religion*, trans. W. Trask (San Diego: Harcourt, 1957), 11.
25. Ibid., 12.
26. Ibid., 11. Cf. Mircea Eliade, *Patterns in Comparative Religion*, trans. R. Sheed (New York: Sheed & Ward, 1958), 7–8.

divine forces.[27] Humans experience the sacred if they are open to such divine revelation; however, humans are not agents in creating the sacred.

Eliade's assertion that anything can be sacred is an important point. He proposes an inherent potential that all spaces possess. In the case of threshing floors, these spaces can change from agricultural spaces (*profane*) to sacred spaces (*sacred*) depending on how they are being used or perceived. Eliade's concept of sacred *versus* profane, however, is probably better understood as sacred *and* profane with regard to threshing floors. Threshing floors can simultaneously be sacred *and* profane as they are used for both cultic and agrarian activities. As will be discussed in chapter 4, in 1 Chron. 21:18–20 an angel appears at a threshing floor and commands an altar to be built while wheat is being threshed there. Concurrently, sacred and profane activity occur on the same threshing floor.

Eliade's theories regarding agency are thought provoking although somewhat inconsistent. As he asserts the divine control over the sacred, Eliade also asserts an object's power in manifesting itself as sacred. Divine revelation and an object's self-revelation appear to be two possible ways for the manifestation of the sacred, although conceptually it is difficult to understand who actually possesses agency in Eliade's model. Eliade's work often minimizes human agency in defining a space as sacred and instead focuses on divine action or self-revelatory actions in revealing sacredness.[28]

---

27. Eliade, *The Sacred and the Profane*, 62–65.
28. One critique of Eliade was that his ideas about sacred space concentrated largely on divine revelation and less on the social action on a space. For instance, Eliade does not focus on rituals and their connections to sacred space. Rather, he sees them as largely meaningless with regard to sacred space; instead, they are often repetitive gestures and imitations of learned behaviors. Mircea Eliade, *The Myth of the Eternal Return: Or, Cosmos and History*, trans. W. Trask (Princeton: Princeton University Press, 1954), 34–35.

Jonathan Z. Smith

Jonathan Z. Smith strongly critiques Eliade for neglecting the social aspects and historical contexts with regard to interpreting space.[29] When discussing sacred space, Smith emphasizes the importance of social action, in particular rituals, happening on a location to make it a sacred space. For Smith, "Ritual is not an expression of or a response to 'the Sacred'; rather, something or someone is made sacred by ritual (the primary sense of *sacrificium*)."[30] Smith underscores how it is the presence of ritual activity that sacralizes a space. The activities that occur on a space are essential to understanding it.

Smith's insights into how ritual/social action on a location aids in defining space are important particularly for the passages that narrate cultic activity on threshing floors (Judg. 6:37–40; 1 Kgs. 22:10 // 2 Chron. 18:9; Gen. 50:10–11; 2 Sam. 6:6–7 // 1 Chron. 13:10–11; 2 Sam. 24:15–25 // 1 Chron. 21:14–27). The presence of cultic activity on threshing floors is an outward sign that the location is considered sacred.

In the case of threshing floors, Smith probably would argue that the cultic activity on threshing floors makes them sacred. However, this study will argue that threshing floors were already considered sacred because of their perceived connection to Yahweh. Though valuable, Smith's definition does not allow for the possibility of idle sacred space without ritual activity. Yet, the intentional selection of threshing floors for ritual shows that there is a notion that these agricultural spaces were considered sacred spaces; namely, they were considered locations connected to the divine and therefore appropriate for ritual activities. Even before rituals occur on these agricultural spaces, the Hebrew Bible reveals a cultural understanding

---

29. Jonathan Z. Smith, *To Take Place: Toward Theory in Ritual* (Chicago: University of Chicago Press, 1987), 1–23.
30. Ibid., 105.

that threshing floors were linked to Yahweh due to the life-sustaining agricultural work that happens on these spaces and the control that Yahweh was thought to have over the survival of Israel and Judah. This perceived relationship explains why cultic activities occur on threshing floors.

The difference between the view presented in this book and Smith's view is like the proverbial chicken or egg. Smith asserts that the cultic activity sacralizes space. This work argues that a space can be considered sacred, thus leading it to being used for cultic activity. The cultic activities are the realization of an innate logic of an agrarian society whose livelihood centered on threshing floors that were wholeheartedly imbued with divine blessings and security.

Sara Japhet

As both Smith and Eliade are useful in contextualizing and defining parameters of sacred space, the work of Sara Japhet is particularly useful in talking about biblical sacred space. Japhet's chapter "Some Biblical Concepts of Sacred Place" outlines the biblical presentation of sacredness and holiness, highlighting the diverse views and concepts in the Hebrew Bible. Recognizing the complexities, Japhet states that "the sanctity of a place is determined exclusively by the existence of a direct and immediate link between that place and God."[31] Japhet notes that this connection can be perceived in two ways: (1) a sacred place is a place where God dwells; (2) a sacred place is one where God reveals himself to humanity.[32]

Japhet stresses the requirement that a sacred space exhibit a connection to God. In the present study of threshing floors, Japhet's two ways of perceiving the link between a sacred place and God are

---

31. Sara Japhet, "Some Biblical Concepts of Sacred Place," in *Sacred Space: Shrine, City, Land*, ed. B. Kedar and R. L. Z. Werblowsky (London: Macmillan, 1998), 57.
32. Ibid., 59.

valuable though not all-encompassing. For instance, regarding point (1), a threshing floor is the location of the temple where Yahweh dwells (2 Chron. 3:1); and, regarding point (2), Yahweh reveals himself to humanity when his anger is kindled and when an angel appears on a threshing floor (2 Sam. 6:6–7 // 1 Chron. 13:9–10; 2 Sam. 24:15–25 // 1 Chron. 21:14–27). However, these ways of determining the link would not address Gideon and the kings of Israel and Judah choosing a threshing floor as a location to contact Yahweh (Judg. 6:37–40; 1 Kgs. 22:10 // 2 Chron. 18:9), nor would it address the cultic rituals offered for Jacob on a threshing floor (Gen. 50:10–11). Perhaps a third way to perceive a link between a place and God might be: (3) a sacred place is a place where God is considered accessible. Such a perception is less recognizable than the other two ways, but equally important, and it enhances the conception of sacred space. To assert that God dwells or reveals himself at a location requires some external sign, whether a temple, cultic object, or a theophany. The additional link suggested here is less visual and more intuitive. It shows the importance of observing an internal understanding of sacred space even without an outward indicator. In this way, a sacred space can be active when there is a temple, cultic object, or theophany on it, but a space can also be sacred and yet inactive if there is a perception that God is potentially reachable on that location.

Another important aspect of Japhet's work is her suggestion that sacredness of a space can be temporary and transient. Unlike Eliade who suggests that once something is sacred it is removed from the profane world, Japhet's view is that there is impermanence to sacred spaces, and they only become permanent when *continued* worship or ritualistic activities occur on those spaces.[33] This is precisely the case

---

33. Ibid., 69–70.

with most threshing floors. While they are agricultural spaces, they can temporarily become sacred spaces associated with theophanies and cultic activities—that is, ad hoc sacred spaces. However, once those cultic activities are complete, threshing floors can once again be used for agricultural activities. This study will demonstrate the fluidity of the various functions that take place on threshing floors. On the one hand, they are spaces used to process crops. On the other hand, they are spaces under the auspices of Yahweh tied to divine blessings and theophanies. There is an inherent seamlessness to these spaces whereby they can instantly be transformed from agricultural to sacred and back to agricultural spaces. There is a level of impermanence to their sacrality. Because threshing floors serve such a fundamental purpose in sustaining life, they do not lose their agricultural nature but instead become temporarily sacred when cultic activities and divine manifestation occur upon them. Only with the construction of the Solomonic temple on a threshing floor, which will be discussed in chapter 5, does a threshing floor completely lose its agrarian function and become a permanent sacred space.

Spatial Theory and Biblical Study

As with the study of sacred space, there are many theorists of space.[34] When trying to understand a particular culture or time period, spatial studies can provide insights into how a society functioned, its values, and its actions. Mark George has aptly noted, "Analysis of the space or spaces produced by a society thus offers another means of studying and understanding the society and culture that produced it."[35] Similarly, Yairah Amit suggests that a biblical location is functional and "understanding its function in the story leads to a deeper, more comprehensive understanding of the narrative."[36] Methodological insights from the spatial theorists Henri Lefebvre and Edward Soja are especially helpful in understanding threshing floors as functional spaces within the society of ancient Israel.[37]

---

34. For studies of spatial theory, see Jon L. Berquist, "Critical Spatiality and the Construction of the Ancient World," in *"Imagining" Biblical Worlds: Studies in Spatial, Social and Historical Constructs in Honor of James W. Flanagan*, ed. D. M. Gunn and P. M. McNutt, JSOTSup 359 (London: Sheffield Academic Press, 2002), 14–29; David Harvey, *The Condition of Postmodernity: An Enquiry into the Origins of Cultural Change* (Oxford: Blackwell, 1989), 201–326; Yi-Fu Tuan, *Space and Place: The Perspective of Experience* (Minneapolis: University of Minnesota Press, 1977), 67–117; Kim Knott, *The Location of Religion: A Spatial Analysis* (London: Equinox, 2005), 1–132; Wesley A. Kort, *Place and Space in Modern Fiction* (Gainesville: University Press of Florida, 2004), 128–72; and Mary R. Huie-Jolly, "Formation of the Self in Construction of Space: Lefebvre in Winnicott's Embrace," in *Constructions of Space I: Theory, Geography, and Narrative*, ed. J. L. Berquist and C. V. Camp (New York: T&T Clark, 2007), 51–67. For more on biblical spatiality, see Thomas B. Dozeman, "Biblical Geography and Critical Spatial Studies," in *Constructions of Space I*, 87–108; Steven James Schweitzer, "Exploring the Utopian Space of Chronicles: Some Spatial Anomalies," in *Constructions of Space I*, 141–56; and Matthew Skinner, *Locating Paul: Places of Custody as Narrative Settings in Acts 21–28*, Academia Biblica (Atlanta: SBL, 2003), 27–56.
35. Mark George, "Space and History: Siting Critical Space for Biblical Studies," in *Constructions of Space I*, 15.
36. Yairah Amit, *Reading Biblical Narratives: Literary Criticism and the Hebrew Bible*, trans. Y. Lotan (Minneapolis: Augsburg Fortress, 2001), 125.
37. See Henri Lefebvre's *The Production of Space*, trans. D. Nicholson-Smith (Malden: Blackwell, 1974), and *Critique of Everyday Life*, vol. 2, *Foundations for a Sociology of the Everyday*, trans. J. Moore (London: Verso, 1961); Edward Soja's *Postmodern Geographies: The Reassertion of Space in Critical Social Theory* (London: Verso, 1989), and *Thirdspace: Journeys to Los Angeles and Other Real-and-Imagined Places* (Cambridge: Blackwell, 1996).

Henri Lefebvre and Edward Soja

Henri Lefebvre's method of analyzing sacred space is with a tripartite understanding. His model includes a distinction between the *physical* (nature, the cosmos), the *mental* (including logical and formal abstractions), and the *social* aspects of space.[38] In characterizing these three, Lefebvre says, "we are concerned with the logico-epistemological space, the space of social practice, the space occupied by sensory phenomena, including products of the imagination."[39] Lefebvre notes that these three ideas must be studied together in order to understand space; one aspect is not more important than another. Physical space would include examining the features of a particular space. Mental space involves ideas and perceptions about the space. Social space refers to the activities and practices of living and experiencing space in relation to other people.

Similar to Lefebvre and influenced by Michel Foucault,[40] Edward Soja suggests that there are also three modes of spatiality. Soja terms these conceptions of space Firstspace (physical space), Secondspace (imagined space), and Thirdspace (experienced space).[41] Soja's Thirdspace is a combination of Firstspace and Secondspace since experienced space is both physical space and imagined space. Soja notes that all three modes are especially useful for the interpreter of space and allow for an examination of space from multiple perspectives.

The tripartite understanding of sacred space proposed by Lefebvre and Soja is an important method for the interpretation of threshing

---

38. Lefebvre, *The Production of Space*, 11.
39. Ibid., 11–12.
40. Soja is especially influenced by Foucault's work on *heterotopia*, which is a concept in human geography that analyzes space as having both physical and mental realities. See Michel Foucault, "Of Other Spaces," *Diacritics* 16 (1986): 22–27.
41. Edward Soja, "Afterword," in *Postmodern Geography: Theory and Praxis*, ed. Claudio Minca (Oxford: Blackwell, 2010), 282–94.

floors in ancient Israel, particularly when the physical spaces themselves are difficult to find archaeologically and may not leave behind clear evidence of activity. The Hebrew Bible provides insights into threshing floors as physical, imagined, experienced spaces. For instance, although the specific size and shape of threshing floors are not included in biblical passages, two large processions (Gen. 50:10–11; 2 Sam. 6:6–7 // 1 Chron. 13:9–10) and a group including 400 unnamed prophets (1 Kgs. 22:10 // 2 Chron. 18:9) are described on threshing floors, so physically these spaces were able to accommodate large groups. There is also an allusion to threshing floors being trodden down (Jer. 51:33), which helps in understanding their physical creation. Additionally, several biblical passages provide information on how threshing floors were imagined and experienced, and consistently a divine connection to these spaces is acknowledged and emphasized. The biblical passages attest a picture of threshing floors as locations thought to be connected to Yahweh and locations where Yahweh is experienced; and Lefebvre and Soja's work will provide insights into the multiple approaches and angles from which to analyze these spaces.

Date, Genre, and Context of Biblical Texts

This study will evaluate passages of the Hebrew Bible that include a reference to a threshing floor (*gōren*).[42] Traditionally, these passages are studied separately, often within biblical commentaries, with the goal of exegeting a particular passage. This study, however, examines references to threshing floors as a collection, side by side, with particular attention to how the Hebrew Bible's various authors and

---

42. Chapters 2–5 will discuss all of the occurrences of threshing floors in the Hebrew Bible except for two: Job 39:12 and Dan. 2:35. These passages are more insightful for understanding threshing and winnowing practices rather than the literary depiction of these spaces; therefore, they were considered above in the section Threshing and Winnowing in the Hebrew Bible.

editors reference these spaces. Because threshing floors are most often depicted as sacred spaces with only minimal references to their agricultural use, a broad look at these passages as a corpus will shed light on this biblical phenomenon.

While the passages treated in this work are from a diverse compositional background spanning several centuries and genres, this study will show overarching similarities in many of the references to threshing floors. As each passage is studied, the date, genre, apparent rhetoric, and *Sitz im Leben* (setting in life) will be noted in order to contextualize the passages and to note the occasions on which threshing floors are mentioned or perceived as sacred spaces. An inherent limitation of a study of this kind is that the Hebrew Bible represents only a glimpse of the world of Israel and Judah. It is the end product of a long history of writing, redacting, and compiling of texts. As biblical traditions are often removed in time and space from the events they purport to depict, the study of these passages brings complexities that will be noted but should not stall the insights that can be garnered. For all of the necessary caveats, complications, and cautions, the Hebrew Bible is the primary literary source about ancient threshing floors in this region, and for that reason it is the central focus of this book. When it is helpful to understanding the passages better from a comparative perspective, literature from the Late Bronze Age city of Ugarit will be noted. Like the Hebrew Bible, Ugaritic literature also includes depictions of threshing floors as locations associated with gods and preternatural beings. Most of these discussions are found in the addendum.

This work does not argue that a particular century, region, social group, or literary genre is responsible for the depictions of threshing floors as sacred spaces. Quite the opposite, the sacrality of threshing floors occurs in passages spanning five hundred years (roughly from 900–400 BCE) and various literary genres, including historical narratives, legends, prophetic poetic oracles, and legal texts. The literary genres often agree on demonstrating a divine association with threshing floors, although they do so in diverse ways. For instance, in narrative contexts threshing floors are portrayed as locations for divine appearances, but in prophetic oracles threshing floors are metaphorically described as under Yahwistic control. Both genres show a connection between Yahweh and threshing floors that permeates many of the biblical references, although they articulate that relationship in different ways. Overall, there does not appear to be a diachronic change in the conception of threshing floors. Perhaps the earliest threshing-floor reference is Genesis 50,[43] which depicts mourning rites occurring on threshing floors; and some of the latest narratives in 1 Chronicles 13 and 21 depict divine manifestation and cultic activities on threshing floors, though these narratives are parallels to earlier accounts from 2 Samuel 6 and 24. The earliest prophetic reference in Isaiah uses threshing imagery in connection to divine power, and the latest prophetic reference in Joel asserts Yahwistic control and blessing of threshing floors. Spanning five hundred years, biblical references to threshing floors often portray them in relation to divine control, blessing, or manifestation.

The present study of threshing floors will provide insights into ancient conceptions of space, particularly the fluidity that spaces can possess. The use of threshing floors in the Hebrew Bible shows their transient quality, where these agricultural spaces have the potential to be used as sacred spaces whether because of divine revelation or human choice. The Hebrew Bible highlights their sacred qualities above their agricultural qualities, which does not negate their vital agricultural function, but instead affirms divine interest, control, and blessing of these important spaces. In what follows, several passages

---

43. This depends on how one dates this passage and the J literary strand. For this discussion, see chapter 4.

will be studied carefully and will illuminate Yahweh's close relationship to threshing floors. Chapter 2 will suggest that Yahweh controls the success or failure of threshing floors. Yahweh's influence over these spaces is visible when he curses (Hosea 9:1–2) and blesses (Joel 2:24) them. In addition, if threshing floors are failing or are under attack, Yahweh can intervene to save them (1 Sam. 23:1–5; 2 Kgs. 6:27; Judg. 6:2–14). Yahweh has a vital interest and concern for sustaining Israel and Judah, and controlling the threshing floors is a way in which Yahweh can support their livelihood (and in the event of unacceptable behavior, Yahweh can punish via the threshing floor). Chapter 2 will also explore prophetic passages that depict Yahweh delivering divine judgment using threshing-floor imagery (Isa. 21:10; Mic. 4:12–13; Jer. 51:33). Chapter 3 will explore the Priestly and Deuteronomic legal perspectives on threshing floors. While the legal corpora do not regulate the use of these spaces for cultic activities, threshing floors are associated with divine offerings (Num. 15:17–20; 18:25–29) and divine blessings (Deut. 15:12–15; 16:13–15). An instance of a legal request and divine invocation on a threshing floor will also be discussed (Ruth 3). Chapter 4 will investigate examples of threshing floors being used as sacred spaces, including instances of cultic activity and divine manifestation. Threshing floors are used as effective locations to communicate with Yahweh (Judg. 6:37–40; 1 Kgs. 22:10 // 2 Chron. 18:9; Gen. 50:10–11). Yahweh's connection to threshing floors manifests itself with divine access and presence on these spaces. In addition, threshing floors are locations associated with theophany (2 Sam. 6:6–7 // 1 Chron. 13:9–10; 2 Sam. 24:15–25 // 1 Chron. 21:14–27). Chapter 4 will also discuss sociological implications regarding which people within the society of ancient Israel are depicted using threshing floors as sacred spaces. Chapters 2–4 will show how Yahweh is connected to threshing floors by illuminating and asserting divine control, accessibility, and blessing of these important agricultural spaces. Furthermore, Yahweh's temple is built on a threshing floor (2 Chron. 3:1), the implications of which will be discussed in chapter 5. This study now turns to chapter 2 to explore divine control and use of threshing floors.

2

Divine Control and Use of Threshing Floors

Three words characterize how Yahweh exhibits control over threshing floors: curse, bless, save. The biblical passages that are explored in the first section of this chapter exemplify divine control over threshing floors and highlight the significant interest that Yahweh has in the failure or success of these agricultural spaces. Prophecies from Hosea and Joel especially illuminate what happens when threshing floors are cursed or blessed. Similarly, three passages (1 Sam. 23:1; 2 Kgs. 6:24; Judg. 6:1–11) provide narrative contexts for Yahweh intervening to save threshing floors when they are under attack by foreigners. In the second section of the chapter, the issue of foreigners arises again. Prophetic oracles from Isaiah, Micah, and Jeremiah describe Yahweh condemning enemies using threshing-floor imagery. All of the passages discussed in this chapter have one overarching theme: Yahweh is intimately linked to threshing floors. These spaces, whether under his control or employed as a literary motif, are connected to the divine, the implications of which will be explored throughout this chapter.

Divine Control of Threshing Floors

Power to Curse: Threshing Floors in Hosea

The book of Hosea includes two references to threshing floors, Hosea 9:1–2 and 13:3. These references are within prophetic oracles that exhibit vivid imagery and parallelism. As oracles, the mention of threshing floors helps in imagining the types of activities that took place on these spaces. The oracles may date to the eighth century BCE, as the superscription of the book of Hosea says that he prophesied during the reign of Jeroboam of Israel and the reigns of Uzziah, Jotham, Ahaz, and Hezekiah of Judah (Hosea 1:1). There are also references to the Assyrians as the dominant power, which supports this eighth century BCE date (Hosea 5:13; 8:9; 10:6; 14:3–4). Geographically, Hosea is a northern prophet prophesying in Israel, though the final editor of the book has a Judean perspective. While not narrative prose, this poetry provides details into what might have occurred historically on these spaces, thus providing insights into the imagined and experienced threshing floors. Moreover, in its poetry Hosea 13:3 uses threshing-floor imagery to describe the destruction of Israel, a motif that occurs in other prophetic books that will be discussed at the end of this chapter.[1]

Hosea 9:1–2

In his prophecies, Hosea exhorts Israel for being disobedient and worshiping other gods. Yahweh is presented metaphorically as a faithful husband, and Israel is an adulterous wife who has "cheated"

---

1. For more on history, textual issues, and editing related to the book of Hosea, see Francis I. Andersen and David Noel Freedman, *Hosea: A New Translation with Introduction and Commentary*, AB 24 (Garden City: Doubleday, 1980), 31–77; C. L. Seow, "Hosea," *ABD* 3:291–97; Roman Vielhauer, "Hosea in the Book of the Twelve," in *Perspectives on the Formation of the Book of the Twelve*, ed. R. Albertz, J. Nogalski, and J. Wöhrle (Berlin: De Gruyter, 2012), 55–75.

by performing non-Yahwistic cultic practices. The following passage notes that Israel's unsanctioned actions occur on threshing floors, and for this reason, Yahweh condemns Israel's harvest and has Hosea deliver this message:

> ¹Do not rejoice, O Israel!
> Do not shout in exultation like the nations,
> because you have played the whore away from your God.
> You have loved for a prostitute's pay
> on all threshing floors of grain.
> ²Threshing floor and wine vat will not feed them,
> and the new wine will fail her.

> ¹'al-tiśmaḥ yiśrā'ēl
> 'el-gîl kā'ammîm
> kî zānîtā mē'al 'ĕlōhêkā
> 'āhabtā 'etnān
> 'al kol-gornōt dāgān²
> ²gōren wāyeqeb lō' yir'ēm
> wĕtîrôš yĕkaḥeš bāh (Hosea 9:1–2)³

This passage effectively curses the sustainability of the land and implies famine in Israel. Israel's threshing floors are cursed because she has "played the whore" and departed from God. Although this literally could indicate sexual indecency on threshing floors, this sexualized language is likely a metaphor for Israel's cultic impropriety,[4] especially with the assertion that she is "away from

---

2. The word for grain, *dāgān*, could be a play on the Canaanite deity Dagan who is associated with grain. If this was the case, it would suggest that these threshing floors were dedicated to Dagan worship. This is an interesting possibility, especially since the oracle focuses on punishment for worship of non-Yahwistic gods. However, throughout Hosea, Baal is repeatedly mentioned in connection to non-Yahwistic cultic activities, so the translation of *dāgān* simply as "grain" seems appropriate, leaving open the possibility that he may have been one of several gods worshiped on threshing floors.
3. In this work, I have produced all of the Hebrew, Greek, and Ugaritic translations and transliterations unless otherwise noted.
4. Andersen and Freedman suggest that this could be literal sexual indecency related to cultic activities at harvest celebrations. They cite Ruth 3, Judges 21, and other passages indicating

God."[5] Elsewhere in Hosea, Israel's religious apostasy is emphasized, as Israel has had festivals and offered incense to the Baals (Hosea 2:13), and Israel has "played the whore" and sacrificed on mountaintops and hills (Hosea 4:12–13). Israel's "whoredom" is directly connected to her performing religious activities to gods other than Yahweh, and the locations of her cultic impropriety are various outdoor spaces, including mountains, hills, and in this account, all threshing floors. With this in mind, the assertion that Israel has "loved for a prostitute's pay on threshing floors" aptly refers to "adulterous" non-Yahwistic cultic activities taking place on these spaces.

Cultic activities offered to the Canaanite deity Baal[6] are mentioned in Hosea in connection with the cursing of foodstuffs, so it may be that Israel was worshiping Baal on threshing floors. For instance, Israel is accused of being unfaithful for not acknowledging that Yahweh has given her grain, wine, and oil; instead, she offered gold and silver to Baal, presumably in thanksgiving or petition for more

---

promiscuous activity related to harvest festivities. Andersen and Freedman, *Hosea*, 523. Though Ruth 3 would be a compelling parallel since the narrative takes place on a threshing floor, sexual activity is not explicitly narrated. If sex is implicit, it is for the purpose of Ruth securing a marriage with Boaz, not because of a harvest celebration. Judges 21 does refer to more explicit sex near vineyards, not threshing floors, but the events are not for the purpose of a harvest celebration. Though the sexual events are at harvest time, they are for the Benjaminites to forcibly acquire women who are performing ritualistic dance. The sexualized language in Hosea 9:1 may merely indicate "unfaithful" non-Yahwistic activities on threshing floors. These cultic improprieties may not include sexual activities, but rather are "adulterous" because they are for other gods.

5. The metaphorical understanding of the marriage of Yahweh to Israel has been noted by several scholars. See Susan Ackerman, "The Personal Is Political: Covenantal and Affectionate Love (*'āhēb, 'ahăbâ*) in the Hebrew Bible," *VT* 52 (2002): 437–58; Peggy Day, "Yahweh's Broken Marriages as Metaphoric Vehicle in the Hebrew Bible Prophets," in *Sacred Marriages: The Divine-Human Sexual Metaphor from Sumer to Early Christianity*, ed. M. Nissinen and R. Uro (Winona Lake: Eisenbrauns, 2008), 219–41.

6. For more on the Baal cult in Hosea, see John Day, "Hosea and the Baal Cult," *Prophecy and the Prophets in Ancient Israel: Proceedings of the Oxford Old Testament Seminar* (New York: T&T Clark, 2010): 202–24. For more on Baal, see Hervé Tremblay, "Yahvé contre Baal? Ou plutot Yahvé a la place de Baal? Jalons pour la naissance d'un monothéisme," *Science et Esprit* 61 (2009): 51–71; Dany Nocquet, *Le livret noir de Baal: La polémique contre le dieu Baal dans la Bible hébraïque et l'ancien Israël* (Genève: Labor et Fides, 2004); and Conrad E. L'Heureux, *Rank among the Canaanite Gods: El, Ba'al, and the Rephaim* (Missoula: Scholars Press, 1979).

foodstuffs. Because of these actions, Yahweh withdraws his support, saying that he will take back his grain and wine when they are in season (Hosea 2:8–9). Yahweh calls the grain and wine *his*, indicating his control over these foodstuffs and thus associating himself with both the survival and demise of Israel. Yahweh's complaints and accusations are in response to Israel's failure to realize and acknowledge that her survival was the result of Yahweh's blessings. Instead of giving offerings to Yahweh, Israel gives offerings to Baal. Such offerings were likely happening on the threshing floors mentioned in Hosea 9:1–2.

Because Baal was an agrarian deity, it is likely that he was petitioned for crop yields at threshing floors, an action that greatly angers Yahweh. In Hosea 9:1–2, the activities that happen on threshing floors could be connected to these requests to Baal for a bountiful harvest. These cultic activities might be in the form of food and drink offerings, which are condemned in the following verses (Hosea 9:4, 10). Because Israel's cultic offerings are non-Yahwistic, they are described as ineffective and cursed.

Israel's iniquity results in a curse of the threshing floors and wine vats, and she is told not to rejoice or shout in exultation. Israel's actions have resulted in a lack of bounty at the harvest, so the typically vibrant harvest festivities must now lack joy. As will be seen in the following chapter, language of joy and celebration is often related to the bounty of the harvest, so this directive not to rejoice is apropos and indicates Yahweh's curse of the threshing floors.

As Hosea 9:1–2 suggests cultic activities were occurring on threshing floors, this obviously supports the notion that threshing floors were used as sacred spaces in addition to their agrarian usage. Because these activities are "away from God," they are condemnable and desecrate these spaces. Fittingly, Yahweh curses the threshing floors, which are the locations of Israel's "whoredom." Yahweh is clearly portrayed as exerting total control and power over threshing floors and, by extension, over Israel's survival. By cursing these essential agricultural spaces and the food supply, Yahweh curses Israel, making survival unlikely. Additionally, in the poetry of Hosea 13:3, threshing-floor imagery is used to describe the destruction of Israel, a motif that occurs in other prophetic books discussed at the end of this chapter.

Hosea 13:3

Hosea 13 also references threshing floors in connection to a curse against Israel. The chapter begins by explaining that the northern tribe of Ephraim has died because it incurred guilt from Baal (Hosea 13:1).[7] Those remaining in Israel continue to sin by making cast images in silver, offering human sacrifices, and kissing calves (Hosea 13:2), each of which is condemnable. Making images is associated with the apostasy at Horeb (Exodus 32), although those were gold images instead of silver. Similarly, image making "for themselves" is a prohibited practice (Exod. 20:4, 23; Deut. 4:16). Human sacrifice is a practice attested and condemned in the Hebrew Bible. Here, it is mentioned in a negative light as it is one of the practices that will lead to the demise of Israel.[8] The practice of ritual kissing is not commonplace, although kissing the image of Baal is attested in the Hebrew Bible (1 Kgs. 19:18).[9] Like the activities of Hosea 9:1, all

---

7. Andersen and Freedman suggest that this Baal is short for Baal Peor mentioned in Hosea 9:10 and may refer to an apostasy at this location that caused many deaths (see Numbers 25). Anderson and Freedman, *Hosea*, 630.

8. For recent treatments of human sacrifice and for bibliography on the subject, see Heath Dewrell, "Child Sacrifice in Ancient Israel and Its Opponents" (PhD diss., The Johns Hopkins University, 2012); Francesca Stavrakopoulou, *King Manasseh and Child Sacrifice: Biblical Distortions of Historical Realities* (Berlin: Walter de Gruyter, 2004); Dieter Hoof, *Opfer, Engel, Menschenkind: Studien zum Kindheitsverständnis in Altertum und früher Neuzeit* (Bochum: Winkler, 1999).

9. For more on Baal iconography see Izak Cornelius, *The Iconography of the Canaanite Gods Reshef and Ba'al: Late Bronze and Iron Age I Periods (c 1500–1000 BCE)* (Fribourg: University Press,

of these actions are portrayed as reprehensible and will result in the demise of Israel; it is even possible that these types of activities were occurring on threshing floors, as they are connected to threshing-floor imagery in the following verse. In Hosea 13:3, such indecent activities lead to a curse of Israel:

> Therefore, they will be like the morning mist
> or like the dew that goes away early,
> like chaff that blows away from the threshing floor
> or like smoke from a window.

> *lākēn yihyû kaʿănan-bōqer*
> *wĕkaṭṭal maśkîm hōlēk*
> *kĕmōṣ yĕsōʿēr miggōren*
> *ûkĕʿāšān mēʾărubbâ* (Hosea 13:3)

Figurative language is used here to express the fleetingness and impermanence of Israel and her imminent destruction on account of her cultic apostasy. Positive images are transformed into negative expressions. Morning mist and dew usually evoke positive sentiments because they provide water, which is vital particularly in Israel's arid regions. For instance, in Judges 6 (a text that will be discussed in chapter 4), Gideon collects dew on a fleece, seeking a divine blessing to go to battle. However, the mist and dew in Hosea 13:3 "leave early," which implies that they are not around long enough to be collected and used. Israel is also described as the chaff that blows away from the threshing floor. Chaff is the part of the crop that is useless. In the winnowing process, the chaff is what blows away because it adds no value and obstructs the grain. Finally, the third image of smoke leaving a window is parallel to the chaff, and it too evokes the fleetingness of Israel, though it breaks with the

---

1994); Nick Wyatt, "On Calves and Kings," in his *The Mythic Mind: Essays on Cosmology and Religion in Ugaritic and Old Testament Literature* (London: Equinox, 2005), 72–91. For treatments of the god Ilu's association with bull imagery, see John Day, "Hosea and the Baal Cult," 215–16.

agrarian imagery. Hosea employs this figurative language associated with environmental and agricultural concerns to assert the ephemerality of Israel and her forthcoming destruction because she has not been faithful to Yahweh. Her apostasy has not only cursed her threshing floors but also ultimately led to her destruction.

Hosea, Sacred Space, and Spatial Theory

In Hosea, the references to threshing floors are illustrative of cultic activities occurring on these spaces as well as the power Yahweh exhibits over these spaces. Hosea alludes to illicit cultic activities happening on threshing floors, which shows a clear instance of these agricultural spaces being used as sacred spaces. Keeping in mind Jonathan Z. Smith's focus on rituals in connection with the sacred, the presence of cultic activities on threshing floors is an indication of the sacrality of these spaces. Moreover, their selection for these cultic activities shows a preconceived notion of the sacredness of these spaces. However, because the cultic activities are non-Yahwistic, these threshing floors are cursed. While the exact nature of these rituals is not specified, the book of Hosea provides examples of apostasy, particularly those associated with the agrarian deity Baal (Hosea 2:10; 13:1). These activities include food and drink offerings for an abundant harvest. Likewise, the creation of silver images, offering of human sacrifices, and kissing of calves are also mentioned in conjunction with threshing-floor imagery and may be hints at the cultic activities that happened on these spaces.

Couched in threshing-floor imagery, Israel's cultic actions on threshing floors lead to punishment from Yahweh, demonstrating the power Yahweh exercises over these essential spaces. Hosea provides insights into what Soja calls "imagined" space and "experienced" space. Even though the poetry of Hosea does not narrate cultic actions on threshing floors, it does provide details into how these spaces were visualized and remembered in the book of Hosea. In Hosea, in contrast to positive *gōren* traditions elsewhere in the Hebrew Bible, all of the threshing floors (*kol-gornōt*) of Israel are associated with, remembered, and imagined as locations of inappropriate cultic experiences. They are divinely condemned spaces because of their association with non-Yahwistic rituals.

Power to Bless: Threshing Floors in Joel

As Hosea shows Yahweh's ability to curse threshing floors, the prophet Joel demonstrates Yahweh's power to bless threshing floors. The book of Joel lacks clear historical references, making it difficult to date. Joel is a Judean prophet who may be dated to the fifth–fourth centuries BCE based on allusions to earlier biblical passages and his postexilic orientation. The reference to threshing floors is within prophetic oracles of lament that exhibit vivid imagery and parallelism. The book is composed of oracles that do not narrate activities on threshing floors but demonstrate a divine interest and blessing of these spaces. As the book of Joel is in the lament genre, many of the oracles focus on mourning as an outward sign of remorse and a gesture in hope of a divine response. The poetry of Joel connects threshing floors with wine and oil vats as signs of the harvest.[10]

Joel 2:23-24

The book of Joel begins with striking imagery about the darkness and gloom that will come upon the land when the Day of Yahweh comes.[11] The Day of Yahweh is a large-scale battle between Israel,

---

10. For more on Joel, see Jörg Jeremias, "The Function of the Book of Joel for Reading the Twelve," in *Perspectives on the Formation of the Book of the Twelve*, ed. R. Albertz, J. Nogalski, and J. Wöhrle (Berlin: De Gruyter, 2012), 77–87; Hans Walter Wolff, *Joel and Amos: A Commentary on the Books of the Prophets Joel and Amos*, ed. S. Dean McBride, Hermeneia (Philadelphia: Fortress Press, 1977), 2–15; and James L. Crenshaw, *Joel: A New Translation with Introduction and Commentary*, AB 24c (New York: Doubleday, 1995), 11–54.

Judah, and her enemies. It includes many apocalyptic elements and may envision a battle at the end of days. The land will be full of locusts, fires, dark clouds, earthquakes, fasting, mourning, and fear (Joel 1–2:20). During all of this turmoil, Joel tells Zion not to fear because their animals, pastures, and fruits will survive and thrive because Yahweh will feed them and tend to their needs (Joel 2:21–22). Then, Joel says:

> [23] O sons of Zion, be glad
> and rejoice in the Lord your God,
> for he has given you the early rain in [his] kindness
> and has poured down for you
> the early and the later rain as before.
> [24] The threshing floors will be full of grain
> and vats will overflow with new wine and oil.

> [23] *ûbnê ṣiyyôn gîlû wĕśimḥû*
> *bayhwh 'ĕlōhêkem kî-nātan lākem 'et-hammôreh liṣdāqâ*[12] *wayyôred lākem*
> *gešem môreh ûmalqôš bāri'šôn*
> [24] *ûmālĕ'û haggŏrānôt bār*
> *wĕhēšîqû hayĕqābîm tîrôš wĕyiṣhār* (Joel 2:23–24)

This prophecy focuses on multiple blessings provided by Yahweh, including abundant rain, grain, wine, and oil. In the midst of dire circumstances, Zion is reminded that Yahweh will sustain them throughout this unrest. Yahweh is in complete control of the natural

---

11. The Day of Yahweh has been understood as a large-scale battle between Israel, Judah, and her enemies. It also has many apocalyptic elements and may envision a battle at the end of days. For more on the Day of Yahweh in Joel, see Barbara Schlenke and Peter Weimar, "'Und JHWH eiferte für sein Land und erbarmte sich seines Volkes' (Joel 2,18): Zu Struktur und Komposition von Joel (II)," *BZ* 53 (2009): 212–37; and Shimon Bakon, "The Day of the Lord," *JBQ* 38 (2010): 149–56.

12. *Liṣdāqâ* has been understood in multiple ways. J. Crenshaw suggests translating it as "in its season" based on his interpretation of Ps. 84:7, which also references early rain. Crenshaw, *Joel*, 154–55. H. Wolff translates it as "according to righteousness," which refers to food provided by Yahweh because of his covenantal relationship with Israel. Wolff, *Joel and Amos*, 63. Along with JPS, I translate it as "in [his] kindness," noting that it is Yahweh's generosity and love of Zion that have prompted him to provide the early rain.

elements; furthermore, Yahweh controls the livelihood of Zion. Because Yahweh will sustain Zion with fullness at threshing floors and vats, Zion is commanded to rejoice. Joel directly connects Yahweh to these blessings of agricultural spaces and products.

These blessings from Joel are reminiscent of the curses from Hosea discussed above. Hosea expresses Yahweh's contempt for Israel's activities and describes her forthcoming demise by saying that she is like the dew that leaves early and by cursing her threshing floors and wine vats. Joel's imagery is strikingly similar except that Zion is blessed by Yahweh with abundant rains and full threshing floors and vats. In Joel's prophecy, the rain does not go away early; instead, rain is poured out for Zion. The rains nourish and sustain the land, causing crops to grow that will feed and maintain Zion. Yahweh's blessing of rain is very effective and results in an overflow of threshing floors and vats. The fullness of the threshing floors and vats is because of Yahweh. Because of this divine gift of abundance, Zion is commanded to rejoice. As mentioned above, rejoicing and celebration are closely linked to harvest festivals. Unlike the harvest in Hosea, which is without joy, the harvest in Joel is abundant and joyful on account of these divine blessings.

While Joel does not explicitly narrate ritual activity on threshing floors, much of his prophecies deal with cult, particularly petitions for sustenance from Yahweh, so it is fitting that Yahweh provides blessings at threshing floors and vats. In laments of the dire conditions in the land, Joel proclaims the sadness of farmers and vine keepers because of their withering crops (Joel 1:11–12). Famine will surely afflict the land, as crops are failing and silos are empty (Joel 1:17). These ominous events lead to mourning, prompting Yahweh to respond by once again filling the threshing floors and wine and oil vats (Joel 2:24), thus sustaining the lives of his people. It is conceivable that Zion's petitions for sustenance took place at threshing floors, as

39

these are locations associated with the harvest. In a similar manner, petitionary prayers occur at a threshing floor in Gen. 50:10–11 when Joseph and his group offer prayers and rituals of mourning for Jacob at a threshing floor. The people of Zion could have used threshing floors in a comparable manner as locations for mourning their famine and locations for seeking a blessing of food.

In Joel, the way in which threshing floors are imagined is present in his prophetic oracles. Though much of the book focuses on lament, the threshing floor emerges as a symbol of survival, the place where Zion will be fed and nourished. Yahweh promises food and satisfaction (Joel 2:26), and the threshing floor is associated both with the prayers of petition and the divine response with the blessing of food.

Power to Save: Threshing Floors in 1 Samuel 23:1–5, 2 Kings 6:24–27, and Judges 6:1–16

Hosea and Joel describe Yahweh cursing and blessing the threshing floors, respectively, but Yahweh also exerts his authority to save threshing floors from attacks. In the following three passages, when the Philistines (1 Sam. 23:1), Assyrians (2 Kgs. 6:24–25), and Midianites (Judg. 6:1–5) attack Israel and her food supply, only Yahweh has the power to save these spaces.

The genre of the books of Samuel and Kings is historical narrative composed of stories about kings of Israel and Judah. The books have a complex literary and textual history containing both preexilic and postexilic material and editing, taking their final form in the southern kingdom. The book of Judges contains narratives about premonarchic Israel. The narratives are of a legendary quality and reflect stories before the development of the monarchy described in Samuel and Kings. Many of the stories in Judges are a product of the northern kingdom, originating before its fall to the Assyrians in the eighth century BCE. The three passages discussed in this section are part of the Deuteronomistic History (DtrH: Deuteronomy, Joshua, Judges, 1–2 Samuel, 1–2 Kings).[13] Scholarship on the DtrH is

---

13. The Deuteronomists have been identified as a school, movement, guild, party, or an individual. For more on Dtr and overviews of scholarship on the DtrH, see Linda S. Schearing and Steven L. McKenzie, eds., *Those Elusive Deuteronomists: The Phenomenon of Pan-Deuteronomism* (Sheffield: Sheffield Academic Press, 1999); Thomas Römer, *The So-Called Deuteronomistic History: A Sociological, Historical and Literary Introduction* (London: T&T Clark, 2005); Brian Peckham, *The Composition of the Deuteronomistic History* (Atlanta: Scholars Press, 1985); R. Polzin, *Moses and the Deuteronomist: A Literary Study of the Deuteronomic History* (New York: Seabury, 1980); R. F. Person Jr., *The Deuteronomic School: History, Social Setting, and Literature*, Studies in Biblical Literature 2 (Atlanta: SBL, 2002); Moshe Weinfeld, *Deuteronomy and the Deuteronomic School* (Oxford: Clarendon Press, 1972); and Gary N. Knoppers, "Deuteronomistic History," in *Eerdmans Dictionary of the Bible*, ed. D. N. Freedman (Grand Rapids: Eerdmans, 2000), 341–42.

Martin Noth hypothesized that there was one Deuteronomist who used older sources and compiled the DtrH during the exile. See Martin Noth, *Überlieferungsgeschichtliche Studien* (Tübingen: Max Niemeyer, 1957), 43–266; Noth, *The Deuteronomistic History*, JSOTSup 15 (Sheffield: JSOT Press, 1991) (translation of pp. 1–110 in 2nd ed. of *Überlieferungsgeschichtliche Studien*); and Noth *Überlieferungsgeschichtes des Pentateuch* (Stuttgart: Kohlhammer, 1948), translated by B. W. Anderson as *A History of Pentateuchal Traditions* (Englewood Cliffs: Prentice Hall, 1972).

Since Noth, there have been scholars who follow his original thesis that the DtrH is the work of one person (Dtr), but consider large portions to be later additions. See J. Van Seters, *In Search of History: Historiography in the Ancient World and the Origins of Biblical History* (New Haven: Yale University Press, 1983); and Steven L. McKenzie, *The Trouble with Kings: The Composition of the Books of Kings in the Deuteronomistic History*, VTSup 42 (Leiden: Brill, 1991).

For discussions of the composition and dating of Samuel, see P. Kyle McCarter Jr. *I Samuel: A New Translation with Introduction and Commentary*, AB 8 (Garden City: Doubleday, 1980), 5–44; A. Graeme Auld, *1 & 2 Samuel*, OTL (Louisville: Westminster John Knox Press, 2011), 1–18; Mary J. Evans, *1 & 2 Samuel* (Grand Rapids: Baker Books, 2012), 18–31; Francesca Aran Murphy, *1 Samuel* (Grand Rapids: Brazos Press, 2010), 23–28; Moses Hirsch Segal, "The Composition of the Books of Samuel," *JQR* 55 (1964): 318–39; Rudolf Smend, "Das Gesetz und die Völker: Ein Beitrag zur deuteronomistischen Redaktionsgeschichte," in *Probleme biblischer Theologie: G. von Rad zum 70. Geburtstag*, ed. H. W. Wolff (Munich: Kaiser, 1971), 494–509.

For discussions of the composition and dating of Kings, see McKenzie, *The Trouble with Kings*, 1–18; Michael Avioz, "The Book of Kings in Recent Research (Part I)," *CBR* 4 (2005): 11–55; Terence E. Fretheim, *First and Second Kings* (Louisville: Westminster John Knox Press, 1999), 1–15; Marvin A. Sweeney, *I & II Kings: A Commentary* (Louisville: Westminster John Knox Press, 2007), 1–44; and Donald J. Wiseman, *1 & 2 Kings: An Introduction & Commentary* (Leicester: Inter-Varsity Press, 1993), 15–59.

For more on Judges in the DtrH, see Römer, *The So-Called Deuteronomistic History*, 90–91; Antony F. Campbell and Mark A. O'Brien, *Unfolding the Deuteronomistic History: Origins, Upgrades, Present Text* (Minneapolis: Augsburg Fortress, 2000), 165–214. For commentaries on the book of Judges and for more on the Gideon narratives, see Yairah Amit, *The Book of Judges:*

grounded and influenced by Martin Noth who hypothesized that one person, the Deuteronomist (Dtr), compiled older traditions, composed and redacted the books of Deuteronomy, Joshua, Judges, 1–2 Samuel, 1–2 Kings. Since Noth, there have been many ways of analyzing the DtrH. Some scholars follow Noth's thesis on one Deuteronomist, although most consider large portions of these books to included later additions.[14] There have also been two common ways of reanalyzing the Deuteronomistic material. The double-redaction theory proposed by Frank Moore Cross is particularly compelling. It dates the first version of the DtrH to the seventh century BCE and ties it to King Josiah, with a second redaction in the exilic period.[15] The second theory advocates several authors of the DtrH, beginning in the exilic period followed by later postexilic redactors such as DtrP (prophetic redactor) and DtrN (legal redactor). This theory was proposed by Rudolph Smend and has found support particularly at the University of Göttingen.[16] The passages discussed in this section

---

The Art of Editing, trans. J. Chipman (Leiden: Brill, 1999); Robert G. Boling, *Judges: A New Translation with Introduction and Commentary*, AB 6a (Garden City: Doubleday, 1975); J. A. Soggin, *Judges: A Commentary*, OTL (Philadelphia: Westminster Press, 1981); Daniel I. Block, "Will the Real Gideon Please Stand Up? Narrative Style and Intention in Judges 6–9," *JETS* 40 (1997): 353–66; Isabelle de Castelbajac, "Le cycle de Gédéon ou la condemnation du refus de la royauté." *VT* 57 (2007): 145–61.

14. See Van Seters, *In Search of History*; and McKenzie, *The Trouble with Kings*.
15. See Frank Moore Cross, *Canaanite Myth and Hebrew Epic: Essays in the History of the Religion of Israel* (Cambridge: Harvard University Press, 1973), 274–89. Other scholars associated with the double-redaction hypothesis include Albert de Pury, Thomas Römer, and Jean-Daniel Maachi, eds., *Israel Constructs Its History: Deuteronomistic Historiography in Recent Research* (Sheffield: Sheffield Academic Press, 2000), 35–38; R. D. Nelson, *The Double Redaction of the Deuteronomistic History*, JSOTSup 18 (Sheffield: JSOT Press, 1981); Gary N. Knoppers, *Two Nations under God: The Deuteronomistic History of Solomon and the Dual Monarchies*, 2 vols. (Atlanta: Scholars Press, 1993–94); J. A. Soggin, *Introduction to the Old Testament: From Its Origins to the Closing of the Alexandrian Canon*, rev. ed., trans. J. Bowden, OTL (Philadelphia: Westminster, 1977), 205; H. Weippert, "Das deuteronomistische Geschichtswerk: Sein Ziel und Ende in der neueren Forschung," *ThR* 50 (1985): 213–49; and R. Rendtorff, *Das Alte Testament: Eine Einführung* (Neukirchen-Vluyn: Neukirchener, 1993).
16. For scholars associated with the exilic dating with several redactional layers, see R. Smend, "Das Gesetz und die Völker," 494–509; W. Dietrich, *Prophetie und Geschichte: Eine redaktionsgeschichtliche Untersuchung zum deuteronomistischen Geschichtswerk*, FRLANT 108

as well as a few in chapter 4 are included in the DtrH, though Samuel and Kings contain the clearest evidence of the Dtr hand while Judges has the fewest Dtr passages.

1 Samuel 23:1

In 1 Samuel 19–26, David is on the run from Saul, who seeks to kill him because he is threatened by David, who will rival him and become the new king. While fleeing Saul, David is informed of a Philistine attack on Keilah, a city that has been identified as the ancient site of Tell Qîlā, roughly eight miles northwest of Hebron (cf. Josh. 15:44, where it is also mentioned in Judah).[17] David is told: "The Philistines are fighting against Keilah, and they are plundering[18] the threshing floors'" (*hinnēh pĕlištîm nilḥāmîm biqʿîlâ wĕhēmmâ šōsîm 'et-haggŏrānôt*) (1 Sam. 23:1b). Upon hearing this, David twice inquires of Yahweh whether he should fight the Philistines, and Yahweh twice affirms that he should attack them and free Keilah (1 Sam. 23:2–4). Yahweh assures David that he should attack "because I am about to give the Philistines into your hand" (*kî-'ănî nōtēn 'et-pĕlištîm bĕyādekā*) (1 Sam. 23:4b). Then, David does as Yahweh instructs, defeating the Philistines and freeing the Keilahites (1 Sam. 23:5).

By attacking Keilah's multiple threshing floors, the Philistines are strategically compromising the sustainability of the city. Attacking these essential food spaces can debilitate a city and lead to famine and city collapse. It is paramount for the survival of Keilah that

---

(Göttingen: Vandenhoeck & Ruprecht, 1972); and T. Veijola, *Die ewige Dynastie: David und die Entstehung seiner Dynastie nach der deuteronomistischen Darstellung*, Toimituksia-Suomalaisen Tiedeakatemian, Annales Academiae Scientiarum Fennicae: Sarja-Ser. B 193 (Helsinki: Suomaleinen Tiedeakatemia, 1975).

17. The city may also be attested in the Amarna Letters as "Qilta." See Nadav Na'aman, "David's Sojourn in Keilah in Light of the Amarna Letters," *VT* 60 (2010): 87–97. The site has not been excavated, so at this point it is unknown whether a threshing floor is preserved.

18. The Hebrew participle *šōsîm*, "plundering," is rendered with two Greek present-tense verbs in the Septuagint: *diarpazousin*, "they plunder," and *katapatousin*, "they trample."

these Philistine attacks be halted. Before attacking the Philistines, however, David seeks approval from Yahweh. Consulting Yahweh before going to battle is an established procedure in ancient Israel, as it was believed that divine approval for battle was needed to ensure victory.[19] David appears well aware that divine approval is needed for his battle. He asks Yahweh binary, yes-or-no questions, an accepted practice associated with divination using the Urim and Thummim.[20] The Urim and Thummim are divinatory objects used to answer yes-or-no questions, traditionally handled by priests and held in a priest's breastplate (Exod. 28:30). Elsewhere in the Hebrew Bible, these items are used at the behest of Yahweh. For instance, Yahweh commands Eleazar the priest to use the Urim and Thummim in order to inquire into whether Joshua is to be Moses's successor (Num. 27:21). Aaron receives the Urim and Thummim as part of his ordination ceremony (Exod. 28:30; Lev. 8:8). In 1 Sam. 23:2–5, David appears to use this priestly divination successfully, likely with the help of the priest Abiathar mentioned in 1 Sam. 23:6–12. As the narrative continues, David also uses the ephod (1 Sam. 23:6), which is a linen garment associated with priests and the Urim and Thummim.[21]

---

19. See Susan Niditch, *War in the Hebrew Bible: A Study in the Ethics of Violence* (Oxford: Oxford University Press, 1993), 137–44. In addition to the Hebrew Bible, the eighteenth-century BCE royal archives from Mari (Tell Hariri) document political authorities consulting prophets to confirm divine approval for campaigns. The Mari archives also attest the need to validate prophetic messages to ensure authenticity. See Herbert B. Huffmon, "A Company of Prophets: Mari, Assyria, Israel," in *Prophecy in Its Ancient Near Eastern Context: Mesopotamian, Biblical, and Arabian Perspectives*, ed. M. Nissinen (Atlanta: SBL, 2000), 48–56; and Martti Nissinen, with contributions by C. L. Seow and Robert K. Ritner, *Prophets and Prophecy in the Ancient Near East*, ed. P. Machinist (Atlanta: SBL, 2003), 13–77.

20. For more on the Urim and Thummim, see Cornelis Van Dam, *The Urim and Thummim: A Means of Revelation in Ancient Israel* (Winona Lake: Eisenbrauns, 1997); Victor Hurowitz, "True Light on the Urim and Thummim," *JQR* 88 (1998): 263–74; and Johann Maier, "Urim und Tummim: Recht und Bund in der Spannung zwischen Königtum und Priestertum im alten Israel," *Kairos* (1969): 22–38.

21. The ephod is a linen garment traditionally worn by priests, and it has the breastplate in which the Urim and Thummim are held. For more on the ephod, see Alicia J. Batten, "Clothing and Adornment," *Biblical Theology Bulletin* 40 (2010): 148–59; Karl Elliger, "Ephod und Choschen:

David's inquiry of Yahweh asserts Yahweh's connection to the success or failure of threshing floors. Yahweh holds the power and authority to save these spaces from their Philistine attackers. David is aware of the practice of consulting Yahweh via priestly divination before embarking on war. Likewise, Yahweh not only confirms David's war, but Yahweh also shows great interest in the people of Keilah and their survival by approving the attack on the Philistines. While the events in 1 Sam. 23:1–5 do not physically happen on threshing floors, they demonstrate insights into how these locations were regarded.

1 Samuel 23:1 and Spatial Theory

The reference to threshing floors in 1 Sam. 23:1 gives insights into the conception and use of these spaces, namely, what Lefebvre terms the *mental* and *social* aspects of space. The passage helps to understand how threshing floors were mentally considered and socially experienced. In this agrarian society, threshing floors were known to be locations of food processing and short-term grain storage, yet here they are also mentally thought to be under the auspices of Yahweh. Cognizant of Yahweh's authority over these locations, the future king David along with the priest Abiathar performs priestly divination to garner Yahwistic support. There is a convergence of royal, priestly, and divine power, the result of which is the securing of these principle spaces. Within this larger discussion of threshing floors, 1 Sam. 23:1 is an important instance where threshing floors are noted as being under divine control and where two social actors, David (future king) and Abiathar (priest) work together in order to secure these important locations.

Ein Beitrag zur Entwicklungsgeschichte des hohepriesterlichen Ornats," *VT* 8 (1958): 19–35; and Andreas Scherer, "Das Ephod im alten Israel," *UF* 35 (2003): 589–604.

2 Kings 6:27

In 2 Kgs. 6:24–25, the Syrian king Ben-Hadad and his army lay siege to Samaria.[22] The Aramaean siege leads to severe famine in the city, and the king of Israel[23] confirms that only Yahweh can provide food, a sentiment that shows a mental understanding of Yahweh's role in the survival of his people. When a city is under siege, people who are being attacked defend themselves by assembling fortifications and obstacles to make hand-to-hand combat difficult. While trying to break down these obstacles, the attacker targets fundamental spaces (like threshing floors) in order to force people out and into combat or defeat. Siege is often associated with starvation, thirst, and disease. The problem of starvation is especially pressing during the Aramaean siege of Samaria. This passage focuses largely on the effects of famine on the city of Samaria. As famine plays a key role in the story, it is very fitting and not surprising that threshing floors are mentioned, as they are locations linked with food and survival.

The attack on Samaria's food supply drastically increases the prices of food (2 Kgs. 6:24–25), which are eventually stabilized by Yahweh through a prophetic intermediary (2 Kgs. 7:1–2, 16). Before Yahweh

---

22. There are three kings with the name Ben-Hadad mentioned in the Hebrew Bible: Ben-Hadad I, son of Tabrimmon, son of Hezion who was a contemporary of Kings Asa of Judah and Baasha of Israel (1 Kgs. 15:18–20); Ben-Hadad II who was contemporary with Ahab of Israel (1 Kings 20); and Ben-Hadad III, son of Hazael (2 Kgs. 13:24–25). Since the name Ben-Hadad may be a Syrian throne name used by various kings, Ben-Hadad in this narrative could be a generic way of saying that this is any Aramaean king. Most scholars doubt the historicity of the event but suggest that this is either Ben-Hadad II or III. Most scholars question the historicity of this siege, but if this were an historical event, it may date to the ninth or eighth centuries BCE, and the composition of the narrative may date to the eighth or seventh centuries BCE. For a discussion of the historical circumstances of this siege, see E. Lipiński, *The Aramaeans* (Leuven: Peeters and Departement Oosterse Studies, 2000), 390–97.
23. The unnamed king in this passage may be Jehoram, who reigns over Israel with his capital in Samaria (849–843 BCE). A regnal account of Jehoram precedes this passage, and he is described as doing evil in the eyes of Yahweh (which may be why his name is omitted) (2 Kgs. 3:1–2). E. Lipiński analyzes the political climate in which Aram may have attacked Samaria and suggests the end of the ninth century BCE as a date and Joash as the Israelite king. Lipiński, *The Aramaeans*, 394–97.

intervenes to save the people and their food, they are in extreme desperation, eating food ritually unclean and unfit for human consumption, such as dove's dung, donkey heads, and even humans.[24]

During the attacks, the king walks along the city wall and sees a woman who cries out to him for help (2 Kgs. 6:26). Before hearing why she is crying out, the king responds to her plea saying, "No, let Yahweh help you! From where can I help you? From the threshing floor or from the wine vat?" (*'al-yôšî'ēk yhwh mē'ayin 'ôšî'ēk hămin-haggōren 'ô min-hayyāqeb*) (2 Kgs. 6:27). The king foreshadows the plea of the woman (which involves food) and proposes that the solution can be found with Yahweh at the threshing floor and the wine vat.

The woman then presents her legal dispute related to a deal she made with another woman that the two of them would eat their sons. The complainant gave her son, and she and the other woman ate him. However, the next day, when the other woman was supposed to give her son, she did not provide him to be eaten. Instead, she hid him (2 Kgs. 6:28b–29). Thus this woman is seeking recompense because she was not able to eat the other woman's son. Upon hearing of this horrific situation, the king tears his clothes and exposes sackcloth on his skin, which are both signs of distress and mourning over the atrocious conditions in Samaria. The Hebrew Bible attests several mourning rituals, including the rending of garments, application of sackcloth, weeping, and wearing black garments (Exod. 33:4; Gen. 50:1–4, 10–11; 2 Sam. 14:2; Jer. 14:2).

In this narrative, the king recognizes the distress of the starving woman as being related to a lack of food, and in total mourning and exasperation, he says that she should consult Yahweh. He cannot help her because the threshing floors and wine vats are empty; rather,

---

24. Cannibalism is attested elsewhere in the Hebrew Bible, especially during the dire conditions of a siege (Deut. 28:55–57; Ezek. 5:10; Lam. 2:20; 4:10).

Yahweh fills (or leaves empty) these spaces. Clearly knowledgeable of the famine, the king declares that only Yahweh can intervene and provide nourishment and sustenance.

According to the author, Yahweh's intervention comes in the following chapter as he eliminates the Syrian threat (2 Kgs. 7:6–7) and stabilizes the exorbitant food prices, an action prophesied by Elisha (2 Kgs. 7:1, 16). Likewise, the captain of the king suggests that Yahweh's intervention could come if he made "windows in the heavens" (*'ărūbbôt baššāmayim*), suggesting that Yahweh can provide the rain needed for crop growth (2 Kgs. 7:2, 19). References to windows in the heavens occur elsewhere in the Hebrew Bible to describe impending rain (Gen. 7:11; Mal. 3:10).

The elements of this narrative in 2 Kings 6 once again address some ideas found in the prophetic passages discussed at the beginning of this chapter. Here there is an assertion that empty threshing floors are the result of Yahweh's intervention, just as in Hosea 9. Empty threshing floors are equivalent to the curse of famine. Similarly, multiple solutions are found in 2 Kings 6–7, and again it is Yahweh who holds the cards. Among other things, Yahweh can provide rain (lacking in Hosea 13 but prominent in Joel 2) to fill the threshing floors.

2 Kings 6:27 and Spatial Theory

While crop growth, processing, and preparation take place on a variety of spaces (fields, silos, kitchens), the threshing floors are at the center of the process, and these spaces represent divine blessings of food and typify livelihood after famine. Instead of emphasizing the fields where crops grow, the author equates survival with crops after they are brought to threshing floors, where the grains are harvested. The author of this text likely imagined the solution to the famine would happen with a combination of military and economic support from Yahweh along with the needed rainfall for crop growth. As Yahweh wielded his power over these affairs, the result could surely fill the threshing floors. Using Lefebvre's ideas about mental space, the threshing floor here is conceived of and equated with divine sustenance and survival. Moreover, Lefebvre's theories on social aspects of spaces are also relevant to this passage. The author of the passage shows how threshing floors were experienced as locations of great concern for various social actors. A royal figure, a military captain and troops, a prophet, and an impoverished woman intersect around the lack of food at threshing floors. By demonstrating the important social role of threshing floors for feeding a society, the author simultaneously highlights the necessity of Yahweh in sustaining and blessing his people at these food-processing locations.

Judges 6:1–16

As in the previous two passages, the narrative in Judges 6 also reflects Yahweh's intervention in saving threshing floors from foreign attacks. The stage is set with the indication that "the Israelites did what was evil in the sight of Yahweh, and Yahweh gave them into the hand of Midian for seven years" (*wayyaʿăśû běnê-yiśrāʾēl hāraʿ běʿênê yhwh wayyittěnēm yhwh běyad-midyān šebaʿ šānîm*) (Judg. 6:1). As in Hosea 9:1–2, the Israelites had been worshiping other gods and doing condemnable activities; such outright apostasy is punishable by Yahweh. In Hosea, Yahweh curses the threshing floors and wine vats. In Judg. 6:1–2, Yahweh punishes Israel by sending the Midianites to attack, which is a punishment analogous to what is described in Hosea since the Midianites attack Israel's food supply (Judg. 6:1–2). The Midianites steal seeds, produce, and animals, leaving Israel without food (Judg. 6:3–6). Like the Philistine and Aramaean attacks, the Midianites focus largely on attacking the food supply, effectively causing famine and unrest. Because of these attacks, the Israelites cry out to Yahweh asking for help, and Yahweh responds in a few ways. He sends an unnamed prophet to remind Israel of the relationship she has with Yahweh who brought her out of Egypt. Yahweh also explains that he is punishing Israel because Israel has not listened to his commands and has worshiped other gods (Judg. 6:8–10). Beyond these reminders and explanations, Yahweh also takes action to save Israel by commissioning Gideon to attack the Midianites.

When Gideon is called by an angel of Yahweh to save Israel, he is described as "beating out wheat on the wine press to hide it from the Midianites" (*ḥōbēṭ ḥiṭṭîm baggat lĕhānîs mippĕnê midyān*) (Judg. 6:11b). As should be clear by now, beating wheat would typically be performed at a threshing floor, but because the Midianites are attacking Israel and her food supply at threshing floors, Gideon instead threshes at the wine press in order to protect the crops from robbery. Having taken Israel's pleas into consideration, Yahweh instructs Gideon to deliver Israel from the hand of Midian. Even though Gideon is doubtful, Yahweh assures him that he will be with him to strike down all of the Midianites (Judg. 6:14–16).

As in 1 Sam. 23:2–5, in Judg. 6:11–15 Yahweh asserts his control over threshing floors when they are under siege. When the Philistines attack threshing floors, David uses priestly divination to contact Yahweh to seek approval to attack, and Yahweh grants his approval. When the Midianites attack, the Israelites cry out for help to Yahweh, and Yahweh sends a prophet to condemn their actions and a warrior to defend them. David and Gideon function in similar manners and are instruments used by Yahweh to save threshing floors. Even though Yahweh punishes Israel by causing famine through outside attacks, Yahweh also has a perpetual concern for Israel; and when they are under siege, Yahweh can intervene to save and nourish them.

Summary

The passages examined in this section illustrate Yahweh's fundamental interest in the failure or success of threshing floors. These floors are essential for Israel and Judah's survival and are dependent upon Yahweh to provide bounty and to safeguard them. Yahweh's will and power are clearly exhibited when he curses the threshing floors in Hosea and blesses the threshing floors in Joel. The passages that describe Yahweh intervening to save threshing floors are especially significant. While cities are under siege from foreign nations, Yahweh acts in order to save the threshing floors, thus providing food for his people. When David hopes to save the threshing floors of the city of Keilah from Philistine attacks, he first consults Yahweh to confirm that this attack is divinely approved and will be successful. David realizes Yahwistic concern and control over these spaces. During the Aramaean siege of Samaria, the king of Israel says that the famine that afflicts the city will end only when Yahweh provides blessings at the threshing floors, which Yahweh does in the form of military and economic relief and rainfall to stimulate crop growth. When the Midianites attack, Israel implores Yahweh to save them and their livelihood, and Yahweh does so by commissioning Gideon to attack the Midianites. Due to Yahweh's close control and authority over threshing floors, these spaces are naturally associated with him. In seeking to provide sustenance to his people, Yahweh blesses Israel and Judah at threshing floors so that they may eat and live.

In the next section, Yahweh declares destruction to come upon Israel and Judah's enemies using graphic threshing-floor imagery. The threshing and trampling that occur on threshing floors are metaphorically employed to describe divine judgment of Israel's enemies.

Divine Use of Threshing Floors

The passages discussed above demonstrate the control and power that Yahweh exhibits over threshing floors. Whether cursing, blessing, or saving threshing floors from attack, Yahweh shows a marked interest in these agricultural spaces. This divine affinity toward threshing floors elucidates why these spaces are typically depicted with some kind of divine connection. The following section will discuss how the prophets Isaiah, Micah, and Jeremiah employ language and imagery related to threshing floors to declare divine destruction of foreign nations. In these prophetic references, threshing floors, which are normally associated with life and livelihood, are used metaphorically to describe death and destruction initiated by divine command.

Isaiah 21:10

Based on internal evidence, historical references, and literary style, the book of Isaiah is typically considered the work of several authors dating from the preexilic to postexilic periods. Isaiah 21 fits within the compositions of First Isaiah (Isaiah 1–39). Like Hosea, the superscription to the book of Isaiah says that he prophesied during the reigns of Uzziah, Jotham, Ahaz, and Hezekiah (Isa. 1:1), which suggests that he was active during the eighth century BCE. The book of Isaiah has a complex textual history including various redactional layers.[25]

---

25. For more on issues of dating and the development of Isaiah, see Joseph Blenkinsopp, *Isaiah 1–39: A New Translation with Introduction and Commentary*, AB 19 (New Haven: Yale University Press, 2000), 74–92; Brevard Childs, *Isaiah: A Commentary*, OTL (Louisville: Westminster John Knox Press, 2001), 1–7; John N. Oswalt, *The Book of Isaiah: Chapters 1–39* (Grand Rapids: William B. Eerdmans, 1986), 3–28; and Hans Wildberger, *Isaiah 13–27*, trans. Thomas H. Trapp (Minneapolis: Fortress Press, 1997).

The oracle in Isa. 21:1–10 proclaims the despair of Babylon. Isaiah recounts attacks that fill the land with anguish, horror, and trembling. Yahweh is actively involved in the destruction while other nations physically deliver the assaults. While the wartime language is throughout the oracle, it ends with destruction of the religious objects of Babylon. The images of her gods are shattered on the ground (Isa. 21:9b). After this oracle of doom, Isaiah then calls Babylon "my threshed one, son of my threshing floor" (*mĕdušātî ûben-gornî*) (Isa. 21:10a), which is a bit cryptic but fitting for this context.

What does it mean to be Yahweh's "threshed one" or to be a "son of a threshing floor"? In an agricultural context, this would be a favorable thing for people. "Threshed ones" are crops that are beaten on threshing floors. This process spawns grains, which might be personified as "sons" or "offspring" of a threshing floor. The physical threshing process is what makes these spaces so important for nourishment. The context in Isaiah 21, however, serves a much different purpose. This passage is not concerned about how threshing occurs. Instead, Isaiah employs threshing-floor imagery to vividly depict the destruction of Babylon while also asserting Yahweh's dominance and power over the Babylonians. The destructive threshing language lends itself well to the vision of Babylon being beaten, but the imagery also serves to assert Yahweh's domination. The shattering of the gods of Babylon is not happenstance; instead, it is another important element that solidifies Yahweh's power over these foreigners and their gods.

The MT of Isa. 21:10 includes the reference to threshing and a threshing floor. Most textual witnesses agree with this reading, but there are two variant traditions that do not mention a threshing floor. These are preserved in the Qumran scroll 4QIsa[a] and the Septuagint. Instead of "threshing floor" (*grn*), 4QIsa[a] reads "wall" (*gdr*), a reading that may have arisen due to *dālet/rêš* confusion of the second letter and *nûn/rêš* confusion of the third letter. The Septuagint has a reading that describes Babylon as "those who have been left and those who are in pain" (*hoi kataleleimmenoi kai hoi odynōmenoi*), though there is not a clear mechanism for such a reading. 4QIsa[a] may reflect an orthographic confusion, and the Septuagint may reflect another tradition regarding this passage.

Threshing language is used elsewhere in the book of Isaiah to describe destruction of enemies. In an oracle against the nations, Yahweh is said to make Israel metaphorically like a threshing sledge with sharp teeth, and the nations, poetically called "mountains" and "hills," are destroyed by the threshing tool (Isa. 41:15–16). Isaiah also describes Yahweh carefully destroying enemies in a manner similar to a farmer carefully threshing crops (Isa. 28:27–28). Both passages use threshing imagery to visualize destruction of foreigners while also asserting Yahweh's power.

In Isaiah, the threshing floor is referenced as an easily imagined agricultural visualization. Although threshing is the process that transforms crops into grain to sustain life, this process is by nature a violent activity that involves beating and trampling. The act of threshing lends itself well to express Yahweh's power and destruction of Babylon.

Micah 4:12-13

The book of Micah is contemporaneous with First Isaiah. Its superscription attests that Micah was active during the reigns of Jotham, Ahaz, and Hezekiah (Mic. 1:1), suggesting an eighth-century BCE date. Some scholars have noted later additions and redactional layers that may date to the postexilic period; this seems especially the case in Micah 4, which talks about life after the exile together with an eschatological orientation.[26] The genre is poetic with vivid imagery and parallelism.

Similar to Isaiah, Micah also uses threshing floor imagery to assert destruction of foreigners and to promote Yahwistic power. The focus of Micah 4 is the restoration of Zion after the exile along with the punishment of foreign nations. Zion is commanded to defeat the nations that have previously gathered against her, and the nations are described as being unaware that Yahweh has "gathered them like sheaves to the threshing floor" (*kî qibbĕṣām keʿāmîr gōrnâ*) (Mic. 4:12b). This image calls to mind how crops are bundled, transported, and laid down on a threshing floor to be threshed, either by beating with a stick or flail or by crushing with an animal or sledge. Just as sheaves are brought to the threshing floor for grain to be harvested, now the nations are brought because they are ripe and ready for their "harvest." In Micah's prophecy, however, this "harvest" is an epic battle that will result in Zion's victory over these nations.

After the nations are primed at the threshing floor, Zion is told to arise and thresh them as if she were an animal stomping upon crops. Figuratively, Zion is described having an iron horn and bronze hoofs (Mic. 4:13a). These metallic features symbolize Zion's strength and guarantee her victory. Although Zion threshes the nations, this is at Yahweh's command. Again Yahweh's control and power over the nations are asserted using graphic threshing imagery.

Several scholars have interpreted this to be a battle between Zion and foreign nations at the end of days based on the language and imagery used in this oracle. Reading this eschatologically is

---

26. For more on the historical considerations and dating of Micah, see Francis I. Andersen and David Noel Freedman, *Micah: A New Translation with Introduction and Commentary*, AB 24e (New York: Doubleday, 2000), 3–29; Delbert R. Hillers, *Micah: A Commentary on the Book of the Prophet Micah*, ed. P. D. Hanson and L. R. Fisher, Hermeneia (Philadelphia: Fortress Press, 1984), 1–10; William McKane, *The Book of Micah: Introduction and Commentary* (Edinburgh: T&T Clark, 1998), 1–26; and Hans Walter Wolff, *Micah: A Commentary*, trans. G. Stansell (Minneapolis: Augsburg, 1990), 1–38.

compelling, as Zion is said to devote (ḥrm) the nations' grain and wealth to Yahweh (Mic. 4:13b), and language of ḥrm is typical in a holy war resulting in the annihilation of enemies and the devotion of their goods to Yahweh. Thus the military battle described by Micah is divinely ordained and has a clear religious focus. This epic holy war is depicted using agricultural terminology and as taking place on a threshing floor. A battle at the end of days on a threshing floor may have influenced later traditions regarding apocalyptic battles. For instance, in the apocryphal book 2 Esdras, an oracle alludes to a battle at the end of the world that will occur on a threshing floor (2 Esd. 4:28–32).

In Micah, the destruction of Zion's enemies is intense and uses threshing-floor imagery to describe a military and religious battle initiated at Yahweh's command. The commonplace activity of threshing on a threshing floor has morphed into a graphic and violent metaphor of destruction. These verses show how threshing imagery lends itself to these depictions; moreover, it once again attaches Yahweh to these threshing-floor activities. Here, Yahweh instructs Zion to defeat the nations on a threshing floor, and Zion is characterized as a destructive animal crushing the nations and devoting their wealth to Yahweh.

Jeremiah 51:33

The book of Jeremiah includes a superscription stating that Jeremiah began prophesying during the reign of Josiah (Jer. 1:1), and his prophetic career lasted through to the Babylonian exile. This internal evidence, along with references to the Babylonians as the dominant power, suggests composition during the seventh–sixth centuries BCE.[27] Jeremiah 51 contains several poems and oracles that prophesy destruction that will come upon Babylon, including crumbling walls, wars, and trembling. Like Micah, Jeremiah references a threshing floor in order to describe destruction initiated by Yahweh. Like Isaiah 21, it is Babylon who is on the receiving end of the attacks:

> For thus says Yahweh of Hosts, the God of Israel:
> the daughter of Babylon is like a threshing floor
> at the time when it is trodden;
> yet a little while
> and the time of her harvest will come.

> *kî kōh 'āmar yhwh ṣĕbā'ôt 'ĕlōhê yiśrā'ēl*
> *bat-bābel kĕgōren*
> *'ēt hidrîkâ*
> *'ôd mĕ'aṭ ûbā'â*
> *'ēt-haqqāṣîr lâ* (Jer. 51:33)

In this passage, Babylon is labeled "as a threshing floor at the time when it is trodden" (*kĕgōren 'ēt hidrîkâ*) (Jer. 51:33a). Describing a city as a trodden threshing floor calls to mind the image of how these floors are created. The earth is trampled, smashed down, and nearly destroyed until a hard floor is formed. Pounding down the earth is necessary to create the stage for threshing. Another time in which a threshing floor is trodden is when threshing is performed by animals. Animals tread upon the crops in order to separate the seeds from the stalks (as referenced in Mic. 4:12 discussed above). This imagery allows the audience to visualize this space and activity, and by analogy visualize the destruction that will befall Babylon.

Jeremiah is visibly prophesying the destruction of Babylon, yet he ends the statement by saying the time of Babylon's harvest will

---

27. Jack Lundbom gives a specific date for this oracle as prior to 594 BCE. Jack Lundbom, *Jeremiah 37–52*, AB 21c (New Haven: Yale University Press, 2004), 469. For more on the complex composition and formation of the book of Jeremiah, see Robert P. Carroll, *Jeremiah: A Commentary* (Philadelphia: The Westminster Press, 1986), 33–88; Jack Lundbom, *Jeremiah 1–20*, AB 21a (New Haven: Yale University Press, 1999), 55–105; and William Lee Holladay, *Jeremiah 1: A Commentary on the Book of the Prophet Jeremiah, Chapters 1–25*, ed. P. D. Hanson, Hermeneia (Philadelphia: Fortress Press, 1986), 1–10.

come (Jer. 51:33b). Since what follows continues to prophesy the annihilation of Babylon, the harvest is unlikely to be a positive omen. Instead, judgment of Babylon is described as a harvest. Babylon's "harvest" will be the time when she is ripe and ready for her forthcoming destruction. Jeremiah then articulates Yahweh's power and control over Babylon's doom by using language related to threshing floors.

Summary

The prophets Isaiah, Micah, and Jeremiah depict Yahweh delivering divine judgment and destruction to foreigners using language relating to threshing floors. By ordering the threshing of nations, Yahweh shows his complete support and devotion to Israel and Judah. By nature, threshing is an intense activity of beating, and yet the destructive process is essential for life. The intense beating that happens at threshing floors allows for and promotes life. Poignantly, the prophets use this vocabulary to provide a graphic visual of destruction, yet the destruction of foreigners allows for the perpetuation of Israel and Judah. For these prophets, the focus is not merely the devastation; but it is also the central role of Yahweh in the process. The threshing motif becomes a way in which to highlight Yahweh's fundamental salvific role in the lives of his people. The language physically represents destruction but spiritually represents divine intercession. Just as destroying crops allows for grains to be harvested to support life, so the destruction of enemies also supports the lives of the people of Israel and Judah. Both of these actions, the processing of crops for food and the destruction of foreigners, are made possible by the actions of Yahweh and allow Israel and Judah to thrive. Once again the biblical authors clearly articulate a connection between threshing floors and Yahweh, as the language of threshing floors allows the prophets to express divine power.

3

Threshing Floors in Legal Contexts

As this study of threshing floors progresses, it should be becoming clear that there is a divine association with threshing floors that is asserted in a variety of texts and in a variety of ways. In the previous chapter, prophetic oracles showed divine control over the failure or success of threshing floors. Prophetic oracles also imagine and articulate divine judgment of foreigners using threshing-floor imagery. Historical narratives revealed divine interest in saving threshing floors from foreign attacks. This belief in a divine link to threshing floors is what makes them logical choices for cultic activity, a phenomenon that will be addressed in the next chapter. One might expect that if threshing floors are considered sacred spaces, they might be regulated in biblical legal texts since that is the locus for cultic guidelines. This is not the case, which is probably because threshing floors are openly accessible to everyone. It would be difficult, if not impossible, to regulate such public space. There are a few references to threshing floors in the legal corpora of the Hebrew Bible, and they highlight an awareness of divine associations to these agricultural spaces. Two Priestly laws (Num. 15:20; 18:27) and two Deuteronomic laws (Deut. 15:14–15; 16:13–15) emphasize links between threshing floors, divine offerings, and divine blessings. These passages will be examined in the first section of this chapter. The second section will consider divine invocations that occur on a threshing floor when a legal request is made in Ruth 3. The use of the threshing floor in Ruth 3 may be happenstance; nevertheless, there is still a divine element.

Laws Concerning Threshing Floors

Numbers 15:17–20

Though there is some scholarly debate about the date, the book of Numbers is a part of Priestly legal material (P) that likely reached its final form in the postexilic period.[1] The Priestly laws include two references to threshing floors, Num. 15:20 and 18:27, laws that are about offerings made to Yahweh. The law stipulated in Num. 15:17–21 is future oriented and takes effect when the Israelites enter the land (Num. 15:18). It requires that: "When you eat the bread of the land, you must offer a *tĕrûmâ* offering[2] to Yahweh. The first

---

1. For scholars who support a preexilic dating, see Yehezkel Kaufmann, *The Religion of Israel: From Its Beginnings to the Babylonian Exile*, trans. M. Greenberg (Chicago: University of Chicago Press, 1960); Avi Hurvitz, *A Linguistic Study of the Relationship between the Priestly Source and the Book of Ezekiel* (Paris: Gabalda, 1982); Menahem Haran, "Behind the Scenes of History: Determining the Date of the Priestly Source," *JBL* 100 (1981): 321–33; Haran, "Ezekiel, P, and the Priestly School," *VT* 58 (2008): 211–18; Jacob Milgrom, *Leviticus 1–16*, AB 3 (New York: Doubleday, 1991), 3–35. For scholars who date P to the exilic or postexilic period, see Joseph Blenkinsopp, "An Assessment of the Alleged Pre-Exilic Date of the Priestly Material in the Pentateuch," *ZAW* 108 (1996): 495–518; Jacob Milgrom, "The Antiquity of the Priestly Source: A Reply to Joseph Blenkinsopp," *ZAW* 111 (1999): 10–22; Frank M. Cross, *Canaanite Myth and Hebrew Epic: Essays in the History of the Religion of Israel* (Cambridge: Harvard University Press), 1973, 291–325; Ludwig Schmidt, *Studien zur Priesterschrift* (Berlin: de Gruyter, 1993), 259; Sarah Shectman and Joel S. Baden, eds., *The Strata of the Priestly Writings: Contemporary Debate and Future Directions*, ATANT 95 (Zurich: Theologischer Verlag, 2009); and Erhard Blum, *Studien zur Komposition des Pentateuch* (Berlin: de Gruyter, 1990), 304–6.

of your dough you will offer as an offering. Like an offering from a threshing floor, so you will offer it" (*wĕhāyâ ba'ăkālkem millehem hā'āreṣ tārîmû tĕrûmâ layhwh. rē'šît 'ărisōtēkem ḥallâ tārîmû tĕrûmâ kitrûmat gōren kēn tārîmû 'ōtāh*) (Num. 15:19–20). This offering is to be performed throughout the generations (Num. 15:21).

This dough offering is to happen when the Israelites eat "the bread of the land" (*leḥem hā'āreṣ*) (Num. 15:19) and is a reminder that Yahweh is bringing Israel to a place that is viable and productive. Because of the sustainability of the land to produce bread, Israel must offer the first of its dough in acknowledgment and thanksgiving for Yahweh's blessing of food.

The exact meaning of *'ărisōtēkem ḥallâ*[3] is complicated and uncertain. Here (and most often) it is translated as "your dough," though it might literally mean "your (unprocessed) grain as a loaf" or "your grain loaf." The difficulty is how to understand unprocessed grain in loaf form since "loaf" implies that it has been processed in some manner. "Dough" may be a close approximation; likewise, this

---

2. *Tĕrûmâ* is a substantive noun which may derive from either the root *rwm* (to lift up, to offer) or *rym* (to present, to give). They may be related biforms of the same root. Typically it is translated "offering, gift, or heave offering."

3. Scholarship is divided on the meaning and etymology of *'rs*. Akkadian *arsanu/arzanu* are a type of groats or grains related to barley (*CAD* A 2:306–7) and *'ărisōtēkem ḥallâ* may be barley loaves. With the Akkadian meaning "groats" in mind, Alan Millard suggests that *'ărisōt* may be "threshed wheat" at the stage before grinding or mixing. Alan Millard, "Two Lexical Explorations," in *The Perfumes of Seven Tamarisks: Studies in Honour of Wilfred G. E. Watson* (eds. G. del Olmo Lete, J. Vidal, and N. Wyatt; Münster: Ugarit-Verlag, 2012), 231–32. Baruch Levine suggests that this law refers to dough that is removed from vessels before baking, based on the meaning of *'arisâ*, which in rabbinic Hebrew means "cradle, bed." Baruch Levine, *Numbers 1–20*, AB 4a (New York: Doubleday, 1993), 394.

Millard's interpretation of *'ărisōtēkem* as "threshed wheat" or "threshed barley" is helpful in translating, but it does not take into account *ḥallâ* (bread, loaf), which directly follows it. With this in mind, I translate *'ărisōtēkem ḥallâ* as "your dough," although literally this may mean "your (unprocessed) grain as a loaf" or "your grain loaf." The difficulty is how to understand an unprocessed grain in loaf form, since "loaf" implies that it has been processed in some manner. I think my translation "dough" may be a close approximation to what this loaf is; likewise, this translation finds support with the Septuagint reading "first dough as a loaf" (*aparchēn phyramatos hymōn arton*) (LXX Num 15:20).

translation finds support with the Septuagint reading "first dough as a loaf" (*aparchēn phyramatos hymōn arton*) (LXX Num. 15:20).

The dough offering is described as being "like an offering from a threshing floor" (*kitrûmat gōren*), which may be a way of stating that this offering is equivalent to grain offerings that come from a threshing floor. Such grain offerings and laws are mentioned elsewhere in Leviticus and Numbers (Lev. 2:1–16; 6:14–18; 7:9–10; 10:12–13; Numbers 28–29). Stating that the dough offering is *like* an offering from a threshing floor implies that it is *not* grain per se, which would *be* an offering from a threshing floor. Instead, this offering is similar to and has the same credence as any grain offering.

Numbers 15:17–21 is often compared to Ezek. 44:30 and Neh. 10:38, which are other so-called dough laws. However, the law in Numbers 15 appears to be the only reference to a true dough law, as it contains the phrase *'ărisōtēkem ḥallâ*, "your dough." Ezekiel and Nehemiah lack the word *ḥallâ* (bread, loaf) and only have the reference to *'ărisōtēkem* (your grain). Likewise, the Septuagint readings also understand these three laws to be different, with the law in Numbers being the only dough law. Mentioned above, the Septuagint reading of Num. 15:20 renders *rē'šît 'ărisōtēkem ḥallâ* as "first dough as a loaf" (*aparchēn phyramatos hymōn arton*). However, the Septuagint reading of Neh. 10:38 renders *'ărisōtēkem* as *sitōn*, "grain," and *'ărisōtēkem* as *prōtogenēmata*, "first fruits," in Ezek. 44:30. Similarly, the laws in Nehemiah and Ezekiel do not say that the *'ărisōtēkem* is like an offering from a threshing floor. This is because grain offerings, such as the ones mentioned in Nehemiah and Ezekiel, are actually *from* the threshing floor, so it would be redundant to say that they are *like* offerings from the threshing floor. Therefore, the dough law in Numbers is unique and should be considered separate from the grain laws of Nehemiah and Ezekiel.

Numbers 18:25-29

The law in Num. 18:25–32 includes a reference to a threshing floor in a similar fashion as the dough law. This law requires Levitical priests to offer a portion of what they receive to Yahweh. The Levites are mandated to give one-tenth of their offerings to Yahweh, namely "a tithe from the tithe" (*ma'ăśēr min-hamma'ăśēr*). The Levitical tithe is equivalent to an offering from the threshing floor or wine vat: "Your offering will be counted like grain from the threshing floor and like the fullness from the wine vat" (*wěneḥšab lākem těrûmatkem kaddāgān min-haggōren wěkamlē'â min-hayyāqeb*) (Num. 18:27). The law continues to state that the Levitical offering is "counted like produce from the threshing floor and produce from the wine vat" (*wěneḥšab lalěwîyyim kitbû'at gōren wěkitbû'at yāqeb*) (Num. 18:30b). Like the first dough, the Levitical offerings carry the same weight and are accepted as standard offerings. Since Levitical offerings could include a variety of items (animals, grain, wine, fruits, oil, etc.), the assertion that they are *like* grain offerings suggests that they are not actually grain but have the same impact.

The laws of Num. 15:17–21 and 18:27–32 provide useful insights into Yahweh's connection to threshing floors. The overall intention of these two laws is to show the importance of being thankful for Yahweh's blessings of food, blessings that are visible in the activities and outcomes that happen on threshing floors. The laws reflect an understanding that the crops that are processed on threshing floors and yield food exist because of Yahweh's actions—Yahweh shows concern for Israel's survival by providing food. As a sign of recognition and gratitude, Israel is commanded to reciprocate with offerings that are like offerings of the threshing floor.

Deuteronomy 15:12–15

Like the books of Judges, Samuel, and Kings discussed in the previous chapter, Deuteronomy is also considered part of the DtrH, which has a complex development that likely reached its final form in the exilic period.[4] The book of Deuteronomy also includes two references to threshing floors, Deut. 15:14–15 and 16:13–15. Like the references in the Priestly laws, these Deuteronomic laws are also concerned about expressing Yahweh's blessings upon Israel.

The law in Deut. 15:12–15 stipulates that male and female Hebrew servants could only be indentured for six years. In the seventh year, Hebrew servants must be released, and they are not to leave empty-handed (Deut. 15:12–13). On the contrary, the Israelites are commanded to:

> [14]Provide liberally to him from your flocks, your threshing floor, and your wine vat, as Yahweh your God has blessed you, so you will give to him. [15]Remember that you were slaves in the land of Egypt, and Yahweh your God redeemed you. Therefore, I am commanding you this word today.

> [14]haʿănêq taʿănîq lô miṣṣōʾnĕkā ûmiggornĕkā ûmîyiqbekā ʾăšer bērakĕkā yhwh ʾĕlōhêkā titten-lô. [15]wĕzākartā kî ʿebed hāyîtā bĕʾereṣ miṣrayim wayyipdĕkā yhwh ʾĕlōhêkā ʿal-kēn ʾānōkî mĕṣawwĕkā ʾet-haddābār hazzeh hayyôm. (Deut. 15:14–15)

This Deuteronomic law limits the amount of time a Hebrew could be indentured, and it requires the owner to be generous when the servant leaves. The threshing floor is mentioned as part of the mandate to provide food to released slaves. The law is not focused on activities on threshing floors but connects these spaces to food and

---

4. For more on the Deuteronomists and the DtrH, see chapter 2. For a recent treatment on Deuteronomy's location in the canon, see Konrad Schmid and Raymond F. Person Jr., eds. *Deuteronomy in the Pentateuch, Hexateuch, and the Deuteronomistic History*, FAT 2/56 (Tübingen: Mohr Siebeck, 2012).

blessings from Yahweh. Generosity is mandated because Yahweh has been generous to Israel. While the Priestly law in Num. 15:17–21 mandates a reciprocal offering given to Yahweh because of the gifts he provides, the law in Deut. 15:14–15 is a law to imitate Yahweh. The importance of sharing Yahweh's blessings as he has shared them with Israel is especially highlighted.

Other manumission laws are attested in Exod. 21:1–6 and Lev. 25:39–41. In the Exodus version (part of the Covenant Code), the law stipulates that male Hebrew servants are to be released after six years (female Hebrew servants are not mentioned). The Leviticus law states that Israelites are not to be slaves. However, if they become poor and sell themselves, they are to be released in the jubilee year, which is every fiftieth year (Lev. 25:10, 39–41). Neither Exodus 21 nor Leviticus 25 requires the owner to provide for the servants when they leave, so there is not a mention of a threshing floor in either law. The Deuteronomic law is unique in its content because it requires the gift of animals, grain, and wine. By reminding the Israelites of their time in captivity, this law mandates the Israelites to be kind to their servants.[5]

---

5. Scholars have suggested various relationships, nonrelationships, and dependencies for these laws. For more on the dating, authorship, and connections between these texts, see Sara Japhet, "The Relationship between the Legal Corpora in the Pentateuch in Light of Manumission Laws," *Studies in Bible, 1986*, ed. S. Japhet, ScrHier 31 (Jerusalem: Magnes, 1986), 68–78; Bernard M. Levinson, *Deuteronomy and the Hermeneutics of Legal Innovation* (New York: Oxford University Press, 1997), 83–84; N. P. Lemche, "The Manumission of Slaves—The Fallow Year—The Sabbatical Year—The Jobel Year," *VT* 26 (1976): 38–59; Mark Leuchter, "The Manumission Laws in Leviticus and Deuteronomy: The Jeremiah Connection," *JBL* 127 (2008): 635–53; Raymond Westbrook, "What Is the Covenant Code?" in *Theory and Method in Biblical and Cuneiform Law*, ed. B. Levinson, JSOTSup 181 (Sheffield: Sheffield Academic Press: 1994), 13–34; Heath D. Dewrell, "Child Sacrifice in Ancient Israel and its Opponents (PhD diss., The Johns Hopkins University, 2012), 133–48; Christophe Nihan, "The Holiness Code between D and P: Some Comments on the Function and Significance of Leviticus 17–26 in the Composition of the Torah," in *Das Deuteronomium zwischen Pentateuch und deuteronomistischem Geschichtswerk*, ed. E. Otto and R. Achenbach, FRLANT 206 (Göttingen: Vandenhoeck & Ruprecht 2004), 81–122; John Sietze Bergsma, *The Jubilee from Leviticus to Qumran: A History of Interpretation*, VTSup 115 (Leiden: Brill, 2007), 40, 143–47; and Jeffrey Stackert, "Rewriting the

Deuteronomy 16:13–15

Deuteronomy 16:13–15 mandates the celebration of the Feast of Booths (Sukkot) "when you have gathered [produce] from your threshing floor and your wine vat. Rejoice during your festival" (*bĕ'ospĕkā miggornĕkā ûmīyyiqbekā wĕśāmaḥtā bĕḥaggekā*) (Deut. 16:13b–14a). The entire community, including children, servants, Levites, foreigners, orphans, and widows are to be joyful during this festival because of the produce from the threshing floor and wine vat (Deut. 16:14b). This joyful festival is commanded for the following reason:

> Seven days you shall celebrate the pilgrimage festival to Yahweh your God at the place that Yahweh will choose because Yahweh your God will bless all your produce and all the work of your hands, and you will indeed be rejoicing.
>
> *šib'at yāmîm tāḥōg layhwh 'ĕlōhêkā bammāqôm 'ăšer-yibḥar yhwh kî yĕbārekĕkā yhwh 'ĕlōhêkā bĕkōl tĕbû'ātĕkā ûbĕkōl ma'ăśēh yādĕkā wĕhāyîtā 'ak śāmēaḥ.* (Deut. 16:15)

This law emphasizes the importance of gathering crops at harvest and the joy and blessings associated with these acts. Unlike the laws discussed above, which involve reciprocity (Num. 15:17–21) or imitation (Deut. 15:13–15), this law is purely celebratory due to Yahweh's blessings.

In Deut. 16:13–15, Yahweh is said to bless the produce from threshing floors and wine vats as well as the work of hands, that is, the labor associated with these spaces. Intriguingly, the author of this law does not state that the agricultural spaces themselves are blessed. One may infer that the threshing floors and wine vats are blessed by

Torah: Literary Revision in Deuteronomy and the Holiness Legislation" (PhD diss., Brandeis University, 2006), 149–219.

default because of their association with these activities, but this is not explicit.

The vibrant, community-wide, seven-day harvest celebration is to happen at Yahweh's "chosen place," which is a requirement found throughout the book of Deuteronomy. As Rannfrid Thelle notes, "the command to bring all sacrifices to, and celebrate feasts at, the 'chosen place' is a distinctive feature of Deuteronomy."[6] Centralization of cultic activities and festivals at a "chosen place" characterizes much of the Deuteronomic program.[7] Consequently, condemning other locations of worship is also important. For example, Deuteronomy 12 condemns places associated with foreign nations—namely, atop mountains and hills and under leafy trees. Moreover, Israel is commanded to break down foreign altars, smash pillars, burn sacred poles, tear down idols, and remove foreign names from these places (Deut. 12:2–3). In addition to foreign-worship locations, other Israelite sanctuaries were also against the Deuteronomic program of centralization. Threshing floors are not mentioned in this list of banned locations, perhaps because they are not associated with foreign worship.

The language of joy occurs throughout Deuteronomy as a rhetorical motif to promote the abandonment of other cult sites; joy is emphasized as an emotion that is experienced at the central sanctuary. Even though local cultic centers are no longer permissible, people are instructed to rejoice that they have a new central location to convene and worship. Bernard Levinson convincingly notes that the joy language in several of Deuteronomy's passages is intentional to promote the abandonment of other cult sites. "Deuteronomy's repeated emphasis on the 'joy' to be experienced at the central

---

6. Rannfrid I. Thelle, *Approaches to the "Chosen Place": Accessing a Biblical Concept* (New York: T&T Clark, 2012), 2.
7. Deut 12:5, 11, 14, 18, 21, 26; 14:23–25; 15:20; 16:2, 6, 7, 11, 15, 16; 17:8, 10; 18:6; 26:2; 31:11.

sanctuary might well represent an attempt to provide compensation for the loss of the local cultic sites, where the people would more conventionally have gained access to the deity."[8] Interestingly, Hosea 9:1–2 is in harmony with this Deuteronomistic sentiment when Israel is told *not* to rejoice because of her use of threshing floors for unsanctioned cultic acts.

While the law of Deut. 16:13–15 mandates the joyous festival to take place at the chosen place, the implication is that the festival should *not* take place anywhere else, including the threshing floors and wine vats that are the sites of the harvest. As threshing floors and wine vats are especially fitting locations for a harvest festival, the location may be omitted intentionally from the blessing so as not to suggest their possible use for the celebration.

The two Deuteronomic laws discussed above are full of insights into the conception of threshing floors. Like the author of the Priestly laws, these Deuteronomic laws do not regulate threshing floors. Instead, these laws assert the connection between threshing floors and blessings of food from Yahweh. This notion is very helpful in understanding why threshing floors are so closely connected to Yahweh and why they can be used for cultic activities. Beyond this, Deut. 16:13–15 may hint at why Dtr does not say more about threshing floors. Although the produce and work on threshing floors (and in wine vats) are blessed, the lack of blessing of the agricultural spaces themselves may be meaningful, an idea that will be explored in chapter 5. The Deuteronomist may have considered these locations as potential rivals and threats to centralization, so he shrewdly downplays the locations in order to highlight Yahweh's chosen place.

---

8. Levinson, *Deuteronomy and the Hermeneutics of Legal Innovation*, 4–5.

Summary

The references to threshing floors in the legal texts of Numbers and Deuteronomy emphasize the connections between threshing floors and Yahwistic blessings of food. The laws in Numbers mandate that the Israelites and the Levites provide offerings to Yahweh in acknowledgment and thanksgiving for their blessings of food. The Deuteronomic references to threshing floors require the Israelites to share their wealth and revel in their divine blessings provided at threshing floors. While there are only a few references in the legal corpora, they are very helpful in understanding the logic behind the idea of Yahweh's relationship to threshing floors. Yahweh is essentially linked to the produce and activities that happen on threshing floors, and he blesses them, allowing for Israel's survival. The life-sustaining work and food of the threshing floors are blessed, and threshing floors are then locations associated with divine blessings. Rather than strictly regulate the use of these spaces, P and Dtr instead bring the Yahwistic offerings and blessings to the forefront in their threshing-floor references. Beyond these four laws, a threshing floor is also the location for a legal request in the book of Ruth.

Legal Request on a Threshing Floor

The book of Ruth identifies itself as set during the period of the judges before the monarchical period (Ruth 1:1). Composed of four chapters, this is a short prose story that uses poetic and legal language to address a variety of issues of family, legal obligations, and interactions with foreigners. Scholars have proposed dating the composition of the book as early as the mid-tenth century BCE and as late as the Hellenistic period. More convincingly, some scholars note both early and late elements in Ruth and suggest that the book may have originated in an early period, but its editing and embellishments reflect a later date.[9]

Agrarian life is of central importance in the book of Ruth, so it is fitting that an important event occurs on a threshing floor. The background of the narrative is that a Judahite family from Bethlehem migrates to Moab because of a famine in their land. While there, the two sons marry Moabite women. However, the sons along with their father die, leaving three widows—Ruth, Naomi her mother-in-law, and Orpah her sister-in-law. After the deaths of her sons, Naomi encourages her daughters-in-law to return to their families. Orpah leaves, but Ruth stays with Naomi and the two return to Bethlehem since the famine is over (Ruth 1:8–19). Living in Bethlehem, Ruth gleans leftover crops from a field belonging to a man named Boaz who is a relative of Naomi. Boaz encourages Ruth to glean only on his property because he knows she is supporting Naomi (Ruth 2:1–23).

Ruth 3

At Naomi's behest, the relationship between Ruth and Boaz advances to a more intimate level in Ruth 3. With the knowledge that Boaz

---

9. Scholars who propose a preexilic date note literary similarities between Ruth and J and E in the book of Genesis. There also seems to be an acknowledgment of the monarchy and the tradition of Ruth as David's ancestor (Ruth 4:17). See Edward F. Campbell Jr., *Ruth: A New Translation with Introduction, Notes, and Commentary*, AB 7 (Garden City: Doubleday, 1975), 24–28; and O. Loretz, "The Theme of the Ruth Story," *CBQ* 22 (1960): 391–99. Scholars who propose an exilic or later date cite Aramaisms, syntactical changes, Babylonian influences, and themes of marriage with foreigners. See R. Gordis, "Love, Marriage, and Business in the Book of Ruth," in *A Light unto My Path: Old Testament Studies in Honor of Jacob M. Myers*, ed. H. N. Bream, D. Heim, and A. Carey (Philadelphia: Temple University Press, 1974), 243–46. For scholars who observe both early and late elements in Ruth, see G. S. Glanzman, "The Origin and Date of the Book of Ruth," *CBQ* 21 (1959): 201–7; Jack M. Sasson, *Ruth: A New Translation with a Philological Commentary and a Formalist-Folklorist Interpretation* (Baltimore: The Johns Hopkins University Press, 1979). For a brief discussion of the various scholarly opinions, see Alice Laffey, "Ruth," in *The New Jerome Biblical Commentary* (Englewood Cliffs: Prentice Hall, 1990), 553–57.

has been kind and loyal to Ruth, Naomi instructs Ruth to seek security—namely, social, financial, and legal protection—from Boaz because Ruth is a widow and Boaz is her kin. Naomi tells Ruth to prepare herself physically by cleansing and wearing her best clothing in order to request security from Boaz at the threshing floor.

As Ruth readies herself, Boaz is winnowing barley at night (Ruth 3:2). This indication of winnowing at the threshing floor is one of only two biblical references to agricultural activity happening on a threshing floor (see chapter 4 for a discussion of 1 Chron. 21:20). Winnowing is the process of tossing or waving crops in the air to separate the grain from the chaff. Wind is an important element of winnowing and allows the chaff to be blown away and the grain to be released and fall to the ground. Very likely, Boaz winnows his barley at nighttime because there tends to be more wind at this time of day.

Boaz eats and drinks on the threshing floor and then falls asleep at the bottom of his grain heap. He may have planned to stay the night in order to protect the grain that had been winnowed and then transport it elsewhere the next day. While Boaz sleeps, Ruth uncovers his feet and lies down next to him.

Boaz awakens at midnight to find Ruth on the threshing floor with him; startled, he asks for her identity. She states her name and says that she is his servant and then makes her legal request: "Spread your garment over your servant, for you are a kinsman redeemer" (ûpāraśtā kĕnāpekā ʿal-ʾămātĕkā kî gōʾēl ʾāttâ) (Ruth 3:9b). A request to "spread the garment" is typically related to legal protection and responsibility through marriage; it may be akin to a marriage proposal. Similar language is found in the book of Ezekiel. When metaphorically describing Jerusalem as a faithless bride, Yahweh says that when Jerusalem was of the age for love, Yahweh spread his garment over her and covered her nakedness. Yahweh pledged himself and entered into a covenant with Jerusalem whereby Jerusalem then belonged to Yahweh (Ezek. 16:8). Jerusalem is described as bathing, washing, and anointing herself (Ezek. 16:8–9), which is also what Ruth does before going to the threshing floor (Ruth 3:3).

Essentially, Ruth seeks social and financial security along with familial loyalty, especially because she is a foreigner and a widow with minimal rights. Ruth's request is for marriage and inclusion in the Judahite community. In response to the request, Boaz invokes the divine name and asserts that Ruth is blessed by Yahweh:

> [10]Blessed are you by Yahweh, my daughter. You have shown more loyalty in the last instance than the first not going after young men, whether poor or rich. [11]And now, my daughter, do not be afraid. All that you say I will do for you because all the assembly of my people know that you are a worthy woman.

> [10]bĕrûkâ 'att layhwh bittî hêṭabt ḥasdēk hā'aḥărôn min-hāri'šôn lĕbiltî-leket 'aḥărê habbaḥûrîm 'im-dal wĕ'im-'āšîr. [11]wĕ'attâ bittî 'al-tîr'î kōl 'ăšer-tō'mĕrî 'e'ĕšeh-lāk kî yôdēa' kol-ša'ar 'ammî kî 'ēšet ḥayil 'ātt. (Ruth 3:10–11)

In declaring that Yahweh blesses Ruth, Boaz sets the tone for the exchange that follows. He asserts that her virtuous act of loyalty to his kin, namely her mother-in-law, Naomi, has made her blessed. Although not required, Ruth stays with Naomi after the deaths of their husbands. Likewise, Ruth is loyal by not pursuing younger men for marriage; therefore, Boaz will heed her request. However, he then explains that there is a legal problem with him acting as her redeemer because there is another kinsman, a closer relative who is lawfully able to claim her (Ruth 3:12). Though this is a setback, Boaz instructs her, "Remain the night, and in the morning, if he [the other man] will redeem you, good. Let him redeem. If he does not desire to redeem you, I will redeem you, as Yahweh lives. Lie down until the morning" (lînî hallaylâ wĕhāyâ babbōqer 'im-yig'ālēk ṭôb yig'āl wĕ'im-

lōʾ yaḥpōṣ lĕgoʾōlēk ûgĕʾaltîk ʾānōkî ḥay-yhwh šikbî ʿad-habbōqer) (Ruth 3:13).

Just as Ruth was not required to remain loyal to Naomi, Boaz is not required to swear "as Yahweh lives"[10] to redeem her. He goes beyond his obligation and strengthens his pledge. Regarding this invocation, Moshe Greenberg states:

> One of the ways in which the Israelite was accustomed to validate his oath was to join it to the mention of the name of God, or to some sacred and powerful substitute. The holy being or object was invoked not merely to witness the truth and sincerity of the statement, but chiefly to punish the swearer if he spoke falsely.[11]

By invoking the divine name, Boaz summons Yahweh to witness, validate, and confirm what he is swearing. Moreover, if Boaz does not follow through on his oath, he is bringing divine punishment onto himself. Indeed, in Ruth 4, when the other man declines, Boaz fulfills his oath sworn on the threshing floor by marrying Ruth.

While the primary concern of Ruth 3 is centered on Ruth acquiring legal security from Boaz, the language and activities have a sexual nuance to them, which suggests that this legal request was consummated with a sexual act on the threshing floor.[12] The

---

10. For scholarship on the *ḥay-yhwh* oath formula, see Yael Ziegler, *Promises to Keep: The Oath in Biblical Narrative* (Leiden: Brill, 2008), 81–122; Moshe Greenberg, "The Hebrew Oath Particle ḤAY/ḤĒ," *JBL* 76 (1957): 34–39; and Manfred R. Lehmann, "Biblical Oaths," *ZAW* 81 (1969): 74–92.

11. Greenberg, "The Hebrew Oath Particle ḤAY/ḤĒ," 34.

12. Ruth 3 includes sexualized language that has led some scholars to believe a sexual act occurs on the threshing floor. For more on sex and gender issues in Ruth, see Phyllis Trible, *God and the Rhetoric of Sexuality*, OBT (Philadelphia: Fortress, 1978), 166–99; Esther Fuchs, "The Literary Characterization of Mothers and Sexual Politics in the Hebrew Bible," in *Women in the Hebrew Bible: A Reader*, ed. Alice Bach (New York: Routledge, 1999), 127–40; L. Juliana M. Claassens, "Resisting Dehumanization: Ruth, Tamar, and the Quest for Human Dignity," *CBQ* 75 (2012): 659–74; Dorothea Erbele-Küster, "Immigration and Gender Issues in the Book of Ruth," *Voices from the Third World* 25 (2002): 32–39; André LaCocque, *The Feminine Unconventional: Four Subversive Figures in Israel's Tradition*, OBT (Minneapolis: Fortress, 1990), 84–116; and Mieke Bal, "Heroism and Proper Names, or the Fruits of Analogy," in *A Feminist Companion to Ruth*, ed. A. Brenner (Sheffield: Sheffield Academic Press, 1993), 42–69.

language of Ruth 3 appears to express some sort of sexual act, although there could be conscious use of double entendres and innuendo. For instance, both Naomi and Boaz emphasize the importance of secrecy and discretion throughout this chapter. Naomi says that Ruth is not to let herself *be known*[13] to Boaz until he finishes his meal, which may have sexual connotations. Ruth lies at Boaz's *feet*, which can be used euphemistically to mean male genitals (see Isa. 6:2). After Boaz makes his oath to Yahweh, he tells Ruth *to stay the night* and *lie* with him until morning (Ruth 3:13).[14] In the morning, after Ruth and Boaz have lain together, Boaz instructs her to leave discretely because "it cannot be known that a woman came to the threshing floor" (*'al-yiwwāda' kî-bā'â hā'iššâ haggōren*) (Ruth 3:14b). It is unclear why a woman should not be at the threshing floor. Perhaps men typically performed the laborious work of threshing and winnowing, so a woman's presence could suggest illicit activity.

Summary

On the threshing floor in Ruth 3, several elements converge. Apropos for a threshing floor, winnowing occurs, and yet the heart of the narrative focuses on the legal request and divine invocation that follows. Also on the threshing floor is a convergence of social strata. Boaz, the male landowner, interacts with Ruth, the female foreign widow, and the two physically (and perhaps sexually) interact at the

---

There are arguments against viewing this pericope as a sexual encounter. For instance, Boaz refers to Ruth as "my daughter," emphasizing a familial relationship more than a sexual one. Also, if Boaz and Ruth had engaged in an illicit sexual encounter, sociologically they would be risking both of their reputations as people of *ḥayil*, "worth/respect/admiration." Cf. *'îš gibbôr ḥayil* to describe Boaz (Ruth 2:1) and *'ēšet ḥayil* to describe Ruth (Ruth 3:11). For more on this interpretation, see Robert L. Hubbard Jr., *The Book of Ruth*, NICOT (Grand Rapids: Eerdmans, 1988), 210–26; and Campbell, *Ruth*, 130–38. Cf. JPS's translation of Ruth 3:8 that has a startled Boaz "pulling back" (*wayyillāpēt*) from the woman lying at his feet.

13. The verb *yd'*, meaning "to know," can have sexual connotations (see Gen. 19:5; Num. 31:17).
14. As with the verb "to know," "to lie" (*škb*) can also occur in sexual contexts (see Gen. 19:32–35; 2 Sam. 13:11), and "to spend the night" (*lyn*) may also carry a sexual nuance in this setting.

threshing floor. What would typically be a very public, communal space, here the threshing floor serves as a private locale where a man and woman come together and even in the ordinary, the divine is called upon on the threshing floor. Within the agricultural activity and legal exchange, there is a detectable sacred element with the invocation of the divine name.

4

Threshing Floors as Sacred Spaces

In the two previous chapters, several passages were discussed which elucidate how threshing floors were understood and conceived of in the Hebrew Bible. Chapter 2 asserted that Yahweh has control over and use of threshing floors, with the ability to bless, curse, and save them from attacks. Moreover, prophetic passages depict Yahweh using threshing-floor imagery to metaphorically punish enemies. In chapter 3, legal texts that mention threshing floors were examined. They highlight that these locations are associated with divine offerings and blessings; moreover, the divine name is invoked on a threshing floor. All of this is to suggest that within the Hebrew Bible, biblical writers assert a clear connection between threshing floors and Yahweh that manifests itself in different ways depending on the context and genre of the text. On multiple occasions, threshing floors are associated with the divine because of Yahweh's interest in feeding and nourishing his people at these important agricultural centers. In this chapter, several passages will further demonstrate Yahweh's connection to threshing floors, as they are chosen as effective locations to contact Yahweh, and they are places associated with theophanies. Here, the clearest examples will be discussed that depict divination rituals and prophecy, cultic processions, and even divine manifestations on these spaces. The end of the chapter will survey who in society is depicted using threshing floors for cultic activities. Notably, the social group that typically facilitates the cult, namely the priests, do not engage in cultic practices on threshing floors.[1]

Consulting Yahweh at Threshing Floors

There are two narratives that depict threshing floors as locations to successfully contact Yahweh: Judg. 6:36–40 and 1 Kgs. 22:10 // 2 Chron. 18:9. In theory, any space could be used to contact Yahweh; however, in these narratives, threshing floors are presented as particularly effective places where Yahweh is reachable and provides a divine answer.

Judges 6:36–40

Judges 6:36–40 is situated in the passages about Gideon.[2] In chapter 2, Gideon was introduced because he is called by Yahweh to save Israel and her threshing floors from Midianite attacks. He is uncertain whether his attack on Midian will be successful, but while he is beating wheat at a wine press (not a threshing floor because those are under attack), he receives a divine sign in the form of fire upon offerings. As Gideon readies his troops to prepare to attack the Midianites, he is still unsure if he will be successful. He asks for another sign to know that his battle will be successful, and this sign occurs on a threshing floor. Gideon goes to a threshing floor to

---

1. There is one reference to priests possibly being present for a cultic procession that goes to a threshing floor (1 Chron. 13:2).
2. For a discussion of the date, genre, and context of Judges, see chapter 2.

perform a divination³ ritual in order to confirm the success of his battle. While on the threshing floor, Gideon says:

> I am placing a fleece of wool on the threshing floor; if there is dew on the fleece alone, and all the ground is dry, then I will know that you will deliver Israel by my hand, as you said.
>
> *hinnēh 'ānōkî maṣṣîg 'et-gizzat haṣṣemer baggōren 'im ṭal yihyeh 'al-haggizzâ lĕbaddāh wĕ'al-kol-hā'āreṣ ḥōreb wĕyāda'tî kî-tôšîa' bĕyādî 'et-yiśrā'ēl ka'ăšer dibbartā.* (Judg. 6:37)

The next day Gideon checks the fleece, and he drains enough dew from it to fill a bowl with water (*wayyimeṣ ṭal min-haggizzâ mĕlô' hassēpel māyim*) (Judg. 6:38b). Then Gideon says:

> Do not let your anger be kindled against me, let me speak one more time; let me test with the fleece once more; let it be dry only on the fleece, and on all the ground let there be dew.
>
> *'al-yiḥar 'appĕkā bî wa'ădabbĕrâ 'ak happā'am 'ănasseh nā'-raq-happa'am baggizzâ yĕhî-nā' ḥōreb 'el-haggizzâ lĕbaddāh wĕ'al-kol-hā'āreṣ yihyeh-ṭāl.* (Judg. 6:39)

---

3. Divination is the act of attempting to communicate with the divine by reading signs in order to better understand and manipulate the present and future. In the Hebrew Bible, there are condemnations of divination, but there are also approved forms. Deuteronomy 18:9–14 forbids divination (*qesem*), soothsayers (*mĕ'ônēn*), omen seekers (*mĕnaḥēš*), sorcerers (*mĕkaššēp*), spells (*ḥeber*), consulting mediums (*'ôb*) and spirits (*yiddĕ'ōnî*), and necromancers (*dōrēš 'el-hammētîm*). Leviticus 19:26, 31 has a similar, shorter list of forbidden magic. However, the use of the Urim and Thummim is an acceptable form of divination, which Aaron receives in his ordination ceremony (Exod. 28:30; Lev. 8:8). In Num. 27:21, at Yahweh's command, Eleazar the priest uses the Urim and Thummim in order to inquire whether Joshua is to be Moses's successor. Casting of lots (*gôrāl*) is another method of determining divine will, innocence, or guilt (Lev. 16:8; Joshua 7; 1 Sam. 14:42; Prov. 16:33). Specific vocabulary and practitioners determine whether the form of divination is acceptable or prohibited. For a discussion of magic and divination, see Ann Jeffers, *Magic and Divination in Ancient Palestine and Syria* (Leiden: Brill, 1996). For more details on divination in a larger Near Eastern context, see Amar Annus, ed., *Divination and Interpretation of Signs in the Ancient World* (Chicago: Oriental Institute of the University of Chicago, 2010).

That night Gideon's second request is answered with a dry fleece and dew on all of the ground (Judg. 6:40).

Rituals using dew and fleece are unattested elsewhere in the Hebrew Bible.[4] Fleece is the skin of an animal, usually a sheep (Deut. 18:4; Job 31:20). It is used here as an effective absorbent of dew. Traditionally, dew is associated with divine blessings (Gen. 27:28; Exod. 16:13; Deut. 33:13) because it can serve as a source of water, especially when there is insufficient rainfall. John Beck asserts that "dew is a welcome presence in Israel, for it plays a critical role in the ancient agricultural cycle … the summer months in Israel are nearly rain free."[5] In his divination ritual, Gideon takes a commonplace material (fleece) and asks for God to manipulate nature (dew) in order to know the fate of his battle. Seeking a divine blessing for battle, Gideon chooses the threshing floor as a favorable location to reach God. God twice responds with a successful manipulation of the dew, suggesting that Gideon's choice of the threshing floor is astute, as this is indeed an auspicious location to communicate with God and to receive a divine answer.

In addition to the successful divination, the narrative depicts Gideon's awareness of an apparent danger associated with accessibility of the divine at the threshing floor. In Judg. 6:39, Gideon requests that God's anger *not* be kindled against him. Gideon knows that as an auspicious location to reach God, the threshing floor may be a location of divine manifestation and divine anger. In two other narratives taking place on threshing floors, the danger and power

---

4. In the Late Bronze Age Ugaritic Aqhatu myth, Paghitu's epithet is "Bearer of water, Collector of dew from the fleece, Knower of the course of the stars," which is another Levantine reference to fleece being used as a medium for collecting dew. Likewise, Paghitu's epithet may be related to her performing divination, so this could be a usage similar to what is found in Judg. 6:37–40. See the addendum for a fuller discussion of this reference, which also occurs in close proximity to a threshing floor.
5. John A. Beck, "Gideon, Dew, and the Narrative-Geographical Shaping of Judges 6:33–40," *BSac* 165 (2008): 35.

of God are visible: God strikes and kills Uzzah on a threshing floor (2 Sam. 6:6–7 // 1 Chron. 13:9–10), and God sends destruction and plague on Israel via an angel associated with a threshing floor (2 Sam. 24:15–16 // 1 Chron. 21:14–16). Both narratives will be discussed later in this chapter. Gideon's request that God's anger *not* be kindled reflects a warranted fear of upsetting God, particularly on a location where God is reachable. Because God is accessible at the threshing floor, there is apparent power and danger associated with such direct access. Similarly, Gideon could be generally concerned about invoking divine wrath since he had asked for a divine sign while at the wine press earlier in the narrative (Judg. 6:15–21).

Depictions of the danger and lethality of divine power are pervasive in the Hebrew Bible. Some examples include God taking lethal action when people behave immorally—for example, the flood (Genesis 6) and the cities of Sodom and Gomorrah (Genesis 19). God also strikes people with plagues (Exodus 7–10; Num. 25:9) and fire (Num. 11:1–3). Likewise, wars are fought for and with Yahweh as a divine warrior (Exod. 14:4; 15:2; Num. 21:1–3; Pss. 18; 24:8; 98:1–3; 149:6–9; Isa. 42:10–13; Joshua 6; Judges 7). Gideon's fear of angering God is justified and in line with the many narratives that describe God taking lethal action against people.

Overall, this episode on the threshing floor shows Gideon's particular agrarian context and reflects the concerns of this agrarian community. While tasked with rescuing the food supply of Israel, Gideon uses the threshing floor as a space to contact Yahweh for approval to do so.

The Gideon narrative provides the only extant example of a threshing floor functioning as a private location for divine contact. The other narratives that will be discussed in this chapter describe groups of people and/or preternatural beings present on threshing floors. As it is the sole example of one individual using a threshing floor as a sacred space, an exploration into what Gideon may have been thinking in his selection of it could add further insights into this larger discussion of threshing floors. A few words from Henri Lefebvre on the topic of *mental* space are helpful in better understanding Gideon's choice.

Judges 6:36–40 and Spatial Theory

In his tripartite analysis of space, Lefebvre highlights the *physical*, *mental*, and *social* aspects of space and notes that each is necessary and important to understanding how a space might function in a society. Lefebvre notes that understanding *mental* space is how one can grasp the reality of social and spatial practice. Understanding the thought process used in selecting space assists in understanding the functionality of that space. Moreover, *mental* space is the center of theoretical practice. In the case of Gideon, though his divination ritual theoretically could happen on any outdoor space, Gideon's selection of a threshing floor shows an inclination toward this location as an effective space to contact the divine and to receive a divine answer. His choice suggests that culturally the threshing floor was perceived to be an auspicious location for human-divine communication. Moreover, the words that Gideon uses while on the threshing floor are particularly telling of his thoughts about the space. In requesting divine anger *not* to appear on the threshing floor, Gideon expresses and confirms that he thought a divine manifestation was probable because of the location. According to the author of this Gideon pericope, threshing floors were understood conceptually as more than just agricultural spaces. They were perceived as sacred spaces, and accordingly they are intentionally selected for this cultic activity.[6]

Samuel-Kings and Chronicles Parallels

Just as Gideon goes to the threshing floor for divine approval for war, the narratives in 1 Kgs. 22:10 // 2 Chron. 18:9 depict kings doing the same.[7] These passages are parallel, meaning the same event is found in a similar, though not necessarily identical, form in more than one account. The books of Samuel-Kings and Chronicles record versions of histories of Israel and Judah. Each of the books reveals insights about its compositional date and motivations. Samuel-Kings probably took its final form in the exilic period, while Chronicles is considered of the postexilic/early Persian period. Based on the many parallel passages, almost all scholars agree that large portions of the books of Samuel-Kings were available to the Chronicler as he recorded his history, even though he does make linguistic, textual, and theological emendations of his *Vorlage*.[8]

---

6. As noted in chapter 1, this is contra Jonathan Z. Smith, who states that ritual activities sacralize a space. The argument presented here is that the spaces were mentally perceived as sacred, which is why they are used for ritual activities. Based on cultural understandings and/or personal experiences of the divine, a society sacralizes a space and manifests their ideas by using a space for the cult.

7. For a discussion of the date, genre, and context of Samuel-Kings, see chapter 2. For treatments of the relationship between Samuel-Kings and Chronicles, see Gary Knoppers, "The Relationship of the Deuteronomistic History to Chronicles: Was the Chronicler a Deuteronomist?" in *Congress Volume Helsinki 2010*, ed. M. Nissinen (Leiden: Brill, 2012), 307–42; Raymond F. Person Jr., *The Deuteronomic History and the Book of Chronicles: Scribal Works in an Oral World* (Atlanta: SBL, 2010), 1–22, 69–86; Steven L. McKenzie, *The Chronicler's Use of the Deuteronomistic History*, HSM 33 (Atlanta: Scholars Press, 1984), 1–32; Isaac Kalimi, *An Ancient Israelite Historian: Studies in the Chronicler, His Time, Place, and Writing* (Leiden: Brill, 2005), 33–39; and Yairah Amit, *History and Ideology: An Introduction to Historiography in the Hebrew Bible*, trans. Y. Lotan (Sheffield: Sheffield Academic Press, 1999), 82–98. For discussions of the composition and dating of Chronicles, see Isaac Kalimi, "The Date of the Book of Chronicles," in *God's Word for Our World*, vol. 1, eds. D. Ellens, J. Ellens, I. Kalimi, R. Knierim (London: T&T Clark International, 2004), 347–71; Kalimi, *An Ancient Israelite Historian*; Steven McKenzie, *1–2 Chronicles*, AOTC (Nashville: Abingdon, 2004); McKenzie, *The Chronicler's Use of the Deuteronomistic History*; Rodney Duke, "Recent Research in Chronicles," *CRBS* 8 (2009): 10–50; J. W. Kleinig, "Recent Research in Chronicles," *CRBS* 2 (1994): 43–76; Sara Japhet, *I & II Chronicles: A Commentary*, OTL (Louisville: Westminster/John Knox, 1993); and J. E. Dyck, "Dating Chronicles and the Purpose of Chronicles," *Didaskalia* 6 (1997): 16–29.

8. For more on this, see Duke, "Recent Research in Chronicles," who discusses various scholarly interpretations of Chronicles. There are also scholars who suggest Samuel-Kings was not

While the books of Samuel-Kings focus on both kingdoms, the Chronicler has a particular Judean interest and perspective, so many of the accounts of Israelite kings are not included. The Chronicler is systematic in including many narratives found in Samuel-Kings but also excluding narratives that are problematic or of less concern. For example, the Chronicler is especially interested in presenting David in a positive light, so he often excludes lengthy portions of Samuel-Kings that depict David less favorably. Likewise, the Chronicler includes information not found in Samuel-Kings, including longer genealogies (1 Chronicles 1–8). Each historian has his own interest and style in creating and presenting available material and traditions, which likely accounts for the variant narratives and texts.

Scholars vary on their perceptions of the Chronicler, from devoted historian to creative writer. Gary Knoppers notes that the Chronicler is very faithful to his sources, and discrepancies between Samuel and Chronicles may be due to Samuel's complex textual development as opposed to the Chronicler altering sources.[9] Knoppers also characterizes Chronicles as ancient imitation (*mimesis*) and states that the Chronicler "self-consciously imitates and revises Deuteronomistic texts as one important means to construct his own literary work."[10]

---

available to the Chronicler but that both have a shared source. See David M. Carr, "Empirische Perspektiven auf das Deuteronomistische Geshichtswerk," in *Die deuteronomistischen Geschichtswerke: Redaktions- und religionsgeschichtliche Perspektiven zur "Deuteronomismus"-Diskussion in Tora und Vorderen Propheten*, ed. Markus Witte et al., BZAW 365 (Berlin: Walter de Gruyter, 2006), 1–17. The language, vocabulary, syntax, and Aramaic and Persian loanwords are similar to other Late Biblical Hebrew books, including Ezra, Nehemiah, and Esther. The content of Chronicles evidences both knowledge and use of the books of Samuel-Kings, especially in terms of the many parallel passages, so it was very likely composed after the DtrH was complete. For more on this, see Kalimi, *An Ancient Israelite Historian*, 33–37; and Person, *The Deuteronomic History and the Book of Chronicles*, 23–40.

9. Gary N. Knoppers, *1 Chronicles 10–29: A New Translation with Introduction and Commentary*, AB 12a (New York: Doubleday, 2004), 761.
10. Knoppers, "The Relationship of the Deuteronomistic History to Chronicles," 332. John Van Seters and Norbert Lohfink have also suggested that the Chronicler was an imitator, though Van Seters classifies much of Chr's work as plagiarism. J. Van Seters, "Creative Imitation in the Hebrew Bible," *SR* 29 (2000): 395–409; and N. Lohfink, "Gab es eine deuteronomistische

Steven McKenzie notes that 1 Chronicles relies heavily on Samuel as its major source, but frequently makes changes to introduce his theological ideas.[11] Many of the Chronicler's variants in parallel passages are supported by fragments of 4QSam[a] from Qumran, so variations between the books should not be immediately disregarded and probably reflect the *Vorlage* of the Chronicler, which was not identical to Samuel-Kings. This is especially the case for the ending of 2 Samuel, which will be discussed later in this chapter and in the following chapter.

With regard to threshing floors, up until this point in the study, none of the Samuel-Kings passages have had parallels in Chronicles. First Samuel 23:1–5 and 2 Kgs. 6:27 show divine control of and interest in threshing floors, but there is not a parallel account in Chronicles. In this chapter, however, all of the Samuel-Kings narratives that are discussed have parallels in Chronicles. Conversely, in the following chapter, the discussion of the building of the temple on a threshing floor is found in Chronicles but not in Kings. Though they differ on some of their texts, Samuel-Kings and Chronicles reflect a similar understanding of threshing floors as sacred spaces.

1 Kings 22:10 // 2 Chronicles 18:9

The mention of a threshing floor occurs in the context of kings determining whether they should go to war. The king of Israel (Ahab)[12] seeks to regain control of Ramoth-gilead from the

---

Bewegung?" in *Jeremia und die "Deuteronomistische Bewegung*," ed. W. Groß, BBB 98 (Weinheim: Beltz Athenäum, 1995), 313–82. These assertions have been refuted by Isaac Kalimi, who emphasizes the Chronicler as an artist and historian instead of an imitator/plagiarizer. Kalimi, *An Ancient Israelite Historian*, 19–39.

11. Steven McKenzie, *The Chronicler's Use of the Deuteronomistic History*, 33.
12. The king of Israel is not named throughout much of the Kings account; however, based on what precedes and what is pronounced in a vision, this king is Ahab. Some scholars have suggested that this story may be related to a later Omride king or one from the Jehu dynasty. See Mordechai Cogan, *1 Kings: A New Translation with Introduction and Commentary*, AB 10 (New York: Doubleday, 2001), 496. Ahab is more likely, as his name is in the passage, though

Aramaeans, and he asks for support from the Judean king Jehoshaphat (1 Kgs. 22:1–3 // 2 Chron. 18:2–3). Although he pledges his support, Jehoshaphat says that they should first inquire after the word of Yahweh to confirm that the campaign will be favorable (1 Kgs. 22:5 // 2 Chron. 18:4). As in David's campaign against the Philistines (1 Sam. 23:2–5) and Gideon's battle against the Midianites (Judg. 6:15–21, 37–40), Jehoshaphat is well aware of the importance of divine approval for war.

The king of Israel heeds Jehoshaphat's request and summons four hundred prophets to ask if they should go to war against Ramoth-gilead, and the prophets all say that Yahweh will give the land to the king (1 Kgs. 22:6 // 2 Chron. 18:5). Jehoshaphat is perhaps suspicious or cautious of these positive prophecies and asks if there are any other prophets of Yahweh available for inquiry. The king of Israel says that Micaiah son of Imlah is a prophet, although he always prophesies against the king (1 Kgs. 22:7–8 // 2 Chron. 18:6–7). While Micaiah is summoned:

> The king of Israel and King Jehoshaphat of Judah were each sitting on his throne, clothed in their robes, at the threshing floor at the entrance of the gate of Samaria; and all the prophets were prophesying before them.
>
> *ûmelek yiśrā'ēl wîhôšāpāṭ melek-yĕhûdâ yōšĕbîm 'îš 'al-kis'ô mĕlubbāšîm bĕgādîm bĕgōren petaḥ ša'ar šōmrôn wĕkol-hannĕbî'îm mitnabbĕ'îm lipnêhem.* (1 Kgs. 22:10).[13]
>
> The king of Israel and King Jehoshaphat of Judah were each sitting on his throne, clothed in their robes, sitting at the threshing floor at the entrance of the gate of Samaria; and all the prophets were prophesying before them.

---

not often. Likewise, the Chronicler includes Ahab's name in the beginning of the narrative (2 Chron. 18:1–3).

13. The Septuagint of 1 Kgs. 22:10 says that they are sitting on their thrones "with weapons at the gates" (*enoploi en tais pylais*). Although this is a different reading than the MT, the inclusion of weapons fits the context since the kings are making decisions regarding war.

ûmelek yiśrā'ēl wîhôšāpāṭ melek-yĕhûdâ yōšĕbîm 'îš 'al-kis'ô mĕlubbāšîm bĕgādîm wĕyōšĕbîm bĕgōren petaḥ ša'ar šōmrôn wĕkol-hannĕbî'îm mitnabbĕ'îm lipnêhem. (2 Chron. 18:9)[14]

The 1 Kings and 2 Chronicles accounts are nearly identical, except that the Chronicler has "they were sitting (*yōšĕbîm*) at the threshing floor (*bĕgōren*)," which may be to emphasize that the kings were enthroned, or it may be a dittographic repetition of the *yōšĕbîm* at the beginning of the verse. The threshing floor where the kings are seated listening to the prophets is at the entrance to the city gate of Samaria, a location also mentioned in 2 Kgs. 6:27 connected to a famine in the city. City gates served multiple functions, including being defensive structures to protect a city from outsiders (Josh. 6:5; Neh. 2:17), marketplaces (2 Kgs. 7:1), places of judgment (Deut. 21:19; 22:15), and places for juridical procedures conducted by elders (Ruth 4:1–11) and by royalty (2 Sam. 15:1–6). Archaeology also attests cultic and mercantile practices at city gates.[15] At Tel Dan, there are elaborate cultic features at the city gate, including several standing stone installations, four stone column bases that may have

---

14. The Septuagint of 2 Chron. 18:9 says that they are sitting on their thrones in robes "in a wide space" (*en tō eurychōrō*). *Eurychoro* is typically a translation of the Hebrew lexeme *rĕḥōb*, "a wide space." The notion of a wide space is very close in meaning to that of a threshing floor, though it is not the expected Greek *halōn*, "threshing floor." Because the Septuagint translations of 1 Kgs. 22:10 and 2 Chron. 18:9 do not include *halōn*, some scholars have questioned whether *gōren* sometimes is a generic wide space. In the other occurrences of *gōren* in the MT, the Septuagint consistently translates it as *halōn*, so it is unlikely that *gōren* was not equated with *halōn*. However, neither of the Septuagint renderings of 1 Kgs. 22:10 and 2 Chron. 18:9 agree with the MT versions, which may be a sign of corruption, variant traditions, or intentional edits by the Septuagint translator(s). There is not a clear mechanism for these variants, though both translations are missing the same word, *halōn*. It is possible that the Septuagint tradition reflects some confusion or uncertainty about a threshing floor at a city gate as the location for these juridical decisions and prophecies. Another tradition of this being a generic space at the city gate may have developed in order to better understand these events. Though the Septuagint translations cannot be ignored, they probably just reflect other traditions about these events.
15. For recent research on cultic activity taking place at ancient Near Eastern city gates, see Tina Haettner Blomquist, *Gates and Gods: Cults in the City Gates of Iron Age Palestine; An Investigation of the Archaeological and Biblical Sources* (Stockholm: Almqvist & Wiksell International, 1999).

held a canopy, incense altars, and pillars. Scholars have suggested that these may have been focal points for cult practices at the city gate.[16] Dan's outermost gate also includes two paved plazas and a bazaar (*huṣṣot*) area used for mercantile transactions. At Bethsaida, several standing stones and a stepped cultic niche with a stele of a bull-headed figure with horns and a dagger have been uncovered.[17] The description of a threshing floor at a city gate is both perplexing and practical. As people would typically enter and leave a city through the city gate, it might require workers to temporarily halt threshing for travelers. Another possibility was that the threshing floor was adjacent to the city gate, which would be convenient for transporting grain to homes or storage areas in the city, and it could function as a wide open, clean space for handling nonagricultural activities, as in these passages.

When Micaiah arrives at the threshing floor, the king of Israel asks him if they should go to battle with Ramoth-gilead, and Micaiah mimics the same positive prophecy as the four hundred prophets already on the threshing floor. However, the king of Israel is apprehensive because he knows Micaiah only prophesies against him. After being goaded by the king, Micaiah clues the kings in to why all

---

16. For more on cult at the city gates at Tel Dan, see Avraham Biran, *Biblical Dan* (Jerusalem: Israel Exploration Society/HUR-JIR, 1994); Biran, "Sacred Space: Of Standing Stones, High Places and Cult Objects at Tel Dan," *BAR* 24 (1998): 38–45, 70; and Amihai Mazar, *Archaeology of the Land of the Bible 10,000–586 BCE* (New York: Doubleday, 1990), 469. For a study of the archaeology of Area T and biblical references to Tel Dan, see Andrew R. Davis, "Tel Dan in its Northern Cultic Context" (PhD diss., The Johns Hopkins University, 2010).
17. See Rami Arav, Richard A. Freund, and John F. Shroder Jr., "Bethsaida Rediscovered," *BAR* 26 (2000): 50; Rami Arav, "The Fortified City of Bethsaida: The Case of an Iron Age Capital City," in *Cities through the Looking Glass: Essays on the History and Archaeology of Biblical Urbanism* (Winona Lake: Eisenbrauns, 2008), 83–115. Some scholars have interpreted the bull figure as the moon god or another Aramaean weather god. See M. Bernett and O. Keel, *Mond, Stier und Kult am Stadttor: Die Stele von Betsaida (et-Tell)*, OBO 161 (Fribourg: Universitätsverlag, 1998); O. Keel and C. Uehlinger, *Gods, Goddesses, and Images of God in Ancient Israel*, trans. T. H. Trapp (Minneapolis: Fortress Press, 1998). Tallay Ornan posits the "deliberate dualism" of a storm god with lunar features rather than a lunar god with storm features. T. Ornan, "The Bull and Its Two Masters," *IEJ* 51 (2001): 1–26.

of the prophets are prophesying success: this is a scheme devised by Yahweh to result in the king's death.

While on the threshing floor, Micaiah reveals a prophetic vision in which he sees Yahweh sitting on a throne with all of the hosts of heaven standing before him. Yahweh asks who will entice Ahab to attack Ramoth-gilead, so that he will fail (1 Kgs. 22:20 // 2 Chron. 18:19). A spirit comes before Yahweh and says that he will entice Ahab by going out and being a lying spirit in the mouth of all of Ahab's prophets. Yahweh affirms these actions that will result in disaster for Ahab (1 Kgs. 22:21–23 // 2 Chron. 18:21–22). After relaying his vision, Micaiah is reprimanded and imprisoned. Ahab goes to war with Aram and dies in battle.

In this narrative, the threshing floor is shown to be an effective location where kings seek divine approval for battle. The location is effective, as the four hundred prophets relay their false message from a lying spirit, and Micaiah receives and relays a true, divine message and vision to the kings. Unfortunately for Ahab, because he and his wife Jezebel are responsible for spreading worship of Baal in Israel (1 Kgs. 16:30–34),[18] Yahweh is not with him in war; rather, Yahweh intentionally decrees disaster on Ahab, which comes to fruition when he dies in the subsequent battle (1 Kgs. 22:29–38 // 2 Chron. 18:28–34).

1 Kings 22:10 // 2 Chronicles 18:9 and Social Space

These passages provide insights into Lefebvre's category of *social space*, which encompasses the group, the individual within the

---

18. Because of the Chronicler's particular focus on Judean kings, much of the Ahab narratives are not found in Chronicles, including his marriage to Jezebel and promotion of Baal worship. Second Chronicles 18–19 is the only time in Chronicles where a northern king (Ahab) is included. However, the Chronicler omits some details regarding Ahab's death and final regnal formula. As seen in this discussion, the material related to the kings of Israel and Judah on the threshing floor is included and largely unchanged by the Chronicler, except for the addition of Ahab's name at the beginning of the narrative (2 Chron. 18:1).

group, how they experience a space, and how they interact at that space. Lefebvre notes that space is transformed into "lived experience" by social subjects/actors, and space is governed by the actions that happen on it and the people who use it. In the above narratives, there are two groups of social subjects/actors who demonstrate a transformation of the threshing floor from agricultural to sacred space. Royal and prophetic actors gather at a threshing floor and use it to obtain access to the divine, thus asserting their joint understanding that this location is auspicious for contacting Yahweh. Just as the Gideon narrative showed a threshing floor *mentally* associated with the divine, the use of the threshing floor by kings and prophets shows two groups acknowledging a cultural understanding of a divine connection at threshing floors. By selecting a threshing floor, the kings and prophets demonstrate that threshing floors were "perceived-conceived-lived"[19] as sacred spaces by these social groups. The kings and prophets together perceived the space to have the potential for accessibility to the divine. Socially, they conceived of them to be spaces that could be used for interactive activities beyond their initial agricultural purposes. Because of these perceptions and conceptions, the threshing floor is lived as both an agricultural and a sacred space. Lefebvre notes that how a space is "perceived-conceived-lived" by a group is essential to understanding the space, and these three elements are interconnected with one another. As the following narratives are discussed, various social groups (excluding priests) gather at threshing floors for cultic activities, showing that these spaces were *mentally* understood and *socially* used as sacred spaces.

---

19. Lefebvre notes a threefold division of space, specifically as it relates to spatial practice. These divisions allow for a coherent and logical analysis of how space is experienced. Lefebvre, *The Production of Space*, trans. D. Nicholson-Smith (Malden: Blackwell, 1974), 38–41, 51–53.

Cultic Processions on Threshing Floors

While threshing floors are used as auspicious locations to seek divine approval for war, they are also locations where cultic processions travel before reaching their final destinations. In our extant texts, two cultic processions make stops at threshing floors: the funeral procession for Jacob en route to burial in Canaan and David's procession transporting the ark to Jerusalem.

Genesis 50:10-11

Traditionally, much of Genesis 50 is attributed to the Yahwist (J), which contains oral and written traditions dating to the ninth century BCE, originating from the southern kingdom. With the developments in recent decades in pentateuchal studies, there has been considerable revision of the Documentary Hypothesis, and Genesis 50 may be considered non-P material according to new models of source identification. The narrative in Genesis 50 is in the genre of a historical narrative, though the historicity of the Joseph narrative is debated.[20]

In Genesis 50, the patriarch Jacob dies and his body is readied to be transported to Canaan for burial. After receiving permission from

---

20. For recent treatments of pentateuchal studies, see Jean-Louis Ska, *Introduction to Reading the Pentateuch* (Winona Lake: Eisenbrauns, 2006); Gordon Wenham, "Pondering the Pentateuch: The Search for a New Paradigm," in *The Face of Old Testament Studies: A Survey of Contemporary Approaches*, ed. D. Baker and B. Arnold (Grand Rapids: Baker Books, 1999), 116–44; Cornelis Houtman, *Der Geschichte seiner Erforschung neben einer Auswertung*, CBET 9 (Kampen: Kok Pharos, 1994); Craig A. Evans, Joel N. Lohr, and David L. Petersen, eds., *The Book of Genesis: Composition, Reception, and Interpretation* (Leiden: Brill, 2012); Zvi Adar, *The Book of Genesis: An Introduction to the Biblical World* (Jerusalem: Magnes Press, 1990); John Van Seters, *The Edited Bible: The Curious History of the "Editor" in Biblical Criticism* (Winona Lake: Eisenbrauns, 2006). For more traditional Genesis commentaries, see E. A. Speiser, *Genesis: A New Translation with Introduction and Commentary*, AB 1 (Garden City: Doubleday, 1964); Claus Westermann, *Genesis 37–50*, trans. John J. Scullion (Minneapolis: Fortress Press, 2002); Gerhard von Rad, *Genesis: A Commentary*, OTL (Philadelphia: Westminster Press, 1961); Nahum M. Sarna, *Genesis = Be-Reshit: The Traditional Hebrew Text with New JPS Translation*, JPS Torah Commentary (Philadelphia: JPS, 1989).

Pharaoh, Joseph along with a large group travels from Egypt en route to Canaan to bury his father. In the very large company, there are servants and elders of Pharaoh along with all of the other elders of Egypt, Joseph's brothers and their families, chariots, and horsemen (Gen. 50:7–9). Jacob's funeral is full of important officials, conveying the magnitude and grandeur of this procession. While on the way to Canaan, the procession sojourns on a threshing floor.

> [10] When they came to the threshing floor of Atad, which is near the Jordan, they wailed with very sorrowful mourning rites there, and he performed mourning rituals for his father for seven days. [11] When the Canaanite inhabitants of the land saw the mourning on the threshing floor of Atad, they said, "This is a sorrowful mourning by the Egyptians." Therefore, the place was named Abel-Mizraim, which is near the Jordan.

> [10] wayyābō'û 'ad-gōren hā'āṭād 'ăšer bĕ'ēber hayyardēn wayyispĕdû-šām mispēd gādôl wĕkābēd mĕ'ōd wayya'aś lĕ'ābîw 'ēbel šib'at yāmîm. [11] wayyar' yôšēb hā'āreṣ hakkĕna'ănî 'et-hā'ēbel bĕgōren hā'āṭād wayyō'mĕrû 'ēbel-kābēd zeh lĕmiṣrāyim 'al-kēn qārā' šĕmāh 'ābēl miṣrayim 'ăšer bĕ'ēber hayyardēn. (Gen. 50:10–11)

The location for these mourning rites is called "the threshing floor of Atad," which could literally mean "the threshing floor of bramble," though this translation is unlikely since these floors should not have obstructions such as bramble.[21] The Septuagint suggests

---

21. The Septuagint does not translate this as "bramble" in this passage. The Septuagint translates *gōren hā'āṭād* as *halōna atad*, "threshing floor of Atad." The Septuagint lacks the definite particle and does not translate *'āṭād* as *hramnon*, meaning "bramble," as it does elsewhere. There are two other instances of *'āṭād* in the MT, Judg. 9:14 and Ps. 58:10. In Judg. 9:14, *hā'āṭād* occurs within the context of a parable of trees. The Septuagint translates *hā'āṭād* as *tēn hramnon*, meaning "the bramble." In Ps. 58:10, *'āṭād* occurs without the definite article, but the Septuagint renders it definite, *tēn hramnon*. The translation of *'āṭād* in Genesis 50 as *atad* is a unique rendering of that Hebrew lexeme in the Septuagint. Note also that the meaning of "bramble" or "boxthorn" is based on the Akkadian word *eddetu*, which *CAD* translates as "boxthorn." It occurs primarily in passages dealing with lists of horticulture, especially prickly or thorny vines. However, *CAD* says that the relationship between *eddetu* and *'āṭād* in Hebrew, Syriac, and Arabic is uncertain. *CAD* vol. E, 23.

understanding Atad as a geographic location or personal name, as it transliterates rather than translates the word.²² Though Atad is not attested elsewhere as a geographic or personal name, this designation suggests that at some point this was a known threshing floor identifiable by name and proximity to the Jordan.

The threshing floor is described literally as "beyond the Jordan" (*bě'ēber hayyardēn*), which could mean either east (Transjordan) or west (Canaan) of the river depending on the location of the scribe and audience. Since the following verses refer to Canaanite inhabitants observing the mourning rites, west of the Jordan is implied although there are traditions that connect Jacob to Transjordan (Gen. 32:22–32). The translation "near the Jordan" is an attempt to capture the inherent ambiguity of the phrase.

While on this threshing floor, Joseph and his company sorrowfully mourn and perform mourning rites (*mispēd*), and Joseph performs mourning rituals (*'ēbel*) for seven days. The exact details of these rituals are not included in these verses; however, these *mispēd* and *'ēbel* rituals are mentioned elsewhere in the Hebrew Bible in conjunction with wearing sackcloth (Ezek. 27:31; Jer. 6:26; Pss. 30:11; 35:13; Esther 4:3), rolling in ashes (Ezek. 27:30; Jer. 6:26; Esther 4:3), fasting (Ps. 35:13; Joel 2:12; Esther 4:3), stripping naked (Mic. 1:8), shaving hair (Ezek. 27:31), and intense weeping and wailing (Ezek. 7:31–32; Jer. 6:26; Amos 5:16; Mic. 1:8; Ps. 35:13; Esther 4:3). Mourning rites for such an important figure like Jacob probably encompassed some or all of these traditional acts of mourning.

---

22. Excavations in the Levant have not yielded a city named Atad, and this name does not appear in any extant texts. Scholars have grappled with this issue and presented a variety of options, although most do not suggest that this could be a personal name. Nahum Sarna does not translate *gōren hā'āṭād*, although his commentary says it literally means "the threshing floor of the bramble." Gordon Wenham translates this as "The Bramble Threshing Floor." Claus Westermann translates it as "the Threshing Floor of Atad," which he says may be enclosed by brambles. N. Sarna, *Genesis*, 348; G. J. Wenham, *Genesis 16–50*, WBC 2 (Nashville: Thomas Nelson Publishers, 1994), 489; Westermann, *Genesis 37-50*, 201.

The biblical tradition regarding Jacob's funeral procession twice mentions the threshing floor of Atad as the location for his mourning rituals. The intense, emotional rituals served as outward signs and reminders of loss. The wailing and lamentation were apparently memorable, as they are used as the etiology of the city, "Mourning Egyptians" (*'ābēl miṣrayim*). While sorrowful rituals are signs of mourning to others, they are also cries to Yahweh. According to numerous biblical traditions, when people cry out in mourning or in distress, Yahweh hears, answers, and comforts them (1 Chron. 5:20; Pss. 3:4; 34:4–17; 40:1–2; 119:28; Jer. 31:25). Implicit in these activities is the hope of solace for the mourners and for the deceased. Joseph and his group offer these rituals for Jacob so that Yahweh will hear and answer their cries. The threshing floor is chosen for these seven-day mourning rituals because Yahweh was thought to be especially accessible and more apt to hear and answer their supplications at this location. Just as Gideon performs his divinatory ritual on the threshing floor because Yahweh is accessible and responsive at that location, so Joseph and his group may use the threshing floor with a similar prospect that Yahweh will hear and answer their requests. Similarly, in Joel 2:23–24 (discussed in chapter 2) the threshing floor may be chosen as a location to offer petitions and prayers to Yahweh. In Joel, a threshing floor may be a place for mourning the loss of crops and petitioning for an abundant harvest. In Gen. 50:10–11, the mourning rites that happen are not for a harvest but are more clearly for comfort and support during a time of grief.

Genesis 50:10-11 and Tripartite Aspects of Space

As the group of mourners gather and pray at the threshing floor, elements of the *physical*, *mental*, and *social* understandings of threshing floors are evident. *Physically*, for such a large group to gather at the threshing floor suggests the space was both clear and large enough to accommodate the mourners. *Mentally* and *socially* this threshing floor is thought to be an appropriate place for ritual activity and a suitable location to contact Yahweh. Joseph, accompanied by a diverse group of mourners, uses a threshing floor for ritual activities, illustrating that mentally the group perceived and conceived of it as an appropriate location for these sorrowful rites. Likewise, the members of the group interact with one another in performing these activities. By bonding together in grief, they find human and divine emotional support at the threshing floor. The choice of the threshing floor for these cultic activities lives out this idea and affirms a cultural notion that divine access and ritual activity were possible at these locations.

This account of a procession on a threshing floor occurs also in the books of 2 Samuel and 1 Chronicles. A procession with the holy ark makes a stop on a threshing floor, and the accessibility of Yahweh is especially prominent in the narrative, as Yahweh strikes and kills on the location.

2 Samuel 6:6-7 // 1 Chronicles 13:9-10

2 Samuel 6 // 1 Chronicles 13 are accounts of David and a lively procession transporting the ark of God[23] to Jerusalem.[24] According to 2 Samuel 6, the procession includes thirty thousand chosen men

---

23. The narrative refers to the ark as "the Ark of God called by the name Yahweh of Hosts seated on the cherubim" (*'ărôn hā'ĕlōhîm 'ăšer-niqrā' šēm šēm yhwh ṣĕbā'ôt yōšēb hakkĕrûbîm 'ālāyw*) (2 Sam. 6:2). The ark is attested with various names in the Hebrew Bible: Ark of Yahweh (*'ărôn yhwh*), Ark of the Covenant (*'ărôn bĕrît*), and Ark of Testimony (*'ărôn hā'ēdūt*). C. L. Seow provides a helpful description of the various attestations and notes that the form in 2 Sam. 6:2 may be the fullest and most ancient name for the ark. C. L. Seow, "Ark of the Covenant," in *ABD*, 1:387–89. In addition to different names, there are also different notions of how the ark functioned in ancient Israel. One tradition is that the ark was conceived of as a box or chest to hold holy objects (2 Kgs. 12:10–11 // 2 Chron. 24:8–11). The ark was also conceived of as the seat of God, namely, an empty throne, which is depicted in 2 Samuel 6 // 1 Chronicles 13.

in Israel (2 Sam. 6:1). First Chronicles 13 speaks of these participants but also says that the whole assembly of Israel was involved in the procession, including priests and Levites. The Chronicler presents David inviting everyone to be involved in this joyful procession with the ark, which is transported by two cultic personnel.

A cultic and political object, the ark signifies the presence and power of Yahweh, so this procession is sacred and very important. The ark is transported from the house of Abinadab by his two sons, Uzzah and Ahio (2 Sam. 6:3 // 1 Chron. 13:7). The Samuel account states that the house is on a hill, although this detail is not found in Chronicles. The procession is full of merriment, dancing, and music (2 Sam. 6:5 // 1 Chron. 13:8), elements often mentioned in conjunction with ceremonial and ritual passages (Exod. 15:20; 32:19; Lev. 23:24). While on the way to Jerusalem, the procession makes a stop at a threshing floor where an incident occurs:

> [6]When they came to the threshing floor of Nakon, Uzzah reached out to the ark of God and took hold of it, for the oxen shook it. [7]The anger of Yahweh was kindled against Uzzah, and God struck him there because of the error. And he died there with the ark of God.

---

24. Scholars have proposed many suggestions for what type of procession occurs in these passages. Sigmund Mowinckel suggests that this is the festival of the kingship of Yahweh, an annual ceremony he reconstructs from various psalms. S. Mowinckel, *The Psalms in Israel's Worship* (New York: Abingdon Press, 1962), 106–92. H. Kraus suggests that it is an annual festival commemorating the historical events related to the election of David and choice of Zion as David's capital city. H.-J Kraus, *Worship in Israel: A Cultic History of the Old Testament*, trans. G. Buswell (Richmond: John Knox, 1966), 183–85. Patrick Miller and J. J. M. Roberts have found similarities between the return of the Mesopotamian god Marduk to Babylon from captivity, and the accounts of David moving the ark of God to Jerusalem. P. D. Miller and J. J. M. Roberts, *The Hand of the Lord: A Reassessment of the "Ark Narrative" of 1 Samuel* (Baltimore: Johns Hopkins University Press, 1977), 9–17. P. Kyle McCarter Jr. suggests understanding this as a unique cultic event for the ritual dedication of the city of David, which is quite compelling. P. Kyle McCarter Jr., "The Ritual Dedication of the City of David in 2 Samuel 6," in *The Word of the Lord Shall Go Forth: Essays in Honor of David Noel Freedman in Celebration of His Sixtieth Birthday*, ed. C. L. Meyers, M. P. O'Connor and D. N. Freedman (Winona Lake: Eisenbrauns, 1983), 273–77; and McCarter, *II Samuel: A New Translation with Introduction, Notes, and Commentary*, AB 9 (Garden City: Doubleday, 1984), 178–84.

⁶*wayyābō'û 'ad-gōren nākôn wayyišlaḥ 'uzzā' 'el-'ărôn hā'ĕlōhîm wayyō'ḥez bô kî šāmĕṭû habbāqār.* ⁷*wayyiḥar-'ap yhwh bĕ'uzzāh wayyakkēhû šām hā'ĕlōhîm 'al-haššal wayyāmot šām 'im 'ărôn hā'ĕlōhîm.* (2 Sam. 6:6–7)

⁹When they came to the threshing floor of Kidon, Uzza reached out his hand to the ark of God and took hold of it, for the oxen shook it. ¹⁰The anger of Yahweh was kindled against Uzza and struck him because he reached out his hand to the ark. He died there before God.

⁹*wayyābō'û 'ad-gōren kîdōn wayyišlaḥ 'uzzā' 'et-yādô le'ĕḥōz 'et-hā'ārôn kî šāmĕṭû habbāqār.* ¹⁰*wayyiḥar-'ap yhwh bĕ'uzzā' wayyakkēhû 'al 'ăšer-šālaḥ yādô 'al-hā'ārôn wayyāmot šām lipnê 'ĕlōhîm.* (1 Chron. 13:9–10)

The parallel accounts of these events provide two different names for this threshing floor, and traditions in 4QSamᵃ and the Septuagint also have differing names. The MT of 2 Samuel attests the threshing floor's name as *nākôn*; the Septuagint of 2 Samuel reads *nōdab*; the MT of Chronicles reads *kîdōn*; the Septuagint of Chronicles lacks a name for the threshing floor; and 4QSamᵃ reads *nwdn*. Following 4QSamᵃ, McCarter translates the threshing floor's name as "Nodan," understanding *nākôn*, *nōdab*, and *kîdōn* as corruptions of *nwdn*, which seems probable.[25] Traditionally, this is understood as the personal name of the threshing floor owner,[26] although like the threshing floor of Atad (Gen. 50:10–11), it could also be a geographic marker. In addition to the variant names of this threshing floor, the name of Uzzah is spelled differently in the two accounts (*'uzzāh*, *'uzzā'*), showing that names and spellings can vary in different traditions.[27]

---

25. McCarter, *II Samuel*, 164.
26. Other interpretations have included reading *nākôn* as the noun meaning "stroke" (N. H. Tur-Sinai, "The Ark of God at Beit Shemesh (1 Sam. VI) and Pereṣ 'Uzza (2 Sam. VI; 1 Chron. XIII)," *VT* 1 [1951]: 275–86); or as a *niphal* participle meaning "a certain threshing floor" (J. Morgenstern, "nkwn," *JBL* 37 [1918]: 144–48); "a secure threshing floor" (W. R. Arnold, *Ephod and Ark: A Study in the Records and Religion of the Ancient Hebrews*, HTS 3 [Cambridge: Harvard University Press, 1917], 62); and "a permanent threshing floor" (Arthur W. Marget, "*gwrn nkwn* in 2 Sam. 6:6," *JBL* 39 [1920]: 70–76).

Likewise, within 2 Samuel 6 the name is attested with both spellings. Although there are some variants, the overall account of this event on the threshing floor is similar in both texts.

On the threshing floor, Uzzah touches the ark of God, which is apparently an egregious offense because it is a cultic object only to be touched by approved cultic personnel who have presumably undertaken a series of ritual precautions. There is no clear law forbidding the touching of the ark, although this passage suggests that it was forbidden at least for some people to touch it. Exodus 25:14 describes the ark being handled with poles, which suggests that it should not be touched.[28] Uzzah's action may have been a reflex to ensure that the ark was not damaged; however, though allowed to transport the ark, Uzzah has presumably not taken the proper ritual precautions needed to touch the ark. Uzzah's death on account of his action reiterates the power and danger associated with Yahweh and cultic items. The ark in particular can bring with it lethal divine power, as evidenced in this narrative. The divine punishment that Uzzah receives is in line with the lethal action taken when cultic violations occur.

The Ark: Lethal and Blessed

The ark is an important cultic object associated with Yahweh, making it extremely holy but also very dangerous because of its

---

27. McCarter has used these alternate spellings to suggest the possibility of Uzza being a variant spelling of Eleazar (*'elʿāzār*) based on similar alternations of ʿz and ʿzr. He cites the name Uzziel (*ʿuzzîʾēl*) in 1 Chron. 25:4, spelled *Azaraēl* in LXXB and Azarel (*ʿăzarʾēl*) in 1 Chron. 25:18. McCarter, *II Samuel*, 169.

28. A. A. Anderson suggests that Uzzah may have been consecrated to take responsibility for transporting the ark, and thus he should have known that the ark falling was a sign that Yahweh wanted to stop the procession. Uzzah's attempt to catch the ark may have been disregarding the will of Yahweh, and this might account for why the anger of Yahweh responds in such a severe manner. Anderson, *2 Samuel*, WBC 11 (Nashville: Thomas Nelson, 1989), 104. J. Dus suggests that Uzzah sinned because he did not allow Yahweh the freedom to choose his own resting place. J. Dus, "Der Brauch der Ladewanderung im alten Israel," *TZ* 17 (1961): 7.

connection to divine power. The instance with Uzzah reflects the power and danger associated with cultic objects, and this is not a unique occurrence. The ark is also connected with death in 1 Samuel 5 when it is transported to the house of Dagon in Ashdod, which is considered sacrilege. The ark is said to be responsible for killing many of the inhabitants of Ashdod, and people want it moved because of its destructive powers (1 Sam. 5:1–8). When it is moved to Gath and then Ekron, the ark continues to inflict harm on inhabitants (1 Sam. 5:9–12). After this incident with the ark on the threshing floor (2 Sam. 6:6–7 // 1 Chron. 13:9–10), David halts the procession because he is afraid of the lethal ark. He takes it to the house of Obed-edom to cool off, and the ark blesses the household during its three-month respite (2 Sam. 6:9–11 // 1 Chron. 13:12–14). While connected to curses and death, the ark is also connected to divine blessings. The location and proper handling of the ark are essential to avoid lethal divine action.

The accounts of Uzzah's death are slightly different in 2 Samuel and 1 Chronicles, although the deadly result is the same. Second Samuel notes that Uzzah's error (*šal*) is the reason for his punishment. First Chronicles does not use the same language, but explains that the action of touching the ark is the reason for his punishment. In both accounts the anger of Yahweh is kindled against Uzzah. In 2 Samuel, God smites Uzzah, although in 1 Chronicles the anger of Yahweh smites Uzzah. The different subjects (God; anger of Yahweh) could suggest two different traditions regarding who/what kills Uzzah, but the two subjects reflect the actions of one single deity. The Chronicler may have found it confusing or problematic for the anger of Yahweh and God to act as two separate entities, although this is not a problem in 2 Samuel.[29]

---

29. See P. Kyle McCarter Jr., "When Gods Lose Their Temper: Divine Rage in Ugaritic Myth and the Hypostasis of Anger in Iron Age Religion," in *Divine Wrath and Divine Mercy in the*

In 2 Samuel, Uzzah dies with the ark of God (*'im 'ărôn hā'ĕlōhîm*). In 1 Chronicles (and in 4QSam^a) Uzzah dies before God (*lipnê 'ĕlōhîm*). Though slightly different details are in these traditions, the essence of the narratives is the same: On the threshing floor, the lethal power of Yahweh manifests itself by striking and killing Uzzah on account of his act of touching the ark.

This narrative is illustrative of what has been seen in other threshing-floor passages. Yahweh is especially present and accessible at threshing floors. While there can be benefits to that presence (successful divination, prophecy, and consolation of the bereaved), there are also risks attached to divine accessibility. As noted in Judg. 6:39 when Gideon asks that Yahweh's anger not be kindled on the threshing floor, the narrative in 2 Sam. 6:6–7 // 1 Chron. 13:9–10 shows what happens when the anger of Yahweh is kindled on the threshing floor. The results are lethal. Gideon's concern about Yahweh's anger and the manifestation of that anger directed toward Uzzah indicate a realistic concern about divine presence and power on threshing floors.

2 Samuel 6:6-7 // 1 Chronicles 13:9-10 and Spatial Theory

Edward Soja's scholarship on spatial theory is helpful in ascertaining the significance of this event. Soja highlights the tripartite nature of space with the concepts Firstspace (physical space), Secondspace (imagined space), and Thirdspace (experienced space). He emphasizes Thirdspace as a component that introduces something new and other about a space and highlights the physical and mental construction of a space. When considering Thirdspace, the focus is on the use of and the range of possibilities associated with a given space.

World of Antiquity, ed. R. G. Kratz and H. Spieckermann (Tübingen: Mohr Siebeck, 2008), 88–91. McCarter's chapter is very useful in understanding how the temper of a deity could be understood as within the deity's control but also on its own as a hypostatic entity.

When trying to consider the Thirdspace of threshing floors, a reminder of what exactly threshing floors are is helpful. These are agricultural spaces for threshing and winnowing, but the presence of a ritual procession with a cultic object demonstrates more than one possible usage for these spaces. Not only can they be used for nonagricultural activities, they also can be used for highly important cultic activities. The cultic procession described above not only combines an array of social actors (from officials to ordinary people), but it also combines multiple divine indicators, an element hitherto unseen.

The presence of the ark on the threshing floor is one indicator of divine presence. Divine anger and divine power are also at the threshing floor to strike and kill. The narrative shows that this threshing floor was physically and mentally attached to multiple divine elements. The divine presence represents an "otherness" about this space, an otherness discernible with outward signs of the sacred, namely the ark (cultic symbol) and the theophany (divine manifestation). Divine manifestation on the threshing floor shows a transcendent, otherworldly aspect that interacts with people at a given location. Human and divine presences converge here. In the following section, another divine manifestation occurs on a threshing floor, which again affirms the potential sacrality of these spaces.

Theophany and Sacrifice upon a Threshing Floor

The narratives in 2 Sam. 24:15–25 and 1 Chron. 21:14–27 describe an angel in connection with a threshing floor, which prompts David to build an altar and offer sacrifices on that threshing floor. The angel had come to destroy Israel due to David's action of taking a census. David's census upsets Yahweh, and as punishment Yahweh sends destruction and plague on the land (2 Sam. 24:1–14 // 1 Chron. 21:1–14).

The accounts vary on what causes this census. According to 2 Samuel, the "anger of Yahweh" (*'ap-yhwh*) incites David against Israel and causes him to commit this evil. According to 1 Chronicles, an adversary (*śāṭān*) incites David. The Chronicler may be uncomfortable with God causing David to do something evil. This may be an instance of the Chronicler altering Samuel, particularly as related to the relationship between God and the anger of Yahweh.

A census may have been understood as a negative act because it often led to financial and military reorganization, which could increase taxes and military service. Exodus 30:11–16 supports this idea of a census being associated with additional taxes. Some censuses, however, were sanctioned by Yahweh such that they were not punishable and did not result in more taxes (Numbers 1).[30]

2 Samuel 24:15–25 // 1 Chronicles 21:14–27

Just as the angel is about to destroy Jerusalem, Yahweh instructs him to withdraw his hand (2 Sam. 24:16 // 1 Chron. 21:15a). The narratives describe the location of the angel:

> And the angel of Yahweh was with the threshing floor of Aravnah, the Jebusite.
>
> *ûmal'ak yhwh hāyá 'im-gōren hā'ôrnâ* [Qere:*'ărawnâ*] *hayĕbusî* (2 Sam. 24:16b)

> [15b]And the angel of Yahweh was standing with the threshing floor of Ornan, the Jebusite. [16a]David lifted up his eyes and saw the angel of Yahweh standing between the earth and the heavens.
>
> [15b]*ûmal'ak yhwh 'ōmēd 'im-gōren 'ornān hayĕbûsî.* [16a]*wayyiśśā' dāwîd 'et-'ênāyw wayyar' 'et-mal'ak yhwh 'ōmēd bên hā'āreṣ ûbên haššāmayim.*

---

30. For more on census and plagues, see McCarter, *II Samuel*, 512–14; J. A. Sanders, "Census," *IDB*, 1:547; E. A. Speiser, "Census and Ritual Expiation in Mari and Israel," *BASOR* 149 (1958): 17–25; G. E. Mendenhall, "The Census Lists of Numbers 1 and 26," *JBL* 77 (1958): 52–66.

(1 Chron. 21:15b–16a)

As in the previous passage with David and the ark on a threshing floor, this threshing-floor owner's name has various attestations. In the MT of 2 Samuel, the Ketib reads *h'wrnh* and the Qere has the pronunciation as *'ărawnâ*; the Septuagint of 2 Samuel and 1 Chronicles reads Orna; the MT of 1 Chronicles reads *'ornān*; and 4QSam^a reads *'rn'*. The variants are slight differences in orthography and pronunciation, which often happens with personal names. The name may be further confused as it is non-Semitic, possibly of Hurrian origins.[31]

Aravnah/Ornan is described in both accounts as a Jebusite. The Jebusites were a Canaanite people group living in Jerusalem. Biblical references to the Jebusites describe them as descendants of Canaan (Gen. 10:15–16) and associate them with the Amorites in the hill country (Num. 13:29). In the traditions of Israel conquering the land, the Jebusites could not be driven out and remained inhabitants of Jerusalem (Josh. 15:63; Judg. 1:21; 19:10–12).

While the spelling and orthography of the personal name are complex, the location of the angel vis-à-vis the threshing floor is also somewhat ambiguous. The phrase *'im-gōren* is translated here literally "with the threshing floor," though it is usually translated as "near," "by," or "at" the threshing floor.[32] While these prepositions make logical sense in modern English, they may not capture the deeper meaning of *'im* in biblical Hebrew. Most often, *'im* means "with" or "together with." Beyond these meanings, *'im* can also mark "the locus of psychological interest," according to Waltke and O'Connor.[33]

---

31. Several scholars have suggested the name may be related to the Hurrian word for "lord" or "king." For more on this, see McCarter, *II Samuel*, 512.
32. "near the threshing floor": HarperCollins NRSV (annotated SBL edition); "by the threshing floor": NRSV, RSV, ESV, NKJV, NJPS; "at the threshing floor": NIV.
33. Bruce K. Waltke and M. O'Connor, *An Introduction to Biblical Hebrew Syntax* (Winona Lake: Eisenbrauns, 1990), 219 (11.2.14b, ## 9–10).

They provide two examples of this sense: "Know in (*'im*) your heart" (Deut. 8:5) and "There is another spirit in (*'im*) him" (Num. 14:24). These examples show that "with" someone or something can show a deep internal connection. *'Im* used to show a "psychological interest" is found elsewhere in the Hebrew Bible. Yahweh being "with" chosen people is very common (e.g., Exod. 3:12; 4:12), and the language is used to denote Yahweh's existential presence. The language of Yahweh being "with" a location is less common but may reflect a similar divine approval. For instance, in 1 Sam. 18:28a, "Saul saw and knew that Yahweh was with (*'im*) David." This verse is within a larger narrative of David's succession as king of Israel and Judah, and the affirmation of Yahweh being "with" David shows an intense interest in and approval of David. With this in mind, the angel being "with" the threshing floor may be more than a location marker; rather, it shows a possible divine interest in and approval of this space. Fittingly, the Chronicler says that this threshing floor becomes the foundation on which Yahweh's temple is built (2 Chron. 3:1).

The Chronicler provides additional information about the location of the angel which is also found in 4QSam[a] though not in the MT of Samuel.[34] The angel is described standing between the earth and the heavens. Scholars have suggested that this may be a depiction of the angel hovering or flying in midair over the threshing floor.[35] This is an attractive possibility, and the larger implications are particularly interesting. This angel is described in a liminal space, literally between two realms, an idea that will be discussed in the excursus at the end of this chapter. Although a divine being of some sort, this

---

34. This phrase may have been overlooked in the copying of this verse, likely due to the scribe skipping from *wyš' dwd* to *wy'mr dwd* in v. 17. This has been noted by McCarter, *II Samuel*, 507; and Ralph W. Klein, *1 Chronicles*, ed. T. Krüger (Minneapolis: Fortress Press, 2006), 425.
35. Klein, *1 Chronicles*, 425; McCarter, *II Samuel*, 511.

angel is "with" the threshing floor and is somehow simultaneously between earth and heaven. These designations may speak more to the essence of this threshing floor as opposed to its physical location. In an intangible way, the angel and the threshing floor are between two realms.

Because this threshing floor is associated with the theophany of the angel of Yahweh, David builds an altar there. Building altars at theophanic locations is attested throughout the Hebrew Bible (Gen. 12:7; 22:9; 35:7; Judg. 6:24). David builds this altar at the command of the prophet Gad (2 Sam. 24:18 // 1 Chron. 21:18), although the Chronicler says that the angel tells Gad to tell David to build the altar, another sign that this angel is particularly interested in this threshing floor. Along with the theophany, David builds an altar to offer sacrifices to end the destruction and plague. Because the threshing floor is owned by Aravnah/Ornan, David must purchase it. The Chronicler notes that when David and his officials approach Ornan, he is threshing wheat on the threshing floor (1 Chron. 21:20b). This detail is lacking in Samuel, but it is in 4QSam^a. That Ornan is threshing wheat should not be overlooked, as this is one of only two occurrences of agricultural activity happening on a threshing floor in the Hebrew Bible.[36] It allows us a window into the transformation and repurposing of nonsacred space into sacred space. Moreover, the threshing supplies, including threshing sledges and yokes, will be burned in the fire for David's offerings (2 Sam. 24:22 // 1 Chron. 21:23). The destruction of the equipment of the former (agrarian) space helps secure the new (sacred) function of the repurposed space. Moreover, this action of ending the use of the threshing floor for agricultural purposes transforms this space from a

---

36. The other occurrence, discussed at the end of chapter 3, is in Ruth 3:7 where Boaz winnows barley on the threshing floor.

temporary sacred space into a *permanent* sacred space, a transformative symbolic gesture that will be discussed in chapter 5.

As David approaches the threshing floor, Aravnah/Ornan greets him by bowing down before him with his face to the ground (2 Sam. 24:20b; 1 Chron. 21:21b). This polite diplomatic gesture sets the tone for the exchange that follows. David offers to purchase the threshing floor at full price (*běkesep mālē'*) (1 Chron. 21:22),[37] along with oxen for the burnt offering and threshing sledges and yokes for wood (2 Sam. 24:22). The Chronicler also says that wheat is purchased for a grain offering, which is probably related to Ornan threshing wheat earlier in the narrative (1 Chron. 21:23). After purchasing the threshing floor and its supplies,

> He [David] built there an altar to Yahweh and offered burnt offerings and peace offerings. So Yahweh answered his request for the land, and the plague was averted from Israel.
>
> *wayyiben šām dāwīd mizbēaḥ layhwh wayyaʻal ʻōlôt ûšělāmîm wayyēʻātēr yhwh lā'āreṣ wattēʻāṣar hammaggēpâ mēʻal yiśrā'ēl.* (2 Sam. 24:25)

> [26]David built there an altar to Yahweh and presented burnt offerings and peace offerings. He called upon Yahweh, and he answered him with fire from the heavens on the altar of burnt offering. [27]And Yahweh commanded the angel, and he put his sword back into its sheath.
>
> [26]*wayyiben šām dāwīd mizbēaḥ layhwh wayyaʻal ʻōlôt ûšělāmîm wayyiqrā' 'el-yhwh wayyaʻănēhû bā'ēš min-haššāmayim ʻal mizbaḥ hāʻōlâ.* [27]*wayyōʼmer yhwh lammal'āk wayyāšeb ḥarbô 'el-nĕdānāh.* (1 Chron. 21:26–27)

---

37. David's insistence upon paying again for the threshing floor owned by Aravnah/Ornan the Jebusite is reminiscent of Abraham's insistence about paying for Sarah's burial plot from Ephron the Hittite. Second Samuel states that David pays fifty shekels of silver, but 1 Chronicles says that he pays six hundred shekels of gold. Jacob Myers suggests that the price difference may be due to the Chronicler not wanting David to pay less for his threshing floor than Abraham paid for the cave of Machpelah (four hundred shekels of silver). Myers, *I Chronicles*, AB 12 (Garden City: Doubleday, 1965), 148–50.

The accounts of David offering sacrifices on the threshing floor are similar, although 1 Chronicles includes some additional information. While both describe David making his offerings, the Chronicler says that David "called upon Yahweh," which is lacking in Samuel perhaps due to haplography.[38] Both accounts assert that Yahweh answers David, but Chronicles says that the answer is with "fire from the heavens." Divine response with fire on offerings occurs when Aaron and his sons use the tabernacle altar for the first time (Lev. 9:24). Similarly, when Elijah calls on Yahweh, he responds with fire over burnt offerings (1 Kgs. 18:24–38). Knoppers rightly notes, "By sanctioning the altar built at the threshing floor of Ornan in a similar way to his sanctioning of the Tabernacle altar, Yhwh publicly designates this place (*māqôm*) as a new sacred precinct."[39] The "fire from the heavens" is the second theophany at this threshing floor, the angel being the first. Just as the angel being "with" the threshing floor is a sign of interest in and approval of this space, so the appearance of fire on the altar is another divine signal supporting this location. The theophanies and the sacrifices are the explicit signs that this is a sacred space; moreover, they help designate this particular threshing floor as the one and only place for cultic activity. These divine actions legitimize Jerusalem above all other contenders—for example, Mt. Ebal (Deut. 27:1–8), Gibeon (1 Kgs. 3:4–5), Mt. Bashan (Ps. 68:16–17).

The Septuagint reading of 2 Sam. 24:25[40] includes an additional note about this altar being in Solomon's temple complex:

> David built there an altar to the Lord and offered up whole burnt offerings and those for peace. And Solomon added onto the altar in the

---

38. This has been suggested by Knoppers as a possible haplography by *homoioarkton* from *wyqr'* to *wy'tr*. Knoppers, *1 Chronicles 10–29*, 750.
39. Ibid., 759.
40. The Septuagint reading of 1 Chron. 21:26–27 is nearly identical to the MT.

end because it was small at first. And the Lord listened to the land, and the destruction was stopped from upon Israel.

kai ōkodomēsan ekei Dauid thysiastērion kyriō kai anēnegken holokautoseis kai eirēnikas kai prosethēken Salōmōn epi to thysiastērion ep' eschatō hoti mikron ēn en prōtois kai epēkousen kyrios tē gē kai syneschethē hē thrausis epanōthen Israēl (LXX 2 Sam. 24:25)

The Septuagint reading "And Solomon added onto the altar in the end because it was small at first"[41] reflects a tradition of this altar becoming the altar of burnt offering in Solomon's temple complex. Interestingly, both Kings and Chronicles preserve the tradition of this altar being too small once the temple is built (1 Kgs. 8:64 // 2 Chron. 7:7); however, neither explicitly says that Solomon enlarged it as found in the Septuagint of 2 Sam. 24:25. This Septuagint reading reflects another aspect of the traditions about the construction of the temple, and it suggests knowledge that the altar originally built by David on this threshing floor is in the Solomonic temple complex.

In this discussion of theophanies and sacrifices on the threshing floor, several elements confirm this location as sacred. The theophany of the angel "with" the threshing floor is a clear manifestation of God. In addition to the angel, the Chronicler notes that fire from the heavens appears on the altar on the threshing floor, which is another manifestation of God on this threshing floor. Because of the events and divine confirmation of this particular space, traditions persist that David's threshing floor purchased from Aravnah/Ornan becomes the location of the temple.

Having considered the types of cultic activities that are situated on threshing floors, the discussion will now shift to look more closely at *who* performs these activities. The following section explores the sociological implications of the use of threshing floors as sacred

---

41. The Septuagint reading suggests that the *Vorlage* of the Septuagint included the Hebrew *wywsp šlmh 'l hmzbḥ 'ḥryt ky qṭwn hyh br'šwnh*, as noted by McCarter, *II Samuel*, 508.

spaces, which will provide additional insights and dimensions to this study and will help to imagine how threshing floors were experienced in ancient Israel.

Social Actors: Who Uses Threshing Floors as Sacred Spaces?

Selecting threshing floors for cultic activities shows a mental understanding of the ability to access and encounter the divine at these locations. Similarly, the social activities that happen on threshing floors are signifiers of the sacredness of the space. The presence of cultic activities shows a mental acknowledgment of the appropriateness of performing rituals on threshing floors. The Hebrew Bible highlights the use of threshing floors as sacred spaces by a variety of social actors: royal officials, prophets under the auspices of kings, nonpriestly officials, and ordinary people. Even a preternatural angel of Yahweh instructs cultic activity to happen on a threshing floor. Though several types of cultic activities (ritual processions, mourning rites, divination rituals, sacrifices) occur on threshing floors, surprisingly priests are rarely, if ever, present for these cultic activities.

Gideon

A warrior and tribal leader divinely commissioned to save Israel from the Midianites, Gideon is a premonarchic leader of Israel who uses a threshing floor as a sacred space. Though he is called by an angel of Yahweh, Gideon is insecure regarding his call and twice seeks divine confirmation for his war, first at a wine press and then at a threshing floor where he performs a divination ritual (Judg. 6:37–40). Gideon seeks a location for access to the divine and goes to the threshing floor in order to find it. Gideon's ritual activity shows that he perceived the threshing floor to be sacred and an auspicious location for contacting Yahweh and receiving a blessing for war. Interestingly, Gideon's divination on the threshing floor is the only narrative that involves a single person using the agricultural space as a sacred space. Most often, there are large groups gathered at threshing floors performing ritual actions, but Gideon's ritual is private and for his personal reassurance.

Ahab, Jehoshaphat, and 402 Prophets

Kings Ahab and Jehoshaphat go to a threshing floor seeking divine approval for their battle against Aram (1 Kgs. 22:10 // 2 Chron. 18:9). Their royal standing is stressed as they are described wearing regalia and seated on thrones. They gather four hundred unnamed prophets to the threshing floor to ascertain a divine message. Additionally, there are two named prophets at this location: Zedekiah, son of Chenaanah, and Micaiah. The kings and prophets use the threshing floor as a way in which to access the divine, and there is a convergence of royal and prophetic authority on this sacred space. Divine presence, divine accessibility, and inquiring after the word of Yahweh occur at the behest of royal officials and in conjunction with prophets.

The four named people, Ahab, Jehoshaphat, Zedekiah, and Micaiah, represent different roles within society. Ahab ruled the northern kingdom during the ninth century BCE and was considered one of the worst kings according to DtrH and prophetic literature (1 Kgs. 16:33; 2 Kgs. 21:3, 13; Mic. 6:16). This is largely because of his marriage to the Phoenician princess Jezebel, who exercised great influence over religious practices in Israel and fostered worship of foreign gods. Ahab is the epitome of a bad, northern ruler. Conversely, Jehoshaphat, a ninth century BCE king of the southern kingdom, is viewed as a pious ruler in 1 Kings and 2 Chronicles, though he did not fully eliminate worship on high places (1 Kgs.

22:41–50; 2 Chron. 17:1–19). The Chronicler includes additional details about Jehoshaphat as a reformer of the military and judicial authority and a faithful leader involved in cultic affairs (2 Chron. 19:1–20:37). Jehoshaphat is a Judean king meeting Ahab in Samaria in Israel to discuss a joint campaign against Aram. While Ahab initiates the discussion, it is Jehoshaphat who suggests to Ahab that they inquire after the word of Yahweh, again highlighting his religious piety. The prophetic intermediary Zedekiah is mentioned in close proximity to the activities on the threshing floor, and he is described making iron horns as a ritual sign-act to portray the destruction of the Aramaeans (1 Kgs. 22:11 // 2 Chron. 18:10). Zedekiah is also in agreement with the four hundred false prophets and reprimands the prophet Micaiah for his negative prophecy. Micaiah is a Yahwistic, non-court-sponsored prophet who is said to regularly prophesy against Ahab. Known only in 1 Kings 22 // 2 Chronicles 18, Micaiah represents true Yahwistic prophecy. Although he initially prophesies in accord with the four hundred unnamed prophets (seemingly in mockery of Ahab or mimicking Ahab's prophets), he then recounts a vision that reveals that Yahweh sent a lying spirit to Ahab's prophets (1 Kgs. 22:20–23 // 2 Chron. 18:19–22) to prophesy in favor of Ahab going to battle in order to bring about his death. In response to Micaiah, Ahab has him imprisoned, asserting his royal power over and above Micaiah's prophetic vision.

The social roles—bad king, pious king, false and true prophets—are all seen united on the threshing floor in hopes of contacting Yahweh, as he is present and reachable at this particular location. This narrative includes several ritual elements: the kings wearing ceremonial robes, Zedekiah making iron horns to symbolize victory, Zedekiah legitimizing his prophetic role and delegitimizing Michaiah's role, four hundred prophets prophesying in unison, and Micaiah receiving a divine vision—all of which add to the ritual activities and sacredness of this location. The use of the threshing floor for such activities is not said to be problematic by Dtr or Chr, even with their strong theologies about centralizing worship in Jerusalem. Within the narrative, Micaiah criticizes Ahab but does not find fault with the use of the threshing floor as a sacred space. This religio-political assembly on the threshing floor is apparently permissible and effective for divine communication. Note once again the absence of priestly actors.

Joseph and a Diverse Group

Joseph performs mourning rituals on a threshing floor accompanied by a diverse funeral procession (Gen. 50:7–11). Having been a successful dream interpreter under the authority of Pharaoh, Joseph ascended to a high status in Egypt. In his departure to bury his father Jacob, Joseph leads a procession of people from various social standings, including servants from his father's house and Pharaoh's house, his brothers and their families, charioteers, and all of the elders of Egypt who exercised great power and authority in the land. People representing those of a lowly status in society, military personnel, and distinguished officials were all present in the ritual activities on the threshing floor. Gathered together, the group performs mourning rites on the threshing floor in order to access Yahweh, who will hear and answer their prayers. By stopping on the threshing floor for such rituals, they reveal their mental inclination towards this space for performing mourning rites. While this procession for Jacob is very large, diverse, and includes people of various social ranks, the author of this passage does not include a priestly presence.

David, Uzzah, and Ahio

On two occasions, King David is depicted in conjunction with cultic activities on threshing floors. The first is soon after he is consecrated as king over Israel and Judah.[42] David gathers military personnel and ordinary people from throughout the land to participate in a cultic procession of the ark to a threshing floor (2 Sam. 6:1–2). The Chronicler's account says that priests and Levites were also involved in the procession (1 Chron. 13:1–2). If they were present, it would be expected for them to handle the ark, and Uzzah's blunder would not have happened. However, like Dtr, Chr does not specify that Uzzah and Ahio are part of the priests or Levites. Chr may note the presence of priests and Levites to draw attention to David's efforts to include all people in his monarchy. Chr meticulously, and in more detail than Dtr, describes David inviting everyone from throughout

---

42. Within the Hebrew Bible, there is an assertion of a united monarchy in the tenth century BCE begun by David and continued with Solomon, and this biblical tradition is what I follow here. This is not to minimize the scholarly questions regarding whether the united monarchy was a historical reality, an ongoing debate without a scholarly consensus. Opinions range from a belief that the Hebrew Bible is historically accurate to a complete denial of the existence of an historical David (a position that has been recently challenged in light of the Tel Dan Stele). I tend to fall somewhere in the middle, finding the person of David to be a historical reality though I question the degree and scope of national unification purported in the Hebrew Bible. For more on the archaeological and historical considerations of this issue, see André Lemaire, "The United Monarchy: Saul, David and Solomon," in *Ancient Israel: From Abraham to the Roman Destruction of the Temple*, ed. H. Shanks (Washington, DC: Biblical Archaeology Society, 1988), 85–108; Israel Finkelstein, "A Great United Monarchy: Archaeological and Historical Perspectives," in *One God-One Cult-One Nation*, ed. R. Kratz and H. Spieckermann (Berlin: de Gruyter, 2010), 1–28; Amihai Mazar, "Archaeology and the Biblical Narrative: The Case of the United Monarchy," in *One God-One Cult-One Nation*, 29–58; Philip R. Davies, *In Search of "Ancient Israel,"* JSOTSup 142 (Sheffield: JSOT Press, 1992), 66–133; William G. Dever, *What Did the Biblical Writers Know & When Did They Know It?* (Grand Rapids: Wm. B. Eerdmans, 2001), 1–158; Thomas L. Thompson, *The Early History of the Israelite People: From the Written and Archaeological Sources* (Leiden: Brill, 1992), 105–26; Israel Finkelstein and Amihai Mazar, *The Quest for the Historical Israel*, ed. B. Schmidt (Atlanta: SBL, 2007), 99–140; Shmuel Ahituv, "The Tel Dan Inscription," in *Echoes from the Past: Hebrew and Cognate Inscriptions from the Biblical Period* (Jerusalem: Carta, 2008), 466–73; P. R. Davies, "'House of David' Built on Sand: The Sins of the Biblical Maximalists," *BAR* 20 (1994): 54–55; and William M. Schniedewind, "Tel Dan Stela: New Light on Aramaic and Jehu's Revolt," *BASOR* 302 (1996): 75–90.

the land to participate in this procession (1 Chron. 13:2). Knoppers aptly notes that this inclusion by Chr is to show David exercising restraint in his use of royal power. He involves everyone, even the priests and Levites, in transferring the cultic symbol to Jerusalem.[43] Additionally, Chr may include the priests and Levites to present a Davidic acknowledgment and assertion of their important role in cultic affairs. This could be why Chr depicts David commanding only the Levites to carry the ark (1 Chron. 15:2), which is similar to Deuteronomic legislation (Deut. 10:8).

In addition to David, there are two other named actors in this procession, Uzzah and Ahio. They are responsible for transporting the ark on a new cart, a job which according to P should have been performed by priests using poles to carry the ark (Exod. 25:10–16). Dtr and Chr do not specify the status of Uzzah and Ahio aside from noting that they transport the ark. However, the brothers are part of a priestly family, as their father Abinadab and brother Eleazar are both priests who previously were in charge of the ark (1 Sam. 7:1). Their priestly heritage could support the notion of Uzzah and Ahio being priests. If they are priests, Chr is explicit that they are not Levitical priests, because after the incident on the threshing floor, he notes that only Levites should transport the ark (1 Chron. 15:2). Uzzah's ineptness in handling the ark, however, lends credence to the idea that he was not a priest, as one would expect him to handle the cultic object properly.

David's large-scale procession includes military personnel and ordinary people (and priests and Levites according to Chr) from throughout Israel and Judah, centered on moving the ark to Jerusalem where it will be housed. This is a militaristic, political, and religious procession designed to promote David as the new

---

43. Knoppers, *1 Chronicles 10–29*, 583.

ruler, bring the ark to the new capital, and bolster and unite the society around David's religious and political agenda. David leads this religio-political, social event to a threshing floor because of its divine connections, which will buttress his bold new monarchy.

If priests and Levites are involved in the procession, this would be our only example of priestly participation in cultic activities at a threshing floor. In the narratives of 2 Samuel 6 // 1 Chronicles 13, large groups composed of various social actors use a threshing floor as a sacred space on which to lead a cultic object and ritual procession. The social actors interacting with each other include a royal official, ordinary people, priests and Levites (only in Chronicles), and two people entrusted with transporting the ark, Uzzah and Ahio. Based on their negligence in handling the ark, it is compelling to presume Uzzah and Ahio were nonpriests given charge over the ark. Based on their father and brother being priests, it has been argued that they are priests, even though this is not stated in the texts. A mix of royal and nonroyal people participate in transforming and substantiating the sacrality of the threshing floor by having their cultic procession at this location.

Angel of Yahweh, Gad, and David

In addition to this procession, David also has an encounter with an angel of Yahweh on a threshing floor where he builds an altar and offers sacrifices (2 Sam. 24:15–25 // 1 Chron. 21:14–27). The angel of Yahweh is described as being in conjunction with the threshing floor. Divine presence and agency are asserted in the angel of Yahweh's manifestation and the activities that occur at the threshing floor. In addition to divine presence, this event also involves prophetic authority.

The prophet Gad is known primarily from David's encounter with the angel of Yahweh on the threshing floor, though he is also mentioned when David is an outlaw in Moab. Advising David to leave Moab to return to Judah (1 Sam. 22:3–5), Gad appears to be David's personal, traveling prophet. Hearing the word of Yahweh, Gad instructs David to build an altar on the threshing floor (Gad hears this from the angel of Yahweh in 1 Chron. 21:18). David follows the divine command, builds an altar, and offers whole burnt offerings and peace offerings on the threshing floor, and according to Chr, divine fire consumes these offerings.

The angel of Yahweh, Gad, and David are agents in the sacrality of the threshing floor. The angel of Yahweh prompts the use of this location as a sacred space, and the prophet delivers a divine word to the king to offer sacrifices, which results in an additional divine manifestation.

This event includes divine presence, prophetic authority, and royal practice of religion on the threshing floor. Ultimately, for Chr this threshing floor becomes the foundation upon which the temple is built. The temple is metaphorically and literally founded on divine, prophetic, and royal religious activity, which will be discussed in chapter 5.

In all of the activities that happen on threshing floors, priests are rarely involved in using threshing floors as sacred spaces. Rather than priests, Uzzah and Ahio appear more as approved cultic functionaries (who recklessly handle the ark); they likely are not priests, despite having priestly family members. People from various social standings—kings, prophets, leaders, soldiers, ordinary people, and servants—are all involved in cultic activities that happen on threshing floors. Even the angel of Yahweh facilitates cultic activity on a threshing floor. Threshing floors are sacred spaces used primarily by groups for nonpriestly cultic activity.

Threshing Floors: Unregulated Sacred Space

In light of this discussion of threshing floors as sacred spaces, one has to wonder why these spaces are not regulated by P or Dtr, considering their special interest in regulating cultic activities. In the previous chapter, legal texts from P and Dtr were analyzed, and there was no mention of threshing floors being used as sacred spaces. If threshing floors are considered under Yahwistic control where cultic activities and divine manifestations can occur, one would expect the Priestly (P) and Deuteronomistic literature (Dtr) to be concerned about regulating the use of threshing floors for cultic activities. Surprisingly, in the legal material of P and Dtr where cultic regulations abound, the topic of threshing floors rarely emerges. As noted in chapter 3, there are only a few mentions of threshing floors in the legal corpora and most focus on the offerings and blessing associated with these spaces. With only a few comments about threshing floors, there is no regulation of these spaces.

Inferior Sacred Space?

The legal material of P, found largely in the books of Leviticus and Numbers, emphasizes purity and holiness as fundamental points of interest. Leviticus is filled with discussions of sacrifices and offerings, the inauguration of the cult, and purity and impurity laws. It is especially concerned with distinguishing Israel from other nations. Numbers is concerned with preparing the Israelites to conquer their promised land. Preparation and execution of their campaign is fundamental as well as laws regarding how to live once in the land. Both legal corpora discuss proper behavior and proper execution of the cult, and P emphasizes the importance of *who* can perform which cultic activities and how they are to be done.

As P is especially concerned with purity, consecration, and proper performance of cultic activities, P places divinatory objects[44] and sacrificial offerings[45] under the auspices of the priests. By doing this, P asserts that the priests are necessary in all cultic affairs. In highlighting the priesthood, P situates priests as conduits for obtaining access to Yahweh, functioning as intermediaries between Israel and Yahweh. While people can obtain divine favor and blessings independent of priests, priests are required in matters such as determining the will of Yahweh through divination and providing offerings to Yahweh through sacrifice. For these cultic activities, P makes it necessary for people to consult the priests.

The emphasis that P places on regulating sacred space is largely in its detailed accounts of how cultic matters are to be handled and who has access to the divine within the sanctuary (Leviticus 1–6; 16; cf. Ezek. 44:1–21, which has Ezekiel's vision of the temple with regulations of the sacred space and gradations of holiness). For instance, priests are permitted entry into certain areas of the sanctuary, and even the Holy of Holies is only accessible to the high priest. The actions of the priests themselves within sacred space reflect carefully controlled gradations of holiness. This emphasis on access to the divine will be explored more in the following chapter on temple construction.

As P is certainly concerned about sacred space and access to the divine, it seems all the more peculiar that they do not regulate threshing floors, as these were "perceived-conceived-lived" as sacred

---

44. These divinatory Urim and Thummim are given to priests at ordination and are held in the priest's breastplate (Exod 28:30; Lev 8:8; Num. 27:21). Priests are also able to cast lots to divine the will of Yahweh (Lev 16:8).

45. In the Hebrew Bible (even within P material) nonpriests are involved in offering sacrifices (Lev. 4:22, 27; 17:3–9). However, the manipulation of sacrificial blood is distinctly a priestly function. See Ziony Zevit, "Israel's Royal Cult in the Ancient Near Eastern Kulturkreis," in *Text, Artifact, and Image: Revealing Ancient Israelite Religion*, ed. G. Beckman and T. Lewis (Providence: Brown Judaic Studies, 2006), 189–200.

spaces. This lack of regulation could be because P did not consider threshing floors of equal status to other sacred spaces such as the tabernacle or the temple. If threshing floors lack the esteem of the priests, this could also explain why priests are rarely, if ever, involved in cultic activities on threshing floors. P may have viewed threshing floors as inferior sacred spaces because of their inability to be carefully regulated, especially with regard to the eradication of impurity. For P, the expiation of impurities is impossible apart from the *ḥaṭṭā't* and *'āšām* rituals provided by the priests.[46] Even if they are effective sacred spaces, threshing floors lack the ability to be controlled and regulated because they still function as open-access agricultural spaces.

Rival Sacred Space?

Dtr is especially concerned with the proper location for cultic activities, so one would expect it to say something about threshing floors since they are used for these activities. As noted in the previous chapter, Deut. 16:13–15 may suggest that threshing floors were potential rivals to Yahweh's chosen place. Beyond the context of that particular pilgrimage law, in general threshing floors may have been viewed as rivals because they are unrestricted and prevalent spaces associated with Yahweh. Every city had at least one threshing floor, and likely more than one in that privately owned threshing floors are attested (2 Sam. 6:6; 24:18–24). As ubiquitous, open-access spaces associated with Yahwistic control and theophany, threshing floors could be viewed as a problem for the Deuteronomist's program of centralization to one sanctuary and his hold on centralized power. If threshing floors were potential threats to centralization, Dtr *should* have banned the use of threshing floors for cultic activities, yet

---

46. For a recent treatment on the *ḥaṭṭā't* and *'āšām* rituals and extensive bibliography, see Isabel Cranz, "Impurity and Ritual in the Priestly Source and Assyro-Babylonian Incantations" (PhD diss., The Johns Hopkins University, 2012), 84–88, 248–71.

there is no such ban. Dtr is elusive on this matter, probably because he is familiar with the tradition found in 2 Chron. 3:1 that the temple is built on a threshing floor (to be discussed in the following chapter and excursus). Because Dtr is especially interested in cultic spaces, the tradition of the temple on a threshing floor is information that was likely available to him. It would be very problematic and contradictory for Dtr to ban the location upon which Solomon builds his temple. Perhaps for this reason, Dtr neither confirms nor condemns threshing floors in the laws of Deuteronomy.

In trying to figure out why neither P nor Dtr regulate these spaces, the answers are slightly different. P focuses largely on who is authorized to perform cultic activities and on maintaining the purity of sacred space. He is especially concerned with priestly eradication of impurity from the sanctuary via the Priestly *ḥaṭṭā't* and *'āšām* rituals. Therefore P has little patience for an openly accessible space that by definition defies regulation. The only way in which a threshing floor could serve as sacred space would be to require a complete overhaul and repurposing—which is precisely what happens when it comes to Aravnah/Ornan's threshing floor. As Dtr is very much focused on the location of cultic activities, his silence is somewhat curious. Confronted with several positive threshing-floor passages within the DtrH (Judg. 6:37–40; 2 Sam. 6:6–7; 24:15–25), it would have been contradictory to condemn these locations as unacceptable for cultic activities. While the killing of Uzzah on the threshing floor is not positive *per se*, the presence of the cultic procession that travels to the threshing floor shows a positive association with ritual activity and highlights the sacrality of this space. Even without a condemnation, Dtr likely found threshing floors to be potential threats on account of their openness, accessibility, prevalence, and connections to Yahweh. Nonetheless, Dtr is silent because a ban on the use of threshing floors for cultic activities would contradict traditions of the Solomonic temple being built on a threshing floor.

Summary

This chapter has argued that cultic activities and divine manifestation occur on threshing floors, suggesting that these spaces are sacred. In comparison to chapter 2, which presented Yahweh as the agent who controlled the success or failure of threshing floors, in this chapter humans are the agents in choosing threshing floors because of their sacred qualities. Yahwistic control over these spaces suggests that these spaces were connected to Yahweh, and the narratives discussed in this chapter show this theory actualized. Gideon and the kings of Israel and Judah go to threshing floors in order to divine the will of God, and both attempts are successful. Rituals are performed on threshing floors because these places were considered appropriate and efficacious for contacting God. With the appearance of the anger of Yahweh, the angel of Yahweh, and fire from the heavens, the divine is made manifest.

Based on these narratives about threshing floors within the biblical corpus, it seems evident that, beyond their use as agricultural spaces, threshing floors were considered locations to be used as sacred spaces. Though an overt revelation is not found in each instance, there does appear to be cultural understanding that these spaces are connected to Yahweh based on his control over and appearance on these spaces. In looking at the social implications of threshing floors as sacred spaces, it is important to note who is involved in cultic activities and how they function in order to understand how threshing floors were experienced in society. Most of the narratives show a combination of various social statuses gathered together to perform cultic activities. The priests, perpetually concerned about cultic affairs, do not engage in this behavior.[47] In fact, the priests may never have been involved in cultic activities on threshing floors, as the Chronicler's inclusion of the priests and Levites in David's cultic procession may serve his Davidic royal ideology rather than reflect historical reality. If that is the case, then the priests never participated in cultic activities on threshing floors likely because they did not see threshing floors as legitimate, priestly sanctioned sacred spaces, and they found problems with nonpriests engaging in unregulated cult activities.

Excursus: Threshing Floors as Liminal Spaces

In addition to the depiction of threshing floors as sacred spaces, a few of the passages discussed above present threshing floors as liminal spaces, namely, locations that are gateways to accessing the divine. This is particularly visible when there are outward signs and divine manifestations on threshing floors.

The term "liminality" (from the Latin *limen* meaning "threshold") was used in the early twentieth century by anthropologist Arnold van Gennep and was later advanced by Victor Turner. In his research on rites of passage, Van Gennep asserted that there is a tripartite structure to such ceremonies, noting that the second stage (the liminal period) is an ambiguous state of transition.[48] Using van Gennep's theoretical framework, Victor Turner incorporated and elaborated on the concept of liminality. Turner emphasized that during the liminal period, individuals are "betwixt and between" stages. The liminal period is when a person "passes through a realm that has few or none of the attributes of the past or coming state."[49] During a liminal phase, a person is often separated from society and enters a time of personal

---

47. If one follows 1 Chronicles 13:2, then that would be the only occurrence of priestly involvement in cultic activities on threshing floors. As discussed above, the historicity of the reference to "priests and Levites" in the procession is in question as they may be listed to establish Davidic openness, inclusion, and promotion of the priests rather than representing an historical reality.
48. See Arnold van Gennep, *The Rites of Passage: A Classic Study of Cultural Celebrations*, trans. M. B. Vizedom and G. L. Caffee (Chicago: The University of Chicago Press, 1960).

growth in a location where they may experience an encounter with a deity or superhuman power in an unbounded way.[50]

Turner's "betwixt and between" language and theory are helpful in conceptualizing what happens on threshing floors when there is simultaneously human and divine presence and communication. Physical spaces possess liminality when they are "betwixt and between" locations. In the case of threshing floors, though physically part of the human world, they are sometimes shown as part of the divine world, particularly with overt indicators of divine presence. For instance, the liminality of threshing floors is discernible when God provides a divine answer of dew to Gideon on the threshing floor (Judg. 6:38–40) and when Micaiah has a prophetic vision (1 Kgs. 22:10 // 2 Chron. 18:9) on the threshing floor at the city gate of Samaria. Also, the divine manifestation of anger that strikes and kills Uzzah and the fire from the heavens (2 Sam. 6:6–7 // 1 Chron. 13:9–10; 2 Sam. 24:15 // 1 Chron. 21:14–15) are manifestations of the liminality of these spaces. While the threshing floor is on earth, these passages reflect a divine display on earth. The most striking example of the liminality of a threshing floor is the presence of the angel of Yahweh between earth and heaven on Ornan's threshing floor (1 Chron. 21:16). In that instance, the angel is literally described in a "betwixt and between" state of being "with" the threshing floor purchased by David.

In the following chapter, the building of the Solomonic temple on David's threshing floor marks a transformation of that space from a temporary sacred and liminal space used by nonpriestly social actors into a permanent sacred and liminal space used primarily by priests in the administration of the cult. The construction of the temple on

---

49. Victor Turner, *The Forest of Symbols: Aspects of Ndembu Ritual* (Ithaca: Cornell University Press, 1967), 94.
50. Ibid., 98.

the threshing floor associated with sacrality and liminality solidifies the idea that threshing floors are locations intimately linked with Yahweh.

5

Temple Construction upon a Threshing Floor

In the previous chapter, the passages discussed very clearly depict threshing floors being used as sacred spaces. From rituals to theophanies, these agricultural spaces are understood and portrayed as sacred locations in several biblical texts. This chapter will present the clearest example of a threshing floor as a sacred space, as it is the foundation on which the Solomonic temple is built.

At the end of 2 Samuel 24 // 1 Chronicles 21,[1] David purchases Aravnah/Ornan's threshing floor and offers burnt offerings to avert destruction and plague. After the catastrophes are avoided, the Chronicler includes additional information about why David sacrifices on this threshing floor. The Chronicler states that David was unable to inquire of God at the high place of Gibeon because of his fear of the angel (1 Chron. 21:29–30).[2] Instead of traveling,

---

1. For more on the date, genre, and context of Samuel and Chronicles, see chapters 2 and 4.
2. Gary Knoppers notes that although the Chronicler can be conservative in quoting sources, he also composes and supplements his *Vorlage*. Knoppers, *1 Chronicles 10–29: A New Translation*

David remains in Jerusalem and sacrifices there at the threshing floor. This detail serves as an explanation for why Gibeon's role as a cult center was to be transferred to Jerusalem. Namely, because David encountered theophanies at the threshing floor in Jerusalem and because Yahweh answered him and affirmed the location, this threshing floor is to be the foundation for the temple. To further legitimize this location, the Chronicler includes an explicit declaration: "Then David said, 'Here will be the house of Yahweh God and here the altar of burnt offering for Israel'" (*wayyōʼmer dāwîd zeh hûʼ bêt yhwh hāʼĕlōhîm wĕzeh-mizbēaḥ lĕʻōlâ lĕyiśrāʼēl*) (1 Chron. 22:1). Subsequently, this is declared with even stronger justification in 2 Chron. 3:1.

2 Chronicles 3:1

> Solomon began to build the House of Yahweh in Jerusalem at Mount Moriah, where Yahweh had appeared to David his father, at the place that David established, on the threshing floor of Ornan the Jebusite.
>
> *wayyāḥel šĕlōmōh libnôt ʼet-bêt-yhwh bîrûšālaim bĕhar hammôrîyā ʼăšer nirʼâ lĕdāwîd ʼābîhû ʼăšer hēkîn bimqôm dāwîd bĕgōren ʼornān hayĕbûsî.* (2 Chron. 3:1)

According to the Chronicler, the temple is built on the threshing floor purchased by David, the same location connected to theophanies of the angel and fire from the heavens and declared by David to be the house of Yahweh. The Chronicler also notes that this threshing floor is associated with Mount Moriah, which seems to be an allusion to Abrahamic traditions in which Abraham took Isaac to the land of Moriah in order to sacrifice him (Gen. 22:2). This allusion to Abraham is likely to further sanctify and legitimize

---

with Introduction and Commentary, AB 12a (New York: Doubleday, 2004), 762. First Chronicles 21:27–22:1 may reflect an original composition of the Chronicler.

the location, a position that has been asserted by others.³ In addition to adding sanctity and history to the location, Theodore Lewis has suggested that the inclusion of the Moriah tradition may harken back to Abraham's sacrifice of a ram, in order to legitimize animal sacrifice at this location that was originally for grain only.⁴ These suggestions are compelling as they connect the foundation of the Solomonic temple to both David and Abraham.

The Chronicler's identification of Yahweh's house with the threshing floor purchased by David is a significant sign that this threshing floor is a sacred space. Moreover, the building of the temple signifies a centralization of all cultic activities at this one location. When considering this larger discussion of threshing floors, situating the temple on a threshing floor is in line with what has been discussed. Chapter 2 showed the great interest and control Yahweh has over threshing floors. He blesses them and intervenes to save them so that they can support life. On the same token, when Yahweh is unhappy with human behavior, he can also curse these locations. In chapter 4, threshing floors are shown to be effective locations to contact Yahweh and places associated with divine manifestation. Rituals are successfully performed on these locations, prophecy is effectual, and divine manifestations (both negative and positive)

---

3. A. Anderson has noted that this inclusion of Moriah may be to add even more sanctity to the location. Anderson, *2 Samuel*, WBC 11 (Nashville: Thomas Nelson, 1989), 283–84. Similarly, Knoppers notes that antiquarian traditions were highly valued, so the Chronicler "draws a straight line from a pivotal area in the ancestral age to the site of the central sanctuary built by David's divinely-chosen heir." Gary Knoppers, "The Relationship of the Deuteronomistic History to Chronicles: Was the Chronicler a Deuteronomist?" in *Congress Volume Helsinki 2010*, ed. M. Nissinen, 307–42 (Leiden: Brill, 2012). Some scholars have questioned the Chronicler's use of the account of the building of the temple in 1 Kings, questioning the historicity and additions within the Chronicler's account. See Isaac Kalimi, "The Land of Moriah, Mount Moriah, and the Site of Solomon's Temple in Biblical Historiography," *HTR* 83 (1990): 345–62; and John Van Seters, "Solomon's Temple: Fact and Ideology in Biblical and Near Eastern Historiography," *CBQ* 59 (1997): 45–57. I think the two accounts of the building of the temple differ in a variety of ways aside from the detail regarding location in 2 Chron. 3:1. The accounts are simply two variant traditions of the building of the temple.
4. Private communication with Theodore J. Lewis.

occur on these locations. With all of this in mind, the tradition of building the temple on a threshing floor is an appropriate and obvious choice because of Yahweh's control over and accessibility at these spaces.

Excursus: The Historicity of the Chronicler's Account of the Temple Construction

While the Chronicler is explicit about the location of the temple on the threshing floor, the narratives of Samuel-Kings are less explicit. The account of the building of the temple in 1 Kings 6 does not specify the location of the temple but instead focuses largely on the precise dimensions, expensive materials, and tools used to build it.[5] Unlike the other parallel accounts in Samuel-Kings and Chronicles discussed in the previous chapter, 1 Kings 6 and 2 Chronicles 3 are not parallel but rather are from independent sources and represent different traditions about the construction of the temple, with only one tradition (2 Chron. 3:1) specifying the location. The Septuagint of Samuel (LXX 2 Sam. 24:25) reflects the tradition of Solomon enlarging the altar for the temple, suggesting that within the Samuel tradition there is an acknowledgment that David's altar that was built on the threshing floor is the one later enlarged to serve the temple. Clearly, there are various details, aspects, and traditions related to the temple construction. Chronicles is considered here because it is the only tradition to preserve a precise location of the temple. There could be a variety of reasons why the Samuel-Kings accounts do not mention the threshing floor (or any location beyond Jerusalem) in the account of the temple construction. Below are a few possible scenarios that might help to explain the differences in the accounts.

---

5. The book of Ezekiel also includes a vision of the temple that focuses heavily on the precise measurements, decorations, and materials. There is not an explicit reference to the temple being on a threshing floor.

Option 1: The Chronicler creates a tradition about the location of the temple by embellishing the story of David's divine encounter at Aravnah/Ornan's threshing floor.

Though not the most compelling possibility, it should be noted that the location of the temple on the threshing floor could be a fictional creation by the Chronicler, but one would have to ask what purpose such an embellished story would serve. Perhaps the Chronicler seeks to endorse threshing floors as sacred spaces. If this were the case, one might expect even more examples of threshing floors in Chronicles, which is not the case. Aside from the location of the temple, the Chronicler does not include any threshing-floor reference that is not also found in Samuel-Kings. In fact, Samuel-Kings has more references to threshing floors than Chronicles (1 Sam. 23:1 and 2 Kgs. 6:27 discussed in chapter 2 do not have parallels in Chronicles). Also, after the building of the temple, threshing floors are rarely mentioned in connection with cultic activities. The kings and prophets seeking divine approval for war (1 Kgs. 22:10 // 2 Chron. 18:9) is the only example of something cultic on a threshing floor after the temple is built, and even in that narrative access to the divine is the focus rather than ritual activity. Like Samuel-Kings, the Chronicler is concerned about perpetuating the tradition of centralization in the Solomonic temple, so he would not want to endorse an alternative sacred space.

Another possible reason for creating an embellished tradition may have been to empower priestly control of the Solomonic temple. The Davidic threshing-floor foundation story may be told not only to link David with the Solomonic temple but also to connect this location with animal sacrifice via the Mount Moriah reference. By situating this threshing floor on Mount Moriah, animal sacrifice becomes the focal point of the cultic activity (replacing the original focus on grain). This emphasis on animal sacrifice may have sought to advance priestly power and prestige at this threshing floor since only priests can manipulate sacrificial blood. If this is fiction by the Chronicler, it is still very telling that at such a late stage the threshing floor was viewed as an appropriate location for cultic activities in the Solomonic temple. Similarly, it provides a way in which priests can assert themselves into the cultic activities that occur on this threshing floor. As was seen in the previous chapter, priests are almost never included in cultic activity on threshing floors, and the only possible occurrence (1 Chron. 13:2 with the reference to the priests and Levites in the cultic procession of the ark) is found in Chronicles. Again, this may be to interject priests into an otherwise nonpriestly sacred space.

Option 2: The author of 1 Kings 6 is unaware of the location of the temple or does not find the detail noteworthy.

The account of the building of the temple in 1 Kings 6 does not specify the location of the temple, but instead focuses largely on the precise dimensions, expensive materials, and tools used to build it. Unlike the other parallel accounts in Samuel-Kings and Chronicles discussed in the previous chapter, 1 Kings 6 and 2 Chronicles 3 are not parallel accounts of the temple construction. For instance, the construction of the temple in Kings includes a longer date formula, more detailed descriptions of the splendor and prestige of the materials used, and more details about the precision of the construction. It is possible that location was not included because other details were deemed more essential. A similar possibility is that the location of the temple was so well-known that the author felt it unnecessary to include it. As Kings was written earlier than Chronicles, perhaps the author felt it more important to highlight lesser-known information. Similarly, the author of Kings does not include the construction of the altar within the Solomonic temple complex. While there surely was an altar, the author does not describe it being built (probably because it had already been constructed by David). As the foundation story of David purchasing the threshing floor and building an altar may have been widespread knowledge, the author of Kings instead focuses on the lesser-known details and on Solomon as David's cultic heir.

Option 3: The author of 1 Kings 6 knows where the temple was built but intentionally omits it.

This is an interesting possibility that was proposed in chapters 3 and 4. If the author of Kings found the threshing floor to be an unacceptable location for the temple, then it is very likely he intentionally omitted this detail. Because threshing floors were ubiquitous throughout the region, confirming that the temple was built on such a commonplace location might inadvertently endorse the use of *any* threshing floor for cultic activity. Thus the author of 1 Kings 6 might have feared that people would use their local threshing floors for cultic activities rather than travel to the Solomonic temple, which is a very dangerous possibility for Dtr who is principally concerned about centralization in the Solomonic temple. As the tradition of the location of the temple was probably known, the author of Kings could not easily create an alternative location; instead, he neither confirms nor denies the location of the temple. Rather, he does not mention its location and highlights other features such as the date, materials, and architecture. Relatedly, the author of 1 Kings 6 may have sought to downplay the Davidic threshing-floor foundation story in order to focus on the new construction that highlighted Solomon's role as temple builder par excellence. Even if he did not find threshing floors to threaten centralization, he still may have sought to minimize their status in order to maximize the importance of Solomon and his temple. Such an omission might date to a preexilic, pro-Solomon redaction layer within the DtrH.[6]

Option 4: The designation of David's threshing floor purchased from Aravnah/Ornan as the future site of the temple is lost in the MT of Samuel, so the author of 1 Kings 6 did not include the location.

The author of 1 Kings 6 may have had a version of Samuel that lacked David's designation of the threshing floor as the location of the temple (cf. 2 Chron. 21:27–22:1, discussed above). The MT of Samuel, when compared to 4QSam^a and Chronicles, may represent a defective text containing extensive haplography. Our data may not reflect a consciously evasive attitude on Dtr's part but rather could just represent a defective text. In short, Dtr may have indeed once had the same longer text as the Chronicler, but what remains has suffered due to mechanical transmission errors.

Option 5: The Chronicler reflects an historical tradition of the location of the temple.

As previously noted, the Chronicler used Samuel-Kings to compose his history, and he also had available other oral and written sources, which could account for his longer genealogies, additional narratives, and details not found in Samuel-Kings. It is also possible that the Chronicler's *Vorlage* of Samuel might have been longer than what is preserved in the MT of Samuel, a *Vorlage* that more closely reflects the traditions found in 4QSam^a. Thus it is conceivable that the

---

6. For more on a possible pro-Solomon layer of the DtrH, see François Langlamet, "Pour ou contre Salomon? La rédaction prosalomonienne de 1 Rois i–ii," Parts 1–2, *RB* 83 (1976): 321–79; 481–528; Timo Veijola, *Die ewige Dynastie: David und die Entstehung seiner Dynastie nach der deuteronomistischen Darstellung*, AASF B 193 (Helsinki: Suomalainen Tiedeakatemia, 1975), 16–30; and Ernst Würthwein, *Die Erzählung von der Thronfolge Davids—theologische oder politische Geschichtsschreibung?* ThSt B 115 (Zürich: Theologischer Verlag, 1974), 7–59.

Chronicler simply includes the threshing-floor detail because he knew such a tradition to exist. Even though Dtr does not connect the Davidic threshing floor to the Solomonic temple, this should not hinder the discussion of the Chronicler's inclusion of the temple location, especially since Dtr does not declare an alternative site.

Temple: *Axis Mundi* on a Threshing Floor

The construction of the temple on the threshing floor purchased by David is the most explicit evidence of a threshing floor being used as a permanent sacred and liminal space. It also represents a transformation within society, in which the once open sacred space becomes a restricted sacred building.

Even with its restrictions, the temple was considered the *axis mundi* of ancient Israel, the spiritual center betwixt and between heaven and earth that was the central location of divine accessibility and presence. As the religious center, the temple exemplified the immanence and transcendence of Yahweh. The terminology used for the temple (*bayit*, "house"; *hêkāl*, "palace") and the elaborate design and fixtures are symbolic declarations of divine presence and residence in the temple. Though a divine house was conceived of in the temple construction, Yahweh's transcendence beyond the physical building is also asserted. For instance, in Ezekiel's visions of the temple, Yahweh's glory (*kābôd yhwh*) resides there, though physically Yahweh is not there (Ezek. 1:1–28; 10:18–19; 40:34–35; 43:1–12). In one of P's *kābôd* texts, Moses requests to see Yahweh's glory (*kābôd yhwh*), and Yahweh equates such an action to seeing his face, which is a dangerous action (Exod. 33:17–23). Likewise, according to Dtr's "name theology," Yahweh's name (*šēm*) is said to dwell within the temple, though not Yahweh physically (Deut. 12:11; 14:23; 16:2–11;

26:2; 2 Sam. 7:12–17).[7] Yahweh's glory and name typify immaterial divine presence.

Yahweh's presence is also symbolized by the ark of the covenant being placed in the inner sanctum, the Holy of Holies (*qōdeš haqqodāšîm*). With its placement in the temple, the ark, the symbol of divine and political power, serves as a reminder of two older traditions in which threshing floors served as sacred spaces. The first, the threshing floor of Nakon/Kidon, was the location where the ark was transported and improperly handled by Uzzah, resulting in his death. The second, the threshing floor of Aravnah/Ornan, was where a theophany occurred and where David subsequently made offerings to Yahweh. Thus it is the location that became the foundation of the temple within which the ark is housed. Now in the temple, the ark is protected by cherubim and properly handled by the high priest.

In the priestly conception of the temple, there are gradations of holiness, and the area deemed most holy (the Holy of Holies) was the closest to the divine and strictly regulated.[8] While priests were permitted in the outer parts of the temple, only the high priest was permitted to enter the Holy of Holies once per year on the Day

---

7. For more on *kābôd* and name theology, see Tryggve N. D. Mettinger, "The Name and the Glory: The Zion-Sabaoth Theology and its Exilic Successors," *JNSL* 24 (1998): 1–24; Mettinger, *The Dethronement of Sabaoth: Studies in the Shem and Kabod Theologies* (Lund: CWK Gleerup, 1982); S. Dean McBride, "The Deuteronomic Name Theology" (PhD diss., Harvard University, 1969); Gerhard von Rad, "Deuteronomy's 'Name' Theology and the Priestly Document's 'Kabod' Theology," in *Studies in Deuteronomy* (London: SCM Press, 1953), 37–44. For a recent challenge to name theology, see Sandra L. Richter, *The Deuteronomistic History and the Name Theology: Lĕšakkēn Šĕmô Šām in the Bible and the Ancient Near East* (Berlin: Walter de Gruyter, 2002). Richter's challenges have also been challenged. See John Van Seters, "Review of S. Richter, The Deuteronomistic History and the Name Theology: Lĕšakkēn Šĕmô Šām in the Bible and the Ancient Near East," *JAOS* 123 (2003): 871–72.
8. See Menahem Haran, *Temples and Temple Service in Ancient Israel: An Enquiry into the Character of Cult Phenomena and the Historical Setting of the Priestly School* (Oxford: Clarendon, 1978), 175–88; Philip Peter Jenson, *Graded Holiness: A Key to the Priestly Conception of the World*, JSOTSup 106 (Sheffield: Sheffield Academic Press, 1992), 56–209; and Seung Il Kang, "Creation, Eden, Temple and Mountain: Textual Presentations of Sacred Space in the Hebrew Bible" (PhD diss., The Johns Hopkins University, 2008), 121–48.

of Atonement (Lev. 16:1–34). In controlling the temple, the priests developed a systematic set of regulations on who gained access to holy areas and cultic objects. Only the high priest had the closest access to the divine. The high priest and other priests were permitted within the outer shrine. Ordinary, nonpriestly people were not permitted to approach the inner or outer shrine but could obtain access to the outer courtyard where sacrifices were offered. The priests insert their presence to such an extent that they alone control access to the divine, with all the power and prestige that this implies. By creating such a systematic set of limits on access to the divine at the temple, the priests effectively took control of a once openly accessible cult and regulated how much access ordinary people were granted to the divine.

While the temple was the religious center, it also played an important political role. In terms of location, the temple was in close proximity to the royal palace, and the building of the temple coincides with the building of the palace and the unification of the national state. The temple was established during a period of sociopolitical transition from a tribal league to a monarchy. Military campaigns and turbulent diplomatic relations surrounded the establishment of the national state, the temple, and the royal palace. In building such extravagant structures, King Solomon, at the command of David, made a bold statement to the people of Israel and Judah and to foreign states of the religious and political strength of the house of David. By situating the palace in close proximity to the temple, Solomon made a declaration that divine support of political affairs was necessary and the two were essentially interconnected.

In addition to close proximity to the temple, kings regularly officiated at cultic affairs. For instance, Solomon expanded the priestly offices (1 Kgs. 4:1–6). He also offered prayer at the dedication of the temple, was involved in the dedicatory sacrifices, and held festivals at the dedication. Deborah Rooke notes that, based on biblical evidence (1 Kgs. 12:26–13:1; 2 Kgs. 16:10–14; 18:1–4; 22:1–23:24), "it seems reasonable to conclude that the king would have had the right, if not the duty, to perform quite a number of ritual observances, but that his responsibilities were largely delegated to the senior priest."[9] While kings participated in sacrifices, they were forbidden from manipulating blood, as this role is strictly for the priests. While kings had involvement in and control over many aspects of the cult, the kings who participated in blood manipulation were condemned. For instance, Ahaz was severely denounced because he sacrificed on forbidden areas and manipulated blood (2 Kgs. 16:12–15).[10]

The temple represented the convergence of the religio-political beliefs of Israel and Judah. Royal officials, though restricted from performing certain activities within the temple proper, were involved in cultic matters and used religion to gain support and show legitimization of their policies. The temple as the *axis mundi* on the threshing floor was a religious, social, and political statement to the people of Israel and Judah and to the outside world. In addition,

---

9. Deborah W. Rooke, "Kingship as Priesthood: The Relationship between the High Priesthood and the Monarchy," in *King and Messiah in Israel and the Ancient Near East: Proceedings of the Oxford Old Testament Seminar*, ed. John Day, JSOTSup 270 (Sheffield: Sheffield Academic Press, 1998), 195. Rooke suggests that the senior priest functioned *in loco regis* to carry out what were technically royal duties.

10. For more on royal involvement in cult see Bernard M. Levinson, "The Reconceptualization of Kingship in Deuteronomy and the Deuteronomistic History's Transformation of Torah," *VT* 51 (2001): 511–34; John Day, "The Canaanite Inheritance of the Israelite Monarchy," in *King and Messiah in Israel and the Ancient Near East*, 72–90; Rooke, "Kingship as Priesthood," 187–208; Gösta W. Ahlström, "Administration of the State in Canaan and Ancient Israel," in *Civilizations of the Ancient Near East*, ed. J. Sasson (New York: Scribner's, 1995), 587–603; J. C. L. Gibson, "The Kingship of Yahweh against Its Canaanite Background," in *Ugarit and the Bible*, ed. G. J. Brooke, A. H. W. Curtis, and J. F. Healey (Münster: Ugarit-Verlag, 1994), 101–12; Zev Falk, "Religion and State in Ancient Israel," in *Politics and Theopolitics in the Bible and Postbiblical Literature*, ed. H. G. Reventlow, Y. Hoffman, and B. Uffenheimeimer (Sheffield: JSOT Press, 1994) 49–54; Susanna Garfein, "Temple-Palace Conflict in Pre-Exilic Judah" (PhD diss., The Johns Hopkins University, 2004).

the temple played an important economic role in society. It was a symbol of wealth with many gold, silver, and bronze furnishings, and it housed the temple treasury. These religio-political dynamics certainly functioned on an economic level as well.

While the temple complex with its inner and outer courtyards united society around worship of Yahweh in one central sanctuary, by design the temple proper (that is, the temple building itself) excluded the majority of societal members. The temple's configuration focused on the exclusion of nonpriests from direct access to the divine. In the building of the temple, the permanent dwelling place for Yahweh, the priests showed extreme concern and care to limit the accessibility to and availability of Yahweh. With several doorways and outer courtyards with the sacrificial altar, people could get in close proximity to the temple proper yet were not permitted entrance.

In a striking twist from the original use of threshing floors as sacred spaces, building the temple on a threshing floor removed many of the basic principles of these spaces and put a tight hold on who could access the divine. For instance, one of the reasons a variety of social actors are able to use the threshing floors is because they are open-access, uncontrolled, and unrestricted spaces with a high potential for divine access. Whether royal official or impoverished servant, the threshing floor was an available space that anyone in society could use as a location where Yahweh was reachable. The narratives that present threshing floors as sacred spaces bring together a wide variety of societal members, united in their knowledge and belief in divine presence and accessibility on threshing floors. While the priests do not condemn these actions outright, they are minimally involved in these activities. Priests are markedly (if not altogether) absent from most cultic events on threshing floors; they likely found these places to be unsuitable, even if effective, sacred spaces because they permitted divine access in an uncontrollable manner. There are no gradations of holiness at a threshing floor. There is no hierarchical design with barriers surrounding the divine. The threshing floor is an open design where all are permitted equal access to the divine, access that is not dependent on a particular social status. The priests made a calculated gesture in transforming an open-access community location into a tightly guarded, hierarchically structured building. In Solomon's construction of the temple, royal and priestly actors elect to give priests control of access to the divine and of cultic activities, an action that excluded most societal members.

Threshing Floor Transformation

How could the once open-access, community space be transformed into a limited access, priestly controlled building? Such a feat was possible and orchestrated with the combined efforts of P and Dtr in repurposing David's threshing floor into the Solomonic temple. The chart below illustrates some significant differences between a threshing floor and a temple.

Threshing Floors	Temples
Open space	Closed building
Open access to all	Restricted access
No gradations of holiness	Gradations of holiness
Inclusive, community-oriented and loosely managed	Exclusive, hierarchically oriented and hyper-managed
Seasonal usage	Year-round usage
Agricultural by design with the potential to be sacred	Sacred by design
Potential for divine accessibility	Near certain divine accessibility

While there clearly are stark differences between these two spaces, there are a few areas of overlap, particularly in sacrality and divine accessibility. While threshing floors were certainly used for their agricultural purposes, their potential for sacredness and divine contact is what led to this type of space being used as the foundation for the temple. Its particular association with David's divine encounter helps solidify why Aravnah/Ornan's threshing floor becomes the foundation for the temple.

Insights from Lefebvre and Japhet

Henri Lefebvre's spatial theory addresses a phenomenon that he calls "contradictory space," which allows for a more varied look at space. Instead of focusing on a space as "transparent, pure, and neutral," contradictory space theory allows for a more complex view based logically on the complexities of a society.[11] As noted above, there are inherent contradictions between a threshing floor and a temple. The works of P and Dtr may be ideological, yet they are nonetheless fleshing out some type of historical reality that tried to make sense of these dichotomies. In reflecting on how the literature and historical circumstances addressed these contradictions, Lefebvre's tripartite spatial theory can help explicate the physical, mental, and social transformation; and Japhet's work on the shift from temporary to permanent sacred space is also informative.

Physically: The most obvious transformative element is that the open-access unrestricted space has a highly restricted building constructed on top of it. The temple construction and regulations that are presented by Dtr highlight the precision and gradations of holiness that were physically absent from the threshing floor (1 Kgs. 6:5, 16, 19; 8:6–10). Likewise, in its conception of the sanctuary,

---

11. Henri Lefebvre, *The Production of Space*, trans. D. Nicholson-Smith (Malden: Blackwell, 1974), 292–96.

P regulates divine accessibility by restricting nearly everyone from direct access to the divine (Exod. 26; 29:30–31; Lev. 16:16–30). By physically separating the Holy of Holies from almost everyone—even most priests—P makes the divine less reachable and positions priests as necessary mediators for divine access.

Sara Japhet suggests there is impermanence to the sanctity of a location, and only continued worship endows a place with permanent sanctity.[12] As part of the transformation, the seasonality of the threshing floor is replaced with a permanent location used year-round. Similarly, as continued cultic activity happens, this necessitates that the former activities physically stop occurring at the location, so the threshing floor could no longer be used for agricultural activities. Very fittingly, when David purchases the threshing floor and its agricultural equipment, the threshing and winnowing tools are burned in the sacrificial fire (2 Sam. 24:22 // 1 Chron. 21:23). While this may have served a pragmatic function of providing the necessary fire, it also serves as a vivid symbolic gesture of the necessary destruction of the former agricultural role of the threshing floor to make room for the brand new exclusively cultic role for this site.

Mentally: Part of the transformation of Aravnah/Ornan's threshing floor into the Solomonic temple is that the past ideas had to be overcome so that the newly transformed could flourish. P and Dtr realize that traditions of an open-access location where Yahweh is reachable could compete with the highly restricted temple. P astutely shifts the focus toward issues of purity and pollution and is especially concerned with who is ritually clean to serve a holy deity. P expresses its mental intolerance with the open-access threshing floor by asserting the necessity of a tightly controlled, ritually pure sanctuary. Dtr mentally shifts the focus away from the threshing floor. Dtr does

---

12. Sara Japhet, "Some Biblical Concepts of Sacred Place," in *Sacred Space: Shrine, City, Land*, ed. B. Kedar and R. L. Z. Werblowsky (London: Macmillan, 1998), 69.

not highlight or mention the Davidic threshing-floor foundation narrative (1 Chron. 22:1) in the description of the temple construction or thereafter. Instead, the emphasis is placed on the conversion of the agricultural space into a sacred building and on Solomon who outshines David as the temple builder par excellence. Dtr spends much time on the architectural design and precise measurements (1 Kgs. 6:2–20), materials used in construction (1 Kgs. 6:7–10, 15–18, 20–22), elaborate furnishings (1 Kgs. 6:23–36), and Solomon's special skills and benevolence (1 Kgs. 8:1–9:10) because the mental focus must turn toward the new construction built by Solomon and away from the former agricultural space purchased by David.

P and Dtr are (re-)writing and editing their received traditions hundreds of years after the construction of the tenth-century BCE Solomonic temple. While they reveal some historical realities, they are also ideological reflections, explanations, and critiques of past events. The emphasis that P places on the high priest's role in the administration of cult (Exodus 28–29; Leviticus 7–8) may have Zadok in mind, the first high priest to serve in the Solomonic temple. According to Deuteronomistic tradition, Zadok, with the prophet Nathan, anoints Solomon as king (1 Kgs. 1:25), and Solomon anoints Zadok as high priest of the temple (1 Kgs. 2:35). As Dtr presents his history vis-à-vis centralized worship of Yahweh in the Solomonic temple, the temple construction is likely an early element, perhaps from preexilic Dtr traditions (Dtr1) of the seventh century BCE. A preexilic date for traditions of Dtr1 seems reasonable since mental refocusing onto the temple would be especially necessary closer to the time of construction. By the time of the Chronicler in the postexilic period, the temple had already been destroyed, and the Chronicler writes his history already knowing the outcome. He may find no clear need to reduce the role of the threshing floor at such a late date. One of the underlying motivations in Dtr's redefinition of the threshing floor was that historically the centralization that was sought was not achieved after the temple construction. Worship at various cult sites persists after the temple is built (1 Kgs. 12:25–33; 16:31–34; 2 Kings 23). As discussed in chapter 3, the eighth-century BCE prophet Hosea includes a condemnation against threshing floors because of their use for non-Yahwistic cultic activities, which may reflect that historically these locations—perhaps even all threshing floors (*kol-gornōt*)—were still used as sacred spaces two hundred years after the building of the temple. Dtr's temple account may reflect the ongoing problems of unsanctioned cultic practices, and his minimization of the threshing floor may actually be to maximize the temple.

Socially: The use of this threshing floor as a place that anyone could visit to obtain access to the divine is drastically changed with the construction of the temple. Yet, the same idea is maintained socially, even if highly restricted. P and Dtr require centralization of all cultic worship at the temple, and socially the temple unites all people from throughout Israel and Judah to worship together. Even though many elements of the threshing floor are altered, the social and communal focus remains constant. Though P and Dtr change who has the direct access to the divine, they maintain the universal, community-focused appeal of the threshing floor.

P and Dtr work together to transform the threshing floor as the Solomonic temple. P takes control of cultic activities and asserts that priests are necessary for accessing the divine in the temple. By promoting the role of the priest, they transform the open-access threshing floor into a sacred space where nonpriests are excluded, with only limited access in the courtyard. Dtr regulates sacred spaces and requires worship to be centralized at the temple, making it socially and culturally unacceptable to worship elsewhere. While Dtr has polemics against other places of worship (Deuteronomy 12), there is no such polemic against threshing floors, which may be further evidence that the temple was located on a threshing floor and a ban would be problematic.

In their successful efforts to transform a threshing floor into a temple, P and Dtr largely fight against what Lefebvre terms the "contradictory space." Their combined efforts eliminate the complexities, multiple functionalities, and inherent contradictions of the space. Instead, P and Dtr transform it into "transparent, pure, and neutral" space. They neutralize the potential for a variety of functions and affirm the new building as the house of Yahweh (*bêt yhwh*). The activities in and use of this space are focused on this location as the central sanctuary and divine dwelling. Cultic matters are handled there, and there is no longer a potential for this threshing floor to be used as an agricultural space. In order to complete their redefinition of this space, they create a stable and permanent building for continued worship. By removing any remnants of a threshing floor and by building a massive temple on top, P and Dtr physically, mentally, and socially supersede its function as an agricultural space with sacred potential, and instead assert its complete sacredness.

The work that these religious leaders needed to do to refocus attention onto the temple and away from the threshing floor is accomplished by making this space a permanent sacred space where everyone in the land is to gather for cultic activities throughout the year. Only this threshing floor purchased by David becomes a place of continued worship, and in fact, once it becomes a permanent sacred space, it ceases being a usable or even a discernable threshing floor.

Summary

Most of the narratives that depict threshing floors as sacred spaces show a variety of people from different social statuses gathered together to perform cultic activities. The priests, perpetually concerned about cultic affairs, do not engage in this behavior, probably because they did not see threshing floors as legitimate, priestly sanctioned sacred spaces.[13] Nonetheless, because of David's actions in purchasing Aravnah/Ornan's threshing floor, the religious leadership (P and Dtr) was confronted with the issue of the threshing floor as a sacred space and responded by redefining the space so that most of the qualities of the threshing floor were no longer perceptible. Instead, they highlight the limitations, gateways, and barriers in keeping people away from the divine presence and assert the priests as necessary in cultic matters. In order to successfully transform the threshing floor into the temple, P and Dtr emphasize this building as the locus of divine accessibility. They physically change the appearance and accessibility of the space, mentally assert its preeminence, and socially promote it as the one and only place for all to gather for cultic activities.

---

13. If one follows 1 Chron. 13:2, then that would be the only occurrence of priestly involvement in cultic activities on threshing floors. As discussed in the previous chapter, the historicity of the reference to "priests and Levites" in the procession is in question, as they may be listed to establish Davidic openness to, inclusion of, and promotion of the priests rather than to represent an historical reality.

Conclusion

In examining threshing floors in the Hebrew Bible, this book has shown that these agricultural spaces are multifaceted. Because ancient Israel was an agrarian society, threshing floors were considered important spaces, pivotal for seasonal activities of threshing and winnowing. Moreover, the basic function of threshing floors is transformative. A person arrives at a threshing floor with sheaves of crops, but through the blessing of Yahweh, that person can leave the threshing floor with grain to sustain life.

Threshing floors played a significant role in food production, as these locations are fundamental for human nourishment and survival. It is only when crops are processed at threshing floors that they truly yield food. Throughout the Hebrew Bible, Israel's belief in Yahweh's important role in life and sustenance is asserted. While Yahweh is described as the creator who gives life (Genesis 1–2), he also sustains it by providing plants, seeds, fruit, and animals as food (Gen. 1:29, 9:3–5). As noted by L. Juliana M. Claassens, the creation and provision of food "[reveal] something of the *intimate nature* of God's relationship with creation. God is personally involved in the life process of what is created."[1] Like a parent nurturing a

---

1. L. Juliana M. Claassens, *The God Who Provides: Biblical Images of Divine Nourishment* (Nashville: Abingdon Press, 2004), 25.

child, Yahweh both creates and facilitates survival with blessings of food. For example, Yahweh promises Israel a land flowing with milk and honey, which is a divine blessing of a fertile and sustainable land (Exod. 3:8, 17).[2] Moreover, as the Israelites complain in the wilderness, God blesses them with manna and quails from heaven to sustain them along the journey (Exod. 16:4–36; Numbers 11). This image of the heavenly blessing of bread reappears in the Hebrew Bible to describe divine food and nourishment during times of need (Ps. 78:24–25; Neh. 9:15). Additionally, several psalms proclaim Yahweh as the source of food and drink, again affirming his critical role in the survival of his people (Pss. 104:10–14, 105:40–41, 136:25).

As Yahweh is considered the originator and sustainer of life, he is depicted as concerned about the health, well-being, and livelihood of creation. Because threshing floors are so fundamental for life, Yahweh's role in controlling and blessing these spaces is emphasized. While their primary function is to serve as clean, flat surfaces for threshing and winnowing, the biblical writers attest a sacral dimension to these spaces. Nearly all of the references to these food-processing locations suggest some type of connection or link between these spaces and Yahweh.

This study has illuminated Yahweh's interest in and control over threshing floors in his ability to curse threshing floors as a punishment for unacceptable behavior (Hosea 9:1–2) or bless threshing floors because of an interest in sustaining a community (Joel 2:23–24). Both Hosea and Joel expound on this divine control by mentioning the rain (or lack of rain) that has an impact on crop growth and ultimately impacts the success or failure of threshing floors. Yahweh's concern for threshing floors is also seen as he

---

2. Similar language of the land flowing with milk and honey can be found in Exod. 13:5; 33:3; Lev. 20:24; Num. 13:27; 14:8; 16:13–14; Deut. 6:3; 11:9; 26:9, 15; 27:3; 31:20; Josh. 5:6; Jer. 11:5; 32:22; Ezek. 20:6, 15.

intercedes to save threshing floors. When the Philistines attack the threshing floors of Keilah, Yahweh grants David permission via priestly divination to attack the Philistines and save the land (1 Sam. 23:1–5). During a famine, the king of Samaria also proclaims that Yahweh is the only one who can fill the empty threshing floors (2 Kgs. 6:27). In the case of the Midianites attacking Israel's land and agricultural areas, Yahweh commissions Gideon to save them (Judg. 6:2–14). These passages demonstrate Yahweh's interest in and connection to sustaining Israel and Judah by protecting and providing at threshing floors, except in the event of reprehensible behavior when Yahweh can punish by not providing at threshing floors. Taking control over threshing floors not only shows a divine interest in these locations, but more specifically it shows Yahweh's interest in feeding and nourishing his people.

In a similar manner, threshing-floor language is used to describe divine destruction of foreigners (Isa. 21:10; Mic. 4:12–13; Jer. 51:33). Though these passages are metaphorical, the threshing-floor motif is used as a way to affirm Yahweh's commitment to his people.

The study of references to threshing floors within the cultic laws provides insights into why threshing floors were thought to be so closely connected to Yahweh: threshing floors are associated with divine offerings (Num. 15:17–20, 18:25–29) and divine blessings (Deut. 15:12–15, 16:13–15). These legal passages aid in understanding the logic behind Yahweh's connection to these space. Once again, Yahweh is linked to the activities that happen on threshing floors and the crops that are processed there, and Yahweh blesses the life-sustaining work and food of the threshing floors. Although these agricultural activities are seasonal, Yahweh's connection to these spaces is constant. The bounty and offerings at the threshing floor are acknowledged as Yahweh's method of sustaining his people. The sacredness of threshing floors persists even when the agricultural activities end.

As locations both under Yahwistic control and associated with offerings and blessings, threshing floors are mentally selected for cultic activities such as rituals and processions (Gen. 50:10–11; Judg. 6:37–40; 2 Sam. 6:6–7 // 1 Chron. 13:9–10). Moreover, threshing floors are utilized as effective locations to communicate with Yahweh (Gen. 50:10–11; Judg. 6:37–40; 1 Kgs. 22:10 // 2 Chron. 18:9). Due to the direct and intimate relationship between threshing floors and Yahweh, threshing floors are shown to be not only sacred but also liminal spaces where theophanies can occur, as in the manifestation of the anger of Yahweh (2 Sam. 6:6–7 // 1 Chron. 13:9–10), the appearance of an angel of Yahweh (2 Sam. 24:15–25 // 1 Chron. 21:14–27), and the appearance of fire from the heavens (1 Chron. 21:26). Furthermore, Yahweh's temple is built on David's threshing floor (2 Chron. 3:1), attesting to both the sacred and liminal qualities of the space. With the construction of the Solomonic temple, there is a change in that particular threshing floor because it becomes a permanent sacred space. Its function as an agricultural space ceases, and instead the most holy location for cultic activity and divine access is situated atop a threshing floor.

Based on the narratives about threshing floors within the biblical corpus, it is evident that beyond their use as agricultural spaces, they were considered sacred spaces in the Hebrew Bible. Though an overt revelation is not found in each instance, there is a detectable cultural understanding that these spaces are connected to Yahweh based on his control over and appearance on these spaces.

The use of threshing floors for cultic activities shows flexibility in these spaces. Threshing floors were seasonally used for agricultural activities, but they have a perceived potential to be effective for cultic activities. Whether blessing the work and produce of the threshing floors or responding to cultic activity, Yahweh is interconnected to both the agricultural and cultic aspects of threshing floors. It is appropriate to characterize threshing floors as agricultural spaces that have the ability and potential to be used for cultic activities due to the perception that Yahweh controls these locations.

The intentional selection of threshing floors for ritual shows that there is a notion that these agricultural spaces were considered ad hoc sacred spaces; namely, they were considered locations connected to the divine and therefore appropriate for ritual activities when needed. Before rituals occur, there is a notion that threshing floors are already linked to Yahweh due to the life-sustaining work that happens on these spaces and the control that Yahweh was thought to have over the survival of Israel and Judah. Thus this perceived relationship explains why repeatedly cultic activities are depicted on threshing floors. The mental association leads to the physical manifestation of the sacredness of these spaces.

The Hebrew Bible places a greater emphasis on the sacrality of threshing floors, particularly as locations for impromptu cultic events. If there were no demand for a sacred space, then threshing floors would simply function as agricultural spaces. However, if there was such a need, threshing floors were considered very effective locations that could immediately become ad hoc sacred spaces. Note that the immediacy in which threshing floors can change from agricultural to sacred spaces is in direct violation of Priestly purity laws, which is probably why priests do not engage in cultic activity on these locations.

When mindful of various biblical passages spanning several centuries, locations, and genres, there is a wealth of information that connects threshing floors with Yahweh. When this insight is understood and acknowledged, the choice of threshing floors for cultic activity is more than practical; it is theological. Imbedded within the core logic of this agrarian society was the belief that threshing floors were more than agricultural spaces; they were sacred spaces controlled and blessed by Yahweh.

This study has shown the manner in which one can analyze literary conceptions of space, using spatial theory to help understand physical, mental, and social aspects. The result shows a more complicated nuance to threshing floors that have a particular fluidity in their function. The use of threshing floors in the Hebrew Bible shows their transient quality, where these agricultural spaces have the potential to be used as sacred spaces whether because of divine revelation or human choice. The Hebrew Bible emphasizes the sacredness of threshing floors and affirms divine interest, control, and blessing of these spaces.

Addendum: Threshing Floors as Sacred Spaces in Ugarit

In this work, several passages affirmed the connection between threshing floors and Yahweh in the Hebrew Bible. From controlling the success or failure of threshing floors to manifesting divine presence on these spaces, the Hebrew Bible presents threshing floors as being used as sacred spaces in addition to agricultural spaces. Similarly, literature from the Late Bronze Age city of Ugarit (Ras Shamra) in ancient Syria depicts threshing floors together with divine and preternatural beings. In this addendum, Ugaritic references to threshing floors (*grn, grnt*) will be surveyed and will show divine control, theophanies, and sacrifice on threshing floors.[1]

In highlighting these Ugaritic threshing floors, this addendum will show that the depiction of threshing floors in close connection to a deity is not unique to ancient Israel. Though caution must be used when comparing two distinct cultures separated geographically and chronologically, it can be helpful to recognize how a particular phenomenon manifests itself in different societies.

---

1. The Ugaritic passages discussed in this addendum represent all of the references to threshing floors (*grn, grnt*) in Ugaritic literature to date. As is the nature of the field, new discoveries could shed a different light on this material.

Israel, Judah, and Ugarit are all West Semitic cultures located in the Levant whose literatures exhibit remarkable similarities. For instance, certain deities appear in both literary traditions: Ilu/El, Athiratu/Asherah, Athtartu/Astarte, Shapshu/Shemesh, Baʻlu/Baʻal, Rashpu/Resheph, and Motu/Mot, among others. Although the Hebrew Bible has polemics against the worship of some of these deities (Deut. 16:21–22; Judg. 6:25–27; 2 Kings 23; Ezek. 8:16), the fact that they are mentioned suggests some overlap with or exposure to those religious traditions, especially since the deities are described with similar imagery and attributes.[2] There are also linguistic similarities between Ugaritic and Hebrew, as both are in the Northwest Semitic language family. While the literary corpora and languages attest similarities, the literature of Ugarit dates to the Late Bronze Age while the Hebrew Bible developed during the Iron Age through the Hellenistic period, hundreds of years after the destruction of Ugarit.

Ugaritic literature provides another Levantine literary corpus that highlights threshing floors as sacred spaces in addition to being agricultural spaces. This is not to suggest direct or indirect dependence between these literary traditions. Instead, this addendum simply shows that both cultures attest a similar understanding of threshing floors as closely connected to deities.

KTU 1.14–1.16

KTU 1.14–1.16 were discovered at Ras Shamra during the 1930–31 expeditions.[3] Written on these tablets is the Kirta story, which begins

---

2. For more on the connections between Yahweh and Ugaritic deities and their attributes, see John Day, *Yahweh and the Gods and Goddesses of Canaan* (New York: Sheffield Academic Press, 2000), 13–225. For more on similarities and differences in Ugaritic and biblical literature, see Frank Moore Cross, *Canaanite Myth and Hebrew Epic: Essays in the History of the Religion of Israel* (Cambridge: Harvard University Press, 1973), 1–75, 145–94.
3. For complete translations of the text, see Edward L. Greenstein, trans., "Kirta" (*CAT* 1.14–1.16), in *UNP*, 1–48; Dennis Pardee, trans., "The Kirta Epic" (1.102), in *COS*, 1:333–43;

with King Kirta suffering the loss of his family (KTU 1.14.1.7–25). While in mourning, he is visited by the god Ilu in a dream, and who instructs him to offer sacrifices to Ilu and Baal, prepare five // six months of food, and ready himself and a large army for battle (KTU 1.14.2.7–50). In this vision, Ilu tells Kirta to lead a battle for six days, and on the seventh day he should arrive at the city of Udum,[4] where he is to attack its outlying towns and villages. "Sweep away its men cutting wood in the fields and women picking straw on the threshing floors" (sʿt. bšdm ḥṭbh. bgrnt. ḥpšt) (KTU 1.14.3.7–8). Kirta is also to attack women drawing water at the well and filling jars at the spring (KTU 1.14.3.9–10). After receiving this vision, Kirta awakens, performs the sacrifices accordingly,[5] and attacks the outlying area of Udum, sweeping away the woodcutters in the fields and straw pickers on the threshing floors (KTU 1.14.4.51–52).

When giving his instruction, Ilu commands a seven-day attack on people involved in agrarian activities. The men in fields and women at threshing floors, wells, and springs are all performing essential tasks that provide food and water for the survival of the city. Attacking them is a tactical maneuver to debilitate the city's inhabitants. Ilu's instruction to attack the women on threshing floors shows he is attentive to the life-sustaining activities that happen on these agricultural spaces.

This Kirta reference may also give a hint regarding who performed agricultural activities and where threshing floors were located within this localized tradition. Women picking straw on threshing floors

---

and Nick Wyatt, *Religious Texts from Ugarit*, The Biblical Seminar 53 (London: Continuum, 2002), 176–245.

4. The location of this city is unknown. Pardee notes that "the root letters are the same as those of the city of Edom." Pardee, "The Kirta Epic," 335n24.

5. After awakening from his dream, Kirta prepares himself and his provisions and makes offerings to Baʿlu and Ilu. As he is then marching to Udum, he stops to visit the shrine of Athiratu and makes a vow concerning his future wife Huraya (KTU 1.14.4.34–43). His failure to fulfill this vow becomes a crucial plot device later in the story when King Kirta becomes deathly ill.

suggests that they were involved in some aspect of threshing and winnowing. Picking straw may have been done after threshing was complete since the straw is already removed from the crop stalks. The women may be cleaning up and removing unnecessary parts of the crops in order to access seeds. Likewise, the threshing floors are reached from outside of the city walls, suggesting that threshing floors may have been especially vulnerable to attack because they were not within the city fortifications.

In this Kirta reference, we see a few divine elements at work in relation to threshing floors. Using a dream revelation, Ilu instructs Kirta to attack women performing agricultural activities on threshing floors. Ilu exhibits divine power and influence over the agricultural work on these spaces. In a similar manner, the city of Udum is owned by Ilu, who gives it to King Pabuli as a gift (KTU 1.14.3.31–32; 5.42–43; 6.12–13). Even though Ilu originally gifts the city to Pabuli, he still exhibits control over the city by instructing Kirta to take over the land.

In comparison to the texts discussed in chapter 2, where Yahweh exhibits power and influence to save threshing floors from attacks, the reverse is found in the story of Kirta, with Ilu *instigating* an attack on workers on threshing floors. Both sets of texts connect the success or failure of threshing floors to a divine power, though Kirta is intentional about attacking the people performing agrarian activities while Yahweh is intentional about saving the agrarian spaces.

KTU 1.20–1.22

The Rapiuma texts are preserved on three tablets, KTU 1.20–1.22. In 1930, KTU 1.21 and 1.22 were discovered during the excavation season at Ras Shamra in the house of the high priest. The following year, KTU 1.20 was discovered in a nearby find spot along with the Kirta text and parts of the Aqhatu text.[6] These texts concern a group known as the Rapiuma, who are spirits of the underworld. The translation of Rapiuma is complex, and there are several scholarly opinions on this elusive group. These are otherworldly beings who sometimes interact with gods. Translating Rapiuma as "spirits" captures their supernatural and ephemeral qualities. Since they are often listed in conjunction with or parallel to apparitions, the term "spirits" reflects their liminal existence between worlds. The ambiguity of "spirits" in English is suitable, as the exact understanding of the Rapiuma is still hazy.[7]

6. Wayne Pitard provides excellent photographs and drawings of the text along with a thorough discussion of the difficulties involved in its interpretation. Wayne Pitard, "A New Edition of the 'Rāpi'ūma' Texts: KTU 1.20–22," *BASOR* 285 (1992): 33–77. For other translations of this text, see Theodore J. Lewis, trans., "The Rapiuma" (*CAT* 1.20–22), in *UNP*, 196–205; and Nick Wyatt, *Religious Texts from Ugarit*, 314–23.

7. The word Rapiuma (*rp'um*) is the plural noun of *rpu*. *Rpu* is defined by Gregorio Del Olmo Lete as a divine ancestral hero/ancestor of the Ugaritic dynasty with a secondary meaning referring to the eponymous deity of this group (see KTU 1.108). *DUL*, 742–43. Throughout the Ugaritic literature, the plural *rp'um* is most common so that the Rapiuma are usually considered one unified group. Dan'ilu, who will be discussed in the section on the story of Aqhatu, is designated with the epithet *rpu*.

There is not a consensus among scholars regarding the Rapiuma because their depictions in Levantine literature are varied. Dussaud, L'Heureux, and Virolleaud have suggested that the Rapiuma were minor deities at the service of Baal. See R. Dussaud, *Les découvertes de Ras Shamra et l'Ancien Testament* (Paris: Geuthner, 1941), 185–88; Conrad L'Heureux, "The Ugaritic and Biblical Rephaim," *HTR* 67 (1974): 265–74; Charles Virolleaud, "Les Rephaïm: Fragments de poèmes de Ras-Shamra," *Syria* 22 (1941): 1–30; and Virolleaud, "Les Rephaïm," *RES* 7 (1940): 77–83. Because they descend into the underworld following Baal, they became closely associated with the shades of the dead, which is one of their depictions in the Hebrew Bible. Gray has suggested that the Rapiuma were divine figures who performed cultic duties for the king. They visit threshing floors and plantations in order to promote fertility. John Gray, "The Rephaim," *PEQ* 81 (1949): 127–39; Gray, "Dtn and Rp'um in Ancient Ugarit," *PEQ* 84 (1952): 39–41. Caquot and Pitard leave *rp'um* untranslated, although they suggest that they are among the shades of the dead. See A. Caquot, "Les Rephaïm ougaritiques," *Syria* 37 (1960): 75–93; and Wayne Pitard, "A New Edition of the 'Rāpi'ūma' Texts," 33–77. Lewis translates *rp'um* as "shades of the dead" and considers them the deceased ancestors who live in the underworld. Theodore J. Lewis, *Cults of the Dead in Ancient Israel and Ugarit*, HSM 39 (Atlanta: Scholars Press, 1989), 95; and Lewis, "The Rapiuma," *UNP*, 196. Pope refers to the Rapiuma as "deified dead." Marvin Pope, "A Divine Banquet at Ugarit," in *The Use of the Old Testament in the New and Other Essays: Studies in Honor of William Franklin Stinespring*, ed. J. M. Efird (Durham: Duke University Press, 1972), 170–203. The Ugaritic Funerary Text, CAT 1.161, suggests that the Rapiuma may have served a role of summoning ancestors to the underworld. For a complete treatment of the Ugaritic Funerary Text, see Lewis, *Cults of the Dead*, 5–46. Although they are described as being in the underworld, they are also depicted as having an active role on earth.

The reference to threshing floors (*grnt*) is in KTU 1.20, which is unfortunately badly damaged. Side 1 of the tablet begins with references to sacrifices, food, and drink. Side 2 describes apparitions // spirits (*'ilm* // *rp'um*) departing their places and preparing for a three-day journey with horses and chariots (KTU 1.20.2.1–5). Then "the spirits arrive at the threshing floors // the apparitions at the planted fields" (*mǵy rp'um. lgrnt.* // *'i[lm l]mṯ't.*) (KTU 1.20.2.6–7). These poetic lines have synonymous parallelism. The spirits // apparitions is a close parallelism as these are two ephemeral, preternatural beings. The threshing floors // planted fields parallelism may envision threshing floors that are covered with gathered crops, analogous

Although there is not complete certainty regarding this elusive group, cognate evidence sheds some light on these characters.

The term *rp'um*, meaning minor deities, shades of the dead, or a tribal group, is restricted to Northwest Semitic languages. Hebrew, Phoenician, Punic, and Amorite are the only languages that attest this group, and this may suggest that they are a particular Levantine phenomenon. Although other ancient Near Eastern societies have very detailed understandings of the afterlife, the *rp'um* are not present. A brief synopsis of some of their Northwest Semitic attestations elucidates this obscure group.

In Phoenician, *rp'm* are attested and usually translated as "shades, shades of the dead." See Richard S. Tomback, *A Comparative Semitic Lexicon of the Phoenician and Punic Languages*, SBL Dissertation Series 32 (Ann Arbor: Edwards Brothers, Inc., 1978), 306. A fifth-century BCE Phoenician tomb inscription from Sidon warns against potential grave robbers and says that one of the punishments for the robbers will be not to dwell with the shades. The inscription ends with a curse saying that the person who disturbs the grave will not have any seed among the living under the sun nor a "resting place together with the shades" (*mškb 't rp'm*). See Ph. Sidon: *KAI* 1:2, ins. #13, line 8; and *ANET*, 662.

In the Hebrew Bible, the Rephaim are mentioned several times. They are sometimes listed with other groups such as the Hittites and the Perizzites (Gen. 15:12; Josh. 17:15), which has led to an understanding of the Rephaim as a primordial group of people who inhabited Canaan before Israel. King Og of Bashan is said be the last of the Rephaim (Deut. 3:11, 13; Josh. 12:4; 13:12), which may link him with the end of this primordial age. There is also a region affiliated with the group. The "land of the Rephaim" occurs once (Deut. 3:13), and the "valley of the Rephaim" occurs eleven times (Josh. 15:8; 18:16; 2 Sam. 5:18, 22; 2 Sam. 23:13; Isa. 17:5; 1 Chron. 11:15; 14:9) and is often connected with a Philistine presence. The biblical occurrences that are most closely related to the Ugaritic depictions are the passages that describe the Rephaim as *below* (Prov. 2:18) or *in Sheol* (Isa. 14:9; Prov. 9:18; 21:16). Rephaim are described as being *dead* and *unable to rise up* (Isa. 26:14; Ps. 88:10), and *beneath the waters* (Job 26:5). The Rephaim are usually passive figures in the Hebrew Bible, while the Ugaritic occurrences describe them as a more active group. The Ugaritic, Phoenician, and Hebrew Bible depictions characterize *rp'um* as dwellers of the underworld, although the Hebrew Bible also maintains traditions of them as primordial dwellers of Canaan.

to the planted fields covered with growing crops. This could also envision empty threshing floors parallel to newly planted/harvested fields without crops. The parallelism could simply be because they are both agricultural spaces associated with food.

After their arrival on the threshing floors // planted fields, Dan'ilu, often designated with the epithet "man of Rapiu" (*mt.rpi*) commands that the spirits // apparitions be fed (KTU 1.20.2.7–10). Words possibly related to the meal are present, including apples (*tph*), delights (*ṯsr*), and a round drinking vessel (*shr*) (KTU 1.20.2.11).[8] The rest of this tablet is missing.

While the tablet has many more lacunae, what is preserved is that spirits // apparitions journey to threshing floors // planted fields, and food is requested on their behalf. Since these locations are vital spaces in food production, Dan'ilu's request is fitting and logical considering the location. The passage may suggest that these preternatural beings journey to food spaces in order to be fed. This is a different idea than what is depicted in the narrative of the preternatural angel of Yahweh associated with Aravnah/Ornan's threshing floor. In the biblical example, the angel of Yahweh is not seeking nourishment at the threshing floor. In KTU 1.20, food appears to be related to the preternatural beings' visit to the threshing floors // planted fields.

KTU 1.17–1.19

KTU 1.17–1.19 was discovered at Ras Shamra in the 1930–31 expedition.[9] The story of Aqhatu begins by introducing Dan'ilu,

---

8. These translations are tenuous. There is Hebrew cognate evidence to support translating *tph* as "apples." Lewis suggests "delights (?)" as a meaning for *ṯsr*. Hebrew *shr* has the meaning of "round goblet" in Song 7:3. For more information on possible translations, see M. Dijkstra and J. D. de Moor, "Problematic Passages in the Legend of Aqhatu," *UF* 7 (1975): 171–215.
9. For complete translations of the text, see Simon B. Parker, trans., "Aqhat" (CAT 1.17–1.19), in *UNP*, 49–80; Dennis Pardee, trans., "The 'Aqhatu Legend" (1.103), in *COS*, 1:343–56; and Nick Wyatt, *Religious Texts from Ugarit*, 246–312.

a legendary figure known for his wisdom. He and his wife have difficulty conceiving a child, so Dan'ilu provides offerings to the gods for six days. On the seventh day, Baal petitions Ilu to bless Dan'ilu with a son. Ilu grants this petition and shortly thereafter Dan'ilu eats and drinks with the Katharatu, goddesses associated with conception and childbirth, and he and his wife conceive. What follows the conception is broken, and when the narrative resumes after some hundred lines,[10] Dan'ilu is at the threshing floor (*grn*).

Dan'ilu goes up and sits at the entrance of the gate (*ṯġr*) among the dignitaries on the threshing floor (*ytš'u. yṯb. b'ap. ṯġr. tḥt. 'adrm. dbgrn*) (KTU 1.17.5.6–7). While there, he judges the cases of the widow and orphan (KTU 1.17.5.7–8). Widows and orphans are disadvantaged groups in society, so the note that Dan'ilu judges their cases could show a particular interest in assisting those who are underprivileged.

While at the threshing floor at the city gate, Dan'ilu sees the god Kotharu-wa-Hasisu en route carrying a bow and arrows, and instructs his wife, Danatiya, to prepare a feast of lamb (KTU 1.17.5.16–19). While on the threshing floor at the city gate (where most travelers would arrive), Dan'ilu awaits Kotharu-wa-Hasisu's arrival. When Kotharu-wa-Hasisu and his party arrive, they hand Dan'ilu the bow and lay the arrows on his lap, and Dan'ilu and his wife provide them with food. The location is not explicit, but the feast could be at the threshing floor since there has not been a stated change in venue (KTU 1.17.5.26–31).

This section of the Aqhatu narrative has a few points of interest, including the threshing floor's location at the city gate and the administration of justice on the threshing floor. As discussed in chapter 4, city gates are locations often associated with justice, so Dan'ilu hearing cases at this location is appropriate. The threshing

---

10. According to Pardee, roughly 100 lines are broken. Pardee, "The 'Aqhatu Legend," 345n23.

floor in connection to a city gate may suggest that the threshing floor was right outside of the gate, which is in line with what was described in the Kirta epic discussed above. In addition, there was a threshing floor in connection with the city gate of Samaria in 1 Kgs. 22:10 // 2 Chron. 18:9, where kings went to determine the will of Yahweh regarding their war against Aram. In the Aqhatu narrative, the placement of the threshing floor at the city gate suggests that this was a threshing floor that was accessible to the community; and when threshing and winnowing practices ceased, this space was used for other community activities, including judicial matters. Also of note is the presence of the god Kotharu-wa-Hasisu who gives Dan'ilu divine weapons.

Near the end of the Aqhatu narrative, a threshing floor is mentioned again. As the city mourns the death of Dan'ilu's son Aqhatu, a severe drought affects the land (KTU 1.19.1.42–46). As if nature and humans are symbiotically related, Aqhatu's death causes the drought. Dan'ilu and the dignitaries are once again portrayed as being at the threshing floor to judge cases of the widow and orphan (KTU 1.19.1.19–25). After a break of about four lines, something dries (*yḥrb*) and withers (*yġly*) on the threshing floor (*bgrn*) (KTU 1.19.1.29–30). The subject of the verbs is in a lacuna, but the next column may help in reconstructing the referent.

In KTU 1.19.2, Dan'ilu calls to his daughter, saying, "Listen, Paghitu, Bearer of water, Collector of dew from the fleece,[11] Knower

---

11. According the Gregorio Del Olmo Lete and Joaquín Sanmartín, the lexeme *šʿr* means 1) "hair, hairs," and 2) "pelisse, fleece," each meaning attested once. With so few occurrences, cognate evidence can be helpful. Hebrew, Syriac, Akkadian, Arabic, and Ethiopic support the translation of "fleece." *DUL*, 798. Hebrew attests *šʿr* referring to human hair (Lev. 14:8; Isa. 7:20; Ezek. 16:7) and a hairy cloak (Gen. 25:25; Zech. 13:4). Parker translates *šʿr* as "fleece (?)," possibly because the lexeme *šʿrm* means "barley," which is how Pardee translates *šʿr*. *DUL*, 798–99; and Pardee, "The 'Aqhatu Legend," 352. While barley on a threshing floor is logical since it would be processed there, the lexeme for "barley" is typically spelled *šʿrm* in Ugaritic texts (see KTU 4.345.6, 4.608.3, 6.19.1, 4.790.14). This passage would account for the only

of the course of the stars" (šmʿ. pǵt. tkmt my/ ḥspt. lšʿr. ṭl. ydʿ[t]/hlk.kbkbm.) (KTU 1.19.2.1–3). These epithets connect Paghitu with carrying water, collecting dew with fleece, and understanding the stars. They could suggest that she was a water gatherer with knowledge of the rainy season, which has been suggested by Jeffrey Cooley: "Because the epithets are used in the context of drought, they would highlight her knowledge of the agricultural situation."[12] Knowing the course of the stars, however, implies more than just collecting rain. It suggests that Paghitu engaged in celestial divination by reading and interpreting the stars. H. L. Ginsberg has characterized Paghitu's activities as "apparently forms of weather-wisdom bordering on divination,"[13] especially because of her knowledge of the stars.

A possible referent for what is drying and withering on the threshing floor is a fleece (šʿr), which is a masculine noun that would agree with yḥrb. A fleece placed on the threshing floor during a drought is a feasible option, as it could absorb whatever small amount of dew is in the atmosphere, even if there is no rain. Paghitu's epithet suggests that fleece was used to collect dew, so it is conceivable that a fleece might be on the threshing floor in order to collect dew. If the fleece has dried and withered, this would demonstrate how dire the conditions were. Not only was there no rain, but there was no naturally occurring dew to sustain the community throughout the drought.

If Ginsberg is correct that Paghitu's epithet is close to describing her as a diviner, then dew and fleece may be elements used in divination, a tempting parallel to Gideon's divination ritual using

---

singular spelling. Based on the cognate evidence and the context of Paghitu's epithet, using fleece to collect dew would be more efficient than barley.
12. Jeffrey Cooley, "Celestial Divination in Ugarit and Ancient Israel: A Reassessment," *JNES* 71 (2012): 25n30.
13. H. L. Ginsberg, trans., "The Tale of Aqhat," in *ANET*, 153nn32, 36.

dew and fleece on a threshing floor discussed in chapter 4. Placing a fleece on a threshing floor might serve a purpose beyond collecting dew. In Gideon's case, the dew and fleece work as divinatory elements from which Gideon receives divine signs regarding his battle. In Paghitu's case, the dew and fleece may also be divinatory, perhaps being used to determine when the drought conditions will end.

KTU 1.116

KTU 1.116 is a bilingual text written in Ugaritic and Hurrian, discovered in the twenty-fourth excavation season at Ras Shamra in 1961.[14] The first two verses written in Ugaritic contain a reference to cultic activity happening on a threshing floor: "Sacrificial meal to Athtartu, communal feast[15] on the threshing floor" (*dbḥ.ʻttrt qrʼat.*

---

14. This text was discovered in the twenty-fourth excavation season at Ras Shamra in 1961, and the *editio princeps* was published by Emmanuel Laroche in 1968. Dennis Pardee has also published an edition of the text. E. Laroche, "Textes hourrites en cunéiformes alphabétiques," *Ugaritica* V (1968): 497–504; D. Pardee, *Les textes rituels*, Ras Shamra-Ougarit XII (Paris: Éditions Recherche sur les Civilizations, 2000), 655–58. This bilingual text was discovered with seven other bilingual Ugaritic-Hurrian texts, which E. Laroche has called "mixed tablets" since each is written in Ugaritic alphabetic script with the beginning lines in Ugaritic and the majority of the tablet in Hurrian. Laroche, "Textes hourrites," 497. Much of the Hurrian is obscure and unable to be translated with the exception of divine names. The Hurrian is especially difficult to translate because it is written in Ugaritic script. The Ugaritic script reduces the Hurrian words to their consonantal roots, so essential parts of words are lacking. Recognizing roots and grammatical morphemes is nearly impossible.
15. There are a few possibilities for the meaning of *qrʼat*, depending on its vocalization. Josef Tropper suggests vocalizing it as *qarīʼatu*, which he translates "Einladung, Gastmahl" (invitation, banquet) based on cognate evidence. J. Tropper, *Kleines Wörterbuch des Ugaritischen*, Elementa Linguarum Orientis 4 (Wiesbaden: Harrassowitz Verlag, 2008), 100. *Qerītu* is attested in Akkadian, meaning "banquet, feast." Akkadian *qerītu* is related to the root *qerû*, which means "to call, invite," and it is especially used in instances of inviting a person to a meal, a deity to an offering, or an enemy to a battle. See CDA, 288. *CAD* lists several examples of *qerītu* being related to divine banquet feasts and ceremonial meals. See *CAD* v. Q, 240–41. Laroche and Pardee do not provide vocalizations for *qrʼat*. Laroche translates it as "rassemblement" (gathering), although he puts a question mark after his translation demonstrating his uncertainty. He provides a footnote saying that this form is unattested at Ugarit, and it may be an abstract noun formed from the root *qrʼ*. Laroche, "Textes hourrites," 501. Pardee translates *qrʼat* as "gathering," and he footnotes that it is literally "a calling together." Pardee, *Les textes*

bgrn) (KTU 1.116.1–2). Though negligible on the details of the sacrifice, this text situates cultic activity on a threshing floor. Here, the threshing floor is more than an agricultural space; it is a sacred space used to offer a sacrifice to a goddess. The communal feast may refer to the people or the gods consuming the meal at the threshing floor. In a similar manner, chapter 4 included a discussion of David offering sacrifices to Yahweh on a threshing floor. Fittingly, this feast is offered on a location associated with food. The threshing floor, typically used to feed people, in this Ugaritic text is used as a location to feed a deity.

Summary

The Ugaritic literature surveyed in this addendum shows threshing floors linked with divine power, divine and preternatural beings, and cultic activity. In the Kirta story, Ilu takes interest in and control over the activities that happen on threshing floors. In the Rapiuma texts, threshing floors are locations where the spirits of the underworld travel, probably for feeding. In the Aqhatu narrative, a threshing floor is located at the city gate and is the location where cases are judged. It could also be a location used for divination with dew and fleece. In the Sacrifice to Athtartu text, a sacrifice is offered on a threshing floor. In two Ugaritic texts (Rapiuma and Sacrifice to Athtartu), divine or preternatural beings are fed on threshing floors. In the four passages, there is only one reference to agricultural activity happening on a threshing floor: the women picking straw in the Kirta epic. Even in that reference, the emphasis is on the divine authority over the

---

rituels, 657. I have followed Tropper's vocalization and translated *qariʾatu* as "communal feast." The root *qrʾ* means "to call together, gather, or summon," and the cognate evidence suggests that this nominal form can refer to gatherings related to food. "Communal feast" is a nuanced translation that is mindful of the primary "gathering" or "calling together" aspects of *qrʾ* while also understanding that within the context of a sacrificial meal, this is a gathering of people or gods to eat the meal.

agrarian activities. Overall, as in the Hebrew Bible passages, Ugaritic literature emphasizes the sacred aspects of threshing floors over their agricultural functions.

Bibliography

Ackerman, Susan. "The Personal Is Political: Covenantal and Affectionate Love (ʾāhēb, ʾahăbâ) in the Hebrew Bible." *Vetus Testamentum* 52 (2002): 437–58.

———. *Under Every Green Tree: Popular Religion in Sixth-Century Judah.* Atlanta: Scholars Press, 1992.

Adar, Zvi. *The Book of Genesis: An Introduction to the Biblical World.* Jerusalem: Magnes Press, 1990.

Adelman, Rachel. "Seduction and Recognition in the Story of Judah and Tamar and the Book of Ruth." *NASHIM* 23 (2012): 87–109.

Aharoni, Yohanan, and Miriam Aharoni. *The Archaeology of the Land of Israel: From the Prehistoric Beginnings to the End of the First Temple Period.* Philadelphia: Westminster, 1982.

Ahituv, Shmuel. "The Tel Dan Inscription." In *Echoes from the Past: Hebrew and Cognate Inscriptions from the Biblical Period*, 466–73. Jerusalem: Carta, 2008.

Ahlström, Gösta W. "Administration of the State in Canaan and Ancient Israel." In *Civilizations of the Ancient Near East*, edited by Jack Sasson, 587–603. New York: Scribner's, 1995.

———. *The History of Ancient Palestine.* Journal for the Study of the Old Testament: Supplement Series. Edited by D. Edelman. Sheffield: Sheffield Academic Press, 1993.

Aitken, Kenneth T. "The Oracles against Babylon in Jeremiah 50–51: Structures and Perspectives." *Tyndale Bulletin* 35 (1984): 25–63.

Albertz, Rainer, and Rüdiger Schmitt. *Family and Household Religion in Ancient Israel and the Levant*. Winona Lake: Eisenbrauns, 2012.

Amit, Yairah. *The Book of Judges: The Art of Editing*. Translated by J. Chipman. Biblical Interpretation Series 38. Leiden: Brill, 1999.

———. *History and Ideology: An Introduction to Historiography in the Hebrew Bible*. Translated by Y. Lotan. Sheffield: Sheffield Academic Press, 1999.

———. *Reading Biblical Narratives: Literary Criticism and the Hebrew Bible*. Translated by Y. Lotan. Minneapolis: Augsburg Fortress, 2001.

Anbar, M. "'L'aire à l'entrée de la porte de Samarie' (1 R. XXII 10)." *Vetus Testamentum* 50 (2000): 121–23.

Andersen, Francis I., and David Noel Freedman. *Hosea: A New Translation with Introduction and Commentary*. Anchor Bible 24. Garden City: Doubleday, 1980.

———. *Micah: A New Translation with Introduction and Commentary*. Anchor Bible 24e. New York: Doubleday, 2000.

Anderson, A. A. *2 Samuel*. Word Biblical Commentary 11. Nashville: Thomas Nelson, 1989.

Anderson, Gary A. *Sacrifices and Offerings in Ancient Israel: Studies in Their Social and Political Importance*. Atlanta: Scholars Press, 1987.

Annus, Amar, ed. *Divination and Interpretation of Signs in the Ancient World*. Chicago: Oriental Institute of the University of Chicago, 2010.

Arav, Rami. *Cities through the Looking Glass: Essays on the History and Archaeology of Biblical Urbanism*. Winona Lake: Eisenbrauns, 2008.

Arav, Rami, Richard A. Freund, and John F. Shroder Jr. "Bethsaida Rediscovered." *Biblical Archaeology Review* 26 (2000): 44–56.

Arnold, W. R. *Ephod and Ark: A Study in the Records and Religion of the Ancient Hebrews*. Harvard Theological Studies 3. Cambridge: Harvard University Press, 1917.

Auld, A. Graeme. *1 & 2 Samuel.* Old Testament Library. Louisville: Westminster John Knox Press, 2011.

Avioz, Michael. "The Book of Kings in Recent Research (Part I)." *Currents in Biblical Research* 4 (2005): 11–55.

Bakon, Shimon. "The Day of the Lord." *Jewish Bible Quarterly* 38 (2010): 149–56.

Bal, Mieke. "Heroism and Proper Names, or the Fruits of Analogy." In *A Feminist Companion to Ruth*, edited by Athalya Brenner, 42–69. Sheffield: Sheffield Academic Press, 1993.

Batten, Alicia J. "Clothing and Adornment." *Biblical Theology Bulletin* 40 (2010): 148–59.

Beck, John A. "Gideon, Dew, and the Narrative-Geographical Shaping of Judges 6:33–40." *Bibliotheca Sacra* 165 (2008): 28–38.

Bell, Catherine. *Ritual Theory, Ritual Practice.* New York: Oxford University Press, 1992.

Ben Meir, Samuel, and Martin I. Lockshin. *Rabbi Samuel Ben Meir's Commentary on Genesis: An Annotated Translation.* Jewish Studies 5. Lewiston: E. Mellen Press, 1989.

Bergsma, John Sietze. *The Jubilee from Leviticus to Qumran: A History of Interpretation.* Supplements to Vetus Testamentum 115. Leiden: Brill, 2007.

Bernett, M. and O. Keel. *Mond, Stier und Kult am Stadttor: Die Stele von Betsaida (et-Tell).* Orbis biblicus et orientalis 161. Fribourg: Universitätsverlag, 1998.

Berquist, Jon L. "Critical Spatiality and the Construction of the Ancient World." In *"Imagining" Biblical Worlds: Studies in Spatial, Social and Historical Constructs in Honor of James W. Flanagan*, edited by David M. Gunn and Paula M. McNutt, 14–29. Journal for the Study of the Old Testament: Supplement Series 359. London: Sheffield Academic Press, 2002.

Biran, Avraham. *Biblical Dan*. Jerusalem: Israel Exploration Society/HUR-JIR, 1994.

———. "Sacred Space: Of Standing Stones, High Places and Cult Objects at Tel Dan." *Biblical Archaeology Review* 24 (1998): 38–45, 70.

Blenkinsopp, Joseph. "An Assessment of the Alleged Pre-Exilic Date of the Priestly Material in the Pentateuch." *Zeitschrift für die alttestamentliche Wissenschaft* 108 (1996): 495–518.

———. *Isaiah 1–39: A New Translation with Introduction and Commentary*. Anchor Bible 19. New Haven: Yale University Press, 2000.

Block, Daniel I. "Will the Real Gideon Please Stand Up? Narrative Style and Intention in Judges 6–9." *Journal of the Evangelical Theological Society* 40 (1997): 353–66.

Blomquist, Tina Haettner. *Gates and Gods: Cults in the City Gates of Iron Age Palestine; An Investigation of the Archaeological and Biblical Sources*. Stockholm: Almqvist & Wiksell International, 1999.

Blum, Erhard. *Studien zur Komposition des Pentateuch*. Berlin: de Gruyter, 1990.

Boling, Robert G. *Judges: A New Translation with Introduction and Commentary*. Anchor Bible 6a. Garden City: Doubleday, 1975.

Borowski, Oded. *Agriculture in Iron Age Israel*. Winona Lake: Eisenbrauns, 1987.

Bottéro, Jean. *Mesopotamia: Writing, Reasoning, and the Gods*. Chicago: University of Chicago Press, 1992.

Bowman, Alan K. *Egypt after the Pharaohs 332 BCE–AD 642: From Alexander to the Arab Conquest*. Berkeley: The University of California Press, 1986.

Bron, Hendrik (Enno). "Sasa." *Hadashot Arkheologiyot: Excavations and Surveys in Israel* 125 (2013): http://www.hadashot-esi.org.il/report_detail_eng.aspx?id=2225.

Campbell, Antony F., and Mark A. O'Brien. *Unfolding the Deuteronomistic History: Origins, Upgrades, Present Text*. Minneapolis: Augsburg Fortress, 2000.

Campbell, Edward F., Jr. *Ruth: A New Translation with Introduction, Notes, and Commentary*. Anchor Bible 7. Garden City: Doubleday, 1975.

Caquot, André. "Les Rephaïm ougaritiques." *Syria* 37 (1960): 75–93.

———. "La tablette RS 24.252 et la question des Rephaïm ougaritiques." *Syria* 53 (1976): 295–304.

Carr, David M. "Empirische Perspektiven auf das Deuteronomistische Geshichtswerk." In *Die deuteronomistischen Geschichtswerke: Redaktions- und religionsgeschichtliche Perspektiven zur "Deuteronomismus"-Diskussion in Tora und Vorderen Propheten*, edited by M. Witte, K. Schmid, D. Prechel, and J. C. Gertz, 1–17. Beihefte zur Zeitschrift für die alttestamentliche Wissenschaft 365. Berlin: Walter de Gruyter, 2006.

Carroll, Robert P. *Jeremiah: A Commentary*. Philadelphia: The Westminster Press, 1986.

Castelbajac, Isabelle de. "Le cycle de Gédéon ou la condemnation du refus de la royauté." *Vetus Testamentum* 57 (2007): 145–61.

Cheetham, Linda. "Threshing and Winnowing—an Ethnographic Study." *Antiquity* 56 (1982): 127–30.

Childs, Brevard. *Isaiah: A Commentary*. Old Testament Library. Louisville: Westminster John Knox Press, 2001.

Claassens, L. Juliana M. *The God Who Provides: Biblical Images of Divine Nourishment*. Nashville: Abingdon Press, 2004.

———. "Resisting Dehumanization: Ruth, Tamar, and the Quest for Human Dignity." *Catholic Biblical Quarterly* 75 (2012): 659–74.

Clifford, Richard. "The Temple in the Ugaritic Myth of Baal." In *Symposia Celebrating the Seventy-Fifth Anniversary of the Founding of the American Schools of Oriental Research (1900–1975)*, 137–45. Cambridge: American Schools of Oriental Research, 1979.

Clines, David. "Sacred Space, Holy Places and Suchlike." In *On the Way to the Postmodern: Old Testament Essays, 1967–1998*, 2:542–54. Journal for the Study of the Old Testament: Supplement Series 293. Sheffield: Sheffield Academic Press, 1998.

Coats, George W. *From Canaan to Egypt: Structural and Theological Context for the Joseph Story*. Catholic Biblical Quarterly Monograph Series 4. Washington: Catholic Biblical Association of America, 1976.

———. "Redactional Unity in Genesis 37–50." *Journal of Biblical Literature* 93 (1974): 15–21.

Cogan, Mordechai. *1 Kings: A New Translation with Introduction and Commentary*. Anchor Bible 10. New York: Doubleday, 2001.

Cohn, Robert L. *The Shape of Sacred Space: Four Biblical Studies*. Studies in Religion 23. Chico: Scholars Press, 1981.

Collins, John Joseph. *Daniel: A Commentary on the Book of Daniel*. Edited by F. M. Cross. Hermeneia. Minneapolis: Fortress Press, 1993.

Coogan, Michael D. "Of Cult and Cultures: Reflections on the Interpretation of Archaeological Evidence." *Palestine Exploration Quarterly* 119 (1987): 1–8.

Cooley, Jeffrey. "Celestial Divination in Ugarit and Ancient Israel: A Reassessment." *Journal of Near Eastern Studies* 71 (2012): 21–30.

Cornelius, Izak. *The Iconography of the Canaanite Gods Reshef and Ba'al: Late Bronze and Iron Age I Periods (c 1500–1000 BCE)*. Fribourg: University Press, 1994.

Cranz, Isabel. "Impurity and Ritual in the Priestly Source and Assyro-Babylonian Incantations." PhD diss., The Johns Hopkins University, 2012.

Crenshaw, James L. *Joel: A New Translation with Introduction and Commentary*. Anchor Bible 24c. New York: Doubleday, 1995.

Cross, Frank Moore. *Canaanite Myth and Hebrew Epic: Essays in the History of the Religion of Israel*. Cambridge: Harvard University Press, 1973.

———. "The Council of Yahweh in Second Isaiah." *Journal of Near Eastern Studies* 12 (1953): 274–77.

Cryer, Frederick H. *Divination in Ancient Israel and Its Near Eastern Environment: A Socio-Historical Investigation.* Sheffield: Sheffield Academic Press, 1994.

———. "The Problem of Dating Biblical Hebrew and the Hebrew of Daniel." In *In the Last Days: On Jewish and Christian Apocalyptic and Its Period*, edited by K. Jeppesen, K. Nielsen, and B. Rosendal, 185–98. Aarhus: Aarhus University Press, 1994.

Dalman, Gustaf. *Arbeit und Sitte in Palästina.* Beiträge zur Förderung christlicher Theologie 2. Reihe: Sammlung wissenschaftlicher Monographien. Gütersloh: C. Bertelsmann, 1928.

Dar, Shimon. *Landscape and Pattern: An Archaeological Survey of Samaria, 800 B.C.E.–636 C.E.* Part i. BAR International Series 308(i). Oxford: B.A.R., 1986.

Davies, Philip R. *In Search of "Ancient Israel."* Journal for the Study of the Old Testament: Supplement Series 142. Sheffield: JSOT Press, 1992.

———. "'House of David' Built on Sand: The Sins of the Biblical Maximizers." *Biblical Archaeology Review* 20 (1994): 54–55.

Davis, Andrew R. "Tel Dan in Its Northern Cultic Context." PhD diss., The Johns Hopkins University, 2010.

Day, John. "Asherah in the Hebrew Bible and Northwest Semitic Literature." *Journal of Biblical Literature* 105 (1986): 385–408.

———. "The Canaanite Inheritance of the Israelite Monarchy." In *King and Messiah in Israel and the Ancient Near East: Proceedings of the Oxford Old Testament Seminar*, edited by J. Day, 72–90. Journal for the Study of the Old Testament: Supplement Series 270. Sheffield: Sheffield Academic Press, 1998.

———. "Hosea and the Baal Cult." In *Prophecy and the Prophets in Ancient Israel: Proceedings of the Oxford Old Testament Seminar*, 202–24. New York: T&T Clark, 2010.

———. *Yahweh and the Gods and Goddesses of Canaan*. New York: Sheffield Academic Press, 2000.

Day, Peggy. "Yahweh's Broken Marriages as Metaphoric Vehicle in the Hebrew Bible Prophets." In *Sacred Marriages: The Divine-Human Sexual Metaphor from Sumer to Early Christianity*, edited by Martti Nissinen and Risto Uro, 219–41. Winona Lake: Eisenbrauns, 2008.

Dever, William G. *Did God Have a Wife? Archaeology and Folk Religion in Ancient Israel*. Grand Rapids: Wm. B. Eerdmans, 2005.

———, ed. *Gezer IV: The 1969–1971 Seasons in Field VI, the "Acropolis," Part I, Text*. Jerusalem: Nelson Glueck School of Biblical Archaeology, 1986.

———. *What Did the Biblical Writers Know & When Did They Know It?* Grand Rapids: Wm. B. Eerdmans, 2001.

Dewrell, Heath D. "Child Sacrifice in Ancient Israel and Its Opponents." PhD diss., The Johns Hopkins University, 2012.

Dietrich, Walter. *Prophetie und Geschichte: Eine redaktionsgeschichtliche Untersuchung zum deuteronomistischen Geschichtswerk*. Forschungen zur Religion und Literatur des Alten und Neuen Testaments 108. Göttingen: Vandenhoeck & Ruprecht, 1972.

Dijkstra, M., and J. C. de Moor. "Problematic Passages in the Legend of Aqhatu." *Ugarit-Forschungen* 7 (1975): 171–215.

Dinur, U., and G. Lipovitz. "A Burial Cave from the 6th Century B.C.E. in Hurvat Almit." *Niqrot Zurim* 14 (1988): 44–51. (Hebrew)

Dobbs-Allsopp, F. W., J. J. M. Roberts, C. L. Seow, and R. E. Whitaker. *Hebrew Inscriptions: Texts from the Biblical Period of the Monarchy with Concordance*. New Haven: Yale University Press, 2005.

Dozeman, Thomas B. "Biblical Geography and Critical Spatial Studies." In *Constructions of Space I: Theory, Geography, and Narrative*, edited by Jon L. Berquist and Claudia V. Camp, 87–108. New York: T&T Clark, 2007.

Drinkard, Joel F. "Threshing Floor." In *The New Interpreter's Dictionary of the Bible*, edited by Katherine Doob Sakenfeld, 588–89. Nashville: Abingdon Press, 2006.

Duke, Rodney. "Recent Research in Chronicles." *Currents in Research: Biblical Studies* 8 (2009): 10–50.

Dus, J. "Der Brauch der Ladewanderung im alten Israel." *Theologische Zeitschrift* 17 (1961): 1–16.

Dussaud, R. *Les découvertes de Ras Shamra et l'Ancien Testament*. Paris: Geuthner, 1941.

Dyck, J. E. "Dating Chronicles and the Purpose of Chronicles." *Didaskalia* 8 (1997): 16–29.

Eliade, Mircea. *The Myth of the Eternal Return: Or, Cosmos and History*. Translated by W. Trask. Princeton: Princeton University Press, 1954.

———. *Patterns in Comparative Religion*. Translated by R. Sheed. New York: Sheed & Ward, 1958.

———. *The Sacred and the Profane: The Nature of Religion*. Translated by W. Trask. San Diego: Harcourt, 1957.

Elliger, Karl. "Ephod und Choschen: Ein Beitrag zur Entwicklungsgeschichte des hohepriesterlichen Ornats." *Vetus Testamentum* 8 (1958): 19–35.

Eph'al, Israel. *The City Besieged: Siege and Its Manifestations in the Ancient Near East*. Leiden: Brill, 2009.

Erbele-Küster, Dorothea. "Immigration and Gender Issues in the Book of Ruth." *Voices from the Third World* 25 (2002): 32–39.

Evans, Craig A., Joel N. Lohr, and David L. Petersen, eds., *The Book of Genesis: Composition, Reception, and Interpretation*. Leiden: Brill, 2012.

Evans, Mary J. *1 & 2 Samuel*. Grand Rapids: Baker Books, 2012.

Falk, Zev. "Religion and State in Ancient Israel." In *Politics and Theopolitics in the Bible and Postbiblical Literature*, edited by Henning Graf Reventlow, Yair Hoffman, and Benjamin Uffenheimer, 49–54. Sheffield: JSOT Press, 1994.

Finkelstein, Israel. "A Great United Monarchy: Archaeological and Historical Perspectives." In *One God-One Cult-One Nation*, edited by Reinhard Kratz and Hermann Spieckermann, 1–28. Berlin: de Gruyter, 2010.

Finkelstein, Israel, and Amihai Mazar. *The Quest for the Historical Israel*. Edited by B. Schmidt. Atlanta: Society of Biblical Literature, 2007.

Finkelstein, Israel, and Neil A. Silberman. *The Bible Unearthed: Archaeology's New Vision of Ancient Israel and the Origin of Its Sacred Texts*. New York: Touchstone, 2002.

Foucault, Michel. "Of Other Spaces." *Diacritics* 16 (1986): 22–27.

Fretheim, Terence E. *First and Second Kings*. Louisville: Westminster John Knox Press, 1999.

Frolov, Serge. "Rethinking Judges." *Catholic Biblical Quarterly* 71 (2009): 24–41.

Fuchs, Esther. "The Literary Characterization of Mothers and Sexual Politics in the Hebrew Bible." In *Women in the Hebrew Bible: A Reader*, edited by A. Bach, 127–40. New York: Routledge, 1999.

Garfein, Susanna. "Temple-Palace Conflict in Pre-Exilic Judah." PhD diss., The Johns Hopkins University, 2004.

Gemser, B. "Beʿēber Hajjardēn: In Jordan's Borderland." *Vetus Testamentum* 2 (1952): 349–55.

Gennep, Arnold van. *The Rites of Passage: A Classic Study of Cultural Celebrations*. Translated by Monika. B. Vizedom and Gabrielle L. Caffee. Chicago: The University of Chicago Press, 1960.

George, Mark. "Space and History: Siting Critical Space for Biblical Studies." In *Constructions of Space I: Theory, Geography, and Narrative*, edited by Jon L. Berquist and Claudia V. Camp, 19–38. New York: T&T Clark, 2007.

Gibson, J. C. L. "The Kingship of Yahweh against Its Canaanite Background." In *Ugarit and the Bible*, edited by G. J. Brooke, A. H. W. Curtis, and J. F. Healey. 101–12. Münster: Ugarit-Verlag, 1994.

Gilmour, Garth. "The Archaeology of Cult in the Period of the Judges: Theory and Practice." *Old Testament Essays* 13 (2000): 283–92.

Ginsberg, H. L. "Job the Patient and Job the Impatient." *Conservative Judaism* 21 (1967): 12–28.

———, trans. "The Tale of Aqhat." In *Ancient Near Eastern Texts Relating to the Old Testament*, edited by J. A. Pritchard, 118–32. Princeton: Princeton University Press, 1969.

Glanzman, G. S. "The Origin and Date of the Book of Ruth." *Catholic Biblical Quarterly* 21 (1959): 201–7.

Gordis, R. *The Book of God and Man: A Study of Job*. Chicago: University of Chicago Press, 1978.

———. "Love, Marriage, and Business in the Book of Ruth." In *A Light unto My Path: Old Testament Studies in Honor of Jacob M. Myers*, edited by H. N. Bream, D. Heim, and A. Carey, 243–46. Philadelphia: Temple University Press, 1974.

Gray, John. "Dtn and Rp'um in Ancient Ugarit." *Palestine Exploration Quarterly* 84 (1952): 39–41.

———. "The *Goren* at the City Gate." *Palestine Exploration Quarterly* 85 (1953): 118–23.

———. "The Rephaim." *Palestine Exploration Quarterly* 81 (1949): 127–39.

Greenberg, Moshe. "The Hebrew Oath Particle ḤAY/ḤĒ." *Journal of Biblical Literature* 76 (1957): 34–39.

Greenstein, Edward L. "Kirta." In *Ugaritic Narrative Poetry*, edited by S. B. Parker, 1–48. Society of Biblical Literature Writings from the Ancient World 9. Atlanta: Scholars Press, 1997.

Griffin, Susan M. "Threshing Floors: A Response to Joanna Brooks." *American Literary History* 22 (2010): 454–58.

Habel, Norman C. *The Book of Job*. Cambridge: Cambridge University Press, 1975.

Hadley, Judith M. *The Cult of Asherah in Ancient Israel and Judah: Evidence for a Hebrew Goddess*. University of Cambridge Oriental Publications 57. Cambridge: Cambridge University Press, 2000.

Hallo, William W., and K. Lawson Younger, eds. *Canonical Compositions from the Biblical World*. Vol. 1 of *The Context of Scripture*. Leiden: Brill, 1997.

Haran, Menahem. "The Ark and the Cherubim: Their Symbolic Significance in Biblical Ritual." *Israel Exploration Journal* 9 (1959): 30–38.

———. "Behind the Scenes of History: Determining the Date of the Priestly Source." *Journal of Biblical Literature* 100 (1981): 321–33.

———. "Ezekiel, P, and the Priestly School." *Vetus Testamentum* 58 (2008): 211–18.

———. *Temples and Temple Service in Ancient Israel: An Enquiry into the Character of Cult Phenomena and the Historical Setting of the Priestly School*. Oxford: Clarendon, 1978.

Harpur, Yvonne. *Decoration in Egyptian Tombs of the Old Kingdom*. London: KPI Limited, 1987.

Harvey, David. *The Condition of Postmodernity: An Enquiry into the Origins of Cultural Change*. Oxford: Blackwell, 1989.

Hearson, Nathanael B. "'Go Now to Shiloh': God's Changing Relationship with Sacred Places in the Hebrew Bible and Early Rabbinic Literature." PhD diss., Hebrew Union College–Jewish Institute of Religion, 2005.

Hendel, Ronald S. "Aniconism and Anthropomorphism in Ancient Israel." In *The Image and the Book: Iconic Cults, Aniconism, and the Rise of Book Religion in Israel and the Ancient Near East*, edited by K. van der Toorn, 205–28. Leuven: Peeters, 1997.

———. *The Epic of the Patriarch: The Jacob Cycle and the Narrative Traditions of Canaan and Israel*. Harvard Semitic Monographs 42. Atlanta: Scholar Press, 1987.

Hess, Richard S., Gordon J. Wenham, and P. E. Satterthwaite. *He Swore an Oath: Biblical Themes from Genesis 12–50*. Carlisle: Paternoster Press, 1994.

Hillers, Delbert R. *Micah: A Commentary on the Book of the Prophet Micah*. Edited by Paul D. Hanson and Loren R. Fisher. Hermeneia. Philadelphia: Fortress Press, 1984.

Hirschfeld, Y., and R. Birger-Calderon. "Early Roman and Byzantine Estates near Caesarea." *Israel Exploration Journal* 41 (1991): 81–111.

Hoffman, Yair. "The Deuteronomistic Concept of the Herem." *Zeitschrift für die alttestamentliche Wissenschaft* 101 (1999): 196–210.

Holladay, William Lee. *Jeremiah 1: A Commentary on the Book of the Prophet Jeremiah, Chapters 1–25*. Edited by Paul D. Hanson. Hermeneia. Philadelphia: Fortress Press, 1986.

———. *Jeremiah 2: A Commentary on the Book of the Prophet Jeremiah, Chapters 26–52*. Edited by Paul D. Hanson. Hermeneia. Minneapolis: Fortress Press, 1989.

Hoof, Dieter. *Opfer, Engel, Menschenkind: Studien zum Kindheitsverständnis in Altertum und früher Neuzeit*. Bochum: Winkler, 1999.

Houtman, Cornelis. *Der Geschichte seiner Erforschung neben einer Auswertung*. Contributions to Biblical Exegesis and Theology 9. Kampen: Kok Pharos, 1994.

Hubbard, Robert L., Jr. *The Book of Ruth*. New International Commentary on the Old Testament. Grand Rapids: Eerdmans, 1988.

Hudson, Don M. "From Chaos to Cosmos: Sacred Space in Genesis." *Zeitschrift für die alttestamentliche Wissenschaft* 108 (1996): 87–97.

Huffmon, Herbert B. "A Company of Prophets: Mari, Assyria, Israel." In *Prophecy in Its Ancient Near Eastern Context: Mesopotamian, Biblical, and*

Arabian Perspectives, edited by M. Nissinen, 47–70. Atlanta: Society of Biblical Literature, 2000.

Huie-Jolly, Mary R. "Formation of the Self in Construction of Space: Lefebvre in Winnicott's Embrace." In *Constructions of Space I: Theory, Geography, and Narrative*, edited by Jon L. Berquist and Claudia V. Camp, 51–67. New York: T&T Clark, 2007.

Hurowitz, Victor. "True Light on the Urim and Thummim." *Jewish Quarterly Review* 88 (1998): 263–74.

Hurvitz, Avi. *A Linguistic Study of the Relationship between the Priestly Source and the Book of Ezekiel*. Paris: Gabalda, 1982.

———. "Once Again: The Linguistic Profile of the Priestly Material in the Pentateuch and Its Historical Age: A Response to J. Blenkinsopp." *Zeitschrift für die alttestamentliche Wissenschaft* 112 (2000): 180–91.

Japhet, Sara. *I & II Chronicles: A Commentary*. Old Testament Library. Louisville: Westminster/John Knox, 1993.

———. "The Relationship between the Legal Corpora in the Pentateuch in Light of Manumission Laws." In *Studies in Bible, 1986*, edited by Sara Japhet, 68–78. Scripta hierosolymitana 31. Jerusalem: Magnes, 1986.

———. "Some Biblical Concepts of Sacred Place." In *Sacred Space: Shrine, City, Land*, edited by B. Kedar and R. L. Z. Werblowsky, 55–71. London: Macmillan, 1998.

Jeffers, Ann. *Magic and Divination in Ancient Palestine and Syria*. Leiden: Brill, 1996.

Jenson, Philip Peter. *Graded Holiness: A Key to the Priestly Conception of the World*. JSOTSup 106. Sheffield: Sheffield Academic Press, 1992.

Jeremias, Jörg. "The Function of the Book of Joel for Reading the Twelve." In *Perspectives on the Formation of the Book of the Twelve*, edited by R. Albertz, J. Nogalski, and J. Wöhrle, 77–87. Berlin: de Gruyter, 2012.

Kalimi, Isaac. *An Ancient Israelite Historian: Studies in the Chronicler, His Time, Place, and Writing*. Leiden: Brill, 2005.

———. "The Date of the Book of Chronicles." In *God's Word for Our World*, vol. 1, edited by D. Ellens, J. Ellens, I. Kalimi, R. Knierim, 347–71. London: T&T Clark International, 2004.

———. "The Land of Moriah, Mount Moriah, and the Site of Solomon's Temple in Biblical Historiography." *Harvard Theological Review* 83 (1990): 345–62.

Kang, Seung Il. "Creation, Eden, Temple and Mountain: Textual Presentations of Sacred Space in the Hebrew Bible." PhD diss., The Johns Hopkins University, 2008.

Kaufmann, Yehezkel. *The Religion of Israel: From Its Beginnings to the Babylonian Exile*. Translated by M. Greenberg. Chicago: University of Chicago Press, 1960.

Keel, O., and C. Uehlinger. *Gods, Goddesses, and Images of God in Ancient Israel*. Translated by T. H. Trapp. Minneapolis: Fortress Press, 1998.

Klein, Ralph W. *1 Chronicles*. Edited by Thomas Krüger. Minneapolis: Fortress Press, 2006

Kleinig, J. W. "Recent Research in Chronicles." *Currents in Research: Biblical Studies* 2 (1994): 43–76.

Knoppers, Gary N. *1 Chronicles 10–29: A New Translation with Introduction and Commentary*. Anchor Bible 12a. New York: Doubleday, 2004.

———. "Deuteronomistic History." In *Eerdmans Dictionary of the Bible*, edited by D. N. Freedman, 341–42. Grand Rapids: Eerdmans, 2000.

———. "Dissonance and Disaster in the Legend of Kirta." *Journal of the American Oriental Society* 11 (1994): 572–82.

———. "The Relationship of the Deuteronomistic History to Chronicles: Was the Chronicler a Deuteronomist?" In *Congress Volume Helsinki 2010*, edited by M. Nissinen, 307–42. Leiden: Brill, 2012.

———. *Two Nations under God: The Deuteronomistic History of Solomon and the Dual Monarchies*. 2 vols. Atlanta: Scholars Press, 1993–94.

Knoppers, Gary N., and J. G. McConville. *Reconsidering Israel and Judah: Recent Studies on the Deuteronomistic History*. Sources for Biblical and Theological Study 8. Winona Lake: Eisenbrauns, 2000.

Knott, Kim. *The Location of Religion: A Spatial Analysis*. London: Equinox, 2005.

Korpel, Marjo Christina Annette. *A Rift in the Clouds: Ugaritic and Hebrew Descriptions of the Divine*. Münster: Ugarit-Verlag, 1990.

Kort, Wesley A. *Place and Space in Modern Fiction*. Gainesville: University Press of Florida, 2004.

Kraus, H.-J. *Worship in Israel: A Cultic History of the Old Testament*. Translated by G. Buswell. Richmond: John Knox, 1966.

LaCocque, André. *The Feminine Unconventional: Four Subversive Figures in Israel's Tradition*. Overtures to Biblical Theology. Minneapolis: Fortress, 1990.

Laffey, Alice. "Ruth." In *The New Jerome Biblical Commentary*, 553–57. Engelwood Cliffs: Prentice Hall, 1990.

Langlamet, François. "Pour ou contre Salomon? La rédaction prosalomonienne de 1 Rois i–ii." Parts 1–2. *Revue biblique* 83 (1976): 321–79; 481–528.

Laroche, Emmanuel. "Textes hourrites en cunéiformes alphabétiques." *Ugaritica* V (1968): 497–504.

Lefebvre, Henri. *Critique of Everyday Life*. Vol. 2, *Foundations for a Sociology of the Everyday*. Translated by John Moore. London: Verso, 1961.

———. *The Production of Space*. Translated by D. Nicholson-Smith. Malden: Blackwell, 1974.

Lehmann, Manfred R. "Biblical Oaths." *Zeitschrift für die alttestamentliche Wissenschaft* 81 (1969): 74–92.

Lemaire, André. "The United Monarchy: Saul, David and Solomon." In *Ancient Israel: From Abraham to the Roman Destruction of the Temple*, edited by Hershel Shanks, 85–108. Washington, DC: Biblical Archaeology Society, 1988.

Lemche, N. P. "The Manumission of Slaves—The Fallow Year—The Sabbatical Year—The Jobel Year." *Vetus Testamentum* 26 (1976): 38–59.

Leuchter, Mark. "The Manumission Laws in Leviticus and Deuteronomy: The Jeremiah Connection." *Journal of Biblical Literature* 127 (2008): 635–53.

Levenson, Jon D. *Sinai and Zion: An Entry into the Jewish Bible.* San Francisco: Harper & Row, 1985.

Levine, Baruch. *Numbers 1–20.* Anchor Bible 4a. New York: Doubleday, 1993.

Levine, Baruch A., and Jean-Michel de Tarragon. "Dead Kings and Rephaim: The Patrons of the Ugaritic Dynasty." *Journal of the American Oriental Society* 104 (1984): 649–59.

Levinson, Bernard M. *Deuteronomy and the Hermeneutics of Legal Innovation.* New York: Oxford University Press, 1997.

———. "The Reconceptualization of Kingship in Deuteronomy and the Deuteronomistic History's Transformation of Torah." *Vetus Testamentum* 51 (2001): 511–34.

Lewis, Theodore J. *Cults of the Dead in Ancient Israel and Ugarit.* Harvard Semitic Monographs 39. Atlanta: Scholars Press, 1989.

———. "The Rapiuma." In *Ugaritic Narrative Poetry*, edited by S. B. Parker, 196–205. Society of Biblical Literature Writings from the Ancient World 9. Atlanta: Scholars Press, 1997.

L'Heureux, Conrad. *Rank among the Canaanite Gods: El, Ba'al, and the Rephaim.* Missoula: Scholars Press, 1979.

———. "The Ugaritic and Biblical Rephaim." *Harvard Theological Review* 67 (1974): 265–74.

Lipiński, E. *The Aramaeans.* Leuven: Peeters and Departement Oosterse Studies, 2000.

Lohfink, Norbert. "*ḥrm*." In *Theological Dictionary of the Old Testament*, 5:186–87. Grand Rapids: Eerdmans, 1986.

———. "Gab es eine deuteronomistische Bewegung?" In *Jeremia und die "Deuteronomistische Bewegung,"* edited by W. Groß, 313–82. BBB 98. Weinheim: Beltz Athenäum, 1995.

———. "'Holy War' and the 'Ban' in the Bible." *Theology Digest* 38 (1991): 109–14.

Loretz, O. "The Theme of the Ruth Story." *Catholic Biblical Quarterly* 22 (1960): 391–99.

Lundbom, Jack. *Jeremiah 1–20*. Anchor Bible 21a. New Haven: Yale University Press, 1999.

———. *Jeremiah 37–52*. Anchor Bible 21c. New Haven: Yale University Press, 2004.

Maier, Johann. "Urim und Tummim: Recht und Bund in der Spannung zwischen Königtum und Priestertum im alten Israel." *Kairos* (1969): 22–38.

Margalit, Baruch. "The Meaning and Significance of Asherah." *Vetus Testamentum* 40 (1990): 264–97.

———. *The Ugaritic Poem of Aqht: Text, Translation, Commentary*. Berlin: Walter de Gruyter, 1989.

Marget, Arthur W. "*gwrn nkwn* in 2 Sam. 6:6." *Journal of Biblical Literature* 39 (1920): 70–76.

Martin, Lee Roy. "'Where Are All His Wonders?': The Exodus Motif in the Book of Judges." *Journal of Biblical and Pneumatological Research* 2 (2010): 87–109.

Matthews, Victor H. "Entrance Ways and Threshing Floors: Legally Significant Sites in the Ancient Near East." *Fides et Historia* 19 (1987): 25–40.

Mazar, Amihai. "Archaeology and the Biblical Narrative: The Case of the United Monarchy." In *One God–One Cult–One Nation*, edited by

Reinhard Kratz and Hermann Spieckermann, 29–58. Berlin: de Gruyter, 2010.

———. *Archaeology of the Land of the Bible 10,000–586 BCE*. The Anchor Bible Reference Library 2. New York: Doubleday, 1990.

———. "On Cult Places and Early Israelites: A Response to Michael Coogan." *Biblical Archaeology Review* 14 (1988): 45.

Mazar, Amihai, and Avraham Biran. "Ritual Dancing in the Iron Age." *Near Eastern Archaeology* 66 (2003): 126–32.

McBride, S. Dean. "The Deuteronomic Name Theology." PhD diss., Harvard University, 1969.

McCarter, P. Kyle, Jr. *I Samuel: A New Translation with Introduction and Commentary*. Anchor Bible 8. Garden City: Doubleday, 1980.

———. *II Samuel: A New Translation with Introduction, Notes, and Commentary*. Anchor Bible 9. Garden City: Doubleday, 1984.

———. "The Ritual Dedication of the City of David in 2 Samuel 6." In *The Word of the Lord Shall Go Forth: Essays in Honor of David Noel Freedman in Celebration of His Sixtieth Birthday*. Edited by C. L. Meyers, M. P. O'Connor and D. N. Freedman, 273–78. Winona Lake: Eisenbrauns, 1983.

———. "When Gods Lose Their Temper: Divine Rage in Ugaritic Myth and the Hypostasis of Anger in Iron Age Religion." In *Divine Wrath and Divine Mercy in the World of Antiquity*, edited by Reinhard G. Kratz and Hermann Spieckermann, 88–91. Tübingen: Mohr Siebeck, 2008.

McKane, William. *The Book of Micah: Introduction and Commentary*. Edinburgh: T&T Clark, 1998.

McKenzie, Steven L. *1–2 Chronicles*. Abingdon Old Testament Commentaries. Nashville: Abingdon, 2004.

———. *The Chronicler's Use of the Deuteronomistic History*. Harvard Semitic Monographs 33. Atlanta: Scholars Press, 1984.

———. *The Trouble with Kings: The Composition of the Books of Kings in the Deuteronomistic History.* Supplements to Vetus Testamentum 42. Leiden: Brill, 1991.

Mendenhall, George E. "The Census Lists of Numbers 1 and 26." *Journal of Biblical Literature* 77 (1958): 52–66.

Mettinger, Tryggve N. D. *The Dethronement of Sabaoth: Studies in the Shem and Kabod Theologies.* Lund: CWK Gleerup, 1982.

———. "The Name and the Glory: The Zion-Sabaoth Theology and its Exilic Successors." *Journal of Northwest Semitic Languages* 24 (1998): 1–24.

Meyers, Carol. "Of Drums and Damsels: Women's Performance in Ancient Israel." *Biblical Archaeologist* 54 (1991): 16–27.

Milgrom, Jacob. "The Antiquity of the Priestly Source: A Reply to Joseph Blenkinsopp." *Zeitschrift für die alttestamentliche Wissenschaft* 111 (1999): 10–22.

———. *Leviticus 1–16.* Anchor Bible 3. New York: Doubleday, 1991.

Millard, Alan. "Two Lexical Explorations." In *The Perfumes of Seven Tamarisks: Studies in Honour of Wilfred G. E. Watson*, edited by Gregorio del Olmo Lete, Jordi Vidal, and Nicolas Wyatt, 231–32. Münster: Ugarit-Verlag, 2012.

Miller, Patrick D., and J. J. M. Roberts. *The Hand of the Lord: A Reassessment of the "Ark Narrative" of 1 Samuel.* Baltimore: Johns Hopkins University Press, 1977.

Minca, Claudio, ed. *Postmodern Geography: Theory and Praxis.* Oxford: Blackwell, 2010.

Mitchell, T. C. "The Music of the Old Testament Reconsidered." *Palestine Exploration Quarterly* 124 (1992): 124–43.

Moor, Johannes C. de. *The Seasonal Pattern in the Ugaritic Myth of Ba'lu according to the Version of Ilimilku.* Herstellung: Verlag Butzon & Bercker Kevelae, 1971.

Morgenstern, J. "nkwn." *Journal of Biblical Literature* 37 (1918): 144–48.

Mowinckel, Sigmund. *The Psalms in Israel's Worship.* New York: Abingdon Press, 1962.

Münderlein, G. "Goren." In *Theological Dictionary of the Old Testament*, translated by J. T. Willis, G. W. Bromiley, and D. E. Green, edited by G. J. Botterweck and H. Ringgren, 3:62–65. Grand Rapids: Eerdmans, 1978.

Murphy, Francesca Aran. *1 Samuel.* Grand Rapids: Brazos Press, 2010.

Myers, Jacob Martin. *I Chronicles.* Anchor Bible 12. Garden City: Doubleday, 1965.

———. *II Chronicles.* Anchor Bible 13. Garden City: Doubleday, 1965.

Na'aman, Nadav. "David's Sojourn in Keilah in Light of the Amarna Letters." *Vetus Testamentum* 60 (2010): 87–97.

Nelson, R. D. *The Double Redaction of the Deuteronomistic History.* Journal for the Study of the Old Testament: Supplement Series 18. Sheffield: JSOT Press, 1981.

Nicholson, Paul, and Ian Shaw, *Ancient Egyptian Material and Technology.* Cambridge: Cambridge University Press, 2000.

Niditch, Susan. *Underdogs and Tricksters: A Prelude to Biblical Folklore.* New Voices in Biblical Studies. San Francisco: Harper & Row, 1987.

———. *War in the Hebrew Bible: A Study in the Ethics of Violence.* Oxford: Oxford University Press, 1993.

Niesiołowski-Spanò, Łukasz. *The Origin Myths and Holy Places in the Old Testament: A Study of Aetiological Narratives.* Translated by J. Laskowski. London: Equinox, 2011.

Nigosian, Solomon A. *Magic and Divination in the Old Testament.* Brighton: Sussex Academic, 2008.

Nihan, Christophe. "The Holiness Code between D and P: Some Comments on the Function and Significance of Leviticus 17–26 in the Composition of the Torah." In *Das Deuteronomium zwischen Pentateuch und deuteronomistischem Geschichtswerk*, edited by Eckart Otto and Reinhard

Achenbach, 81–122. Forschungen zur Religion und Literatur des Alten und Neuen Testaments 206. Göttingen: Vandenhoeck & Ruprecht, 2004.

Nissinen, Martti. *Prophets and Prophecy in the Ancient Near East*. Edited by P. Machinist. Atlanta: Society of Biblical Literature, 2003.

Nocquet, Dany. *Le livret noir de Baal: La polémique contre le dieu Baal dans la Bible hébraïque et l'ancien Israël*. Genève: Labor et Fides, 2004.

Noth, Martin. *The Deuteronomistic History*. Journal for the Study of the Old Testament: Supplement Series 15. Sheffield: JSOT Press, 1991.

———. *Überlieferungsgeschichte des Pentateuch*. Stuttgart: Kohlhammer, 1948. Translated by B. W. Anderson as *A History of Pentateuchal Traditions*. Englewood Cliffs: Prentice Hall, 1972.

———. *Überlieferungsgeschichtliche Studien*. 2nd ed. Tübingen: Max Niemeyer, 1957.

Nwaoru, Emmanuel. "The Motif 'Food of Life' in Biblical and Extra Biblical Traditions." *Biblische Notizen* 105 (2000): 16–27.

Obermann, J. "YHWH's Victory over the Babylonian Pantheon: The Archetype of Isaiah 21 1–10." *Journal of Biblical Literature* 48 (1929): 307–28.

Ornan, Tallay. "The Bull and Its Two Masters." *Israel Exploration Journal* 51 (2001): 1–26.

Oswalt, John. *The Book of Isaiah: Chapters 1–39*. Grand Rapids: William B. Eerdmans, 1986.

Pardee, Dennis, trans. "The 'Aqhatu Legend." In *The Context of Scripture*, edited by William Hallo and K. Lawson Younger, 1:343–56. Leiden: Brill, 1997.

———, trans. "The Kirta Epic." In *The Context of Scripture*, edited by William Hallo and K. Lawson Younger, 1:333–43. Leiden: Brill, 1997.

———. *Ritual and Cult at Ugarit*. Writings from the Ancient World 10. Edited by T. J. Lewis. Leiden: Brill, 2002.

———. *Les textes rituels*. 2 vols. Ras Shamra-Ougarit XII. Paris: Éditions Recherche sur les Civilizations, 2000.

Park, Sung Jin. "The Cultic Identity of Asherah in Deuteronomistic Ideology of Israel." *Zeitschrift für die alttestamentliche Wissenschaft* 123 (2011): 553–64.

Parker, Simon B. "Aqhat." In *Ugaritic Narrative Poetry*, edited by S. B. Parker, 49–80. Society of Biblical Literature Writings from the Ancient World 9. Atlanta: Scholars Press, 1997.

Patai, Raphael. "The 'Control of Rain' in Ancient Palestine: A Study in Comparative Religion." *Hebrew Union College Annual* 14 (1939): 251–86.

Peckham, Brian. *The Composition of the Deuteronomistic History*. Harvard Semitic Monographs 35. Atlanta: Scholars Press, 1985.

Peleg, Y., and I. Yezerski. "A Dwelling and Burial Cave at Kh. Abu-Musarraḥ in the Land of Benjamin." In *Burial Caves and Sites in Judea and Samaria from the Bronze and Iron Ages*, edited by H. Hizmi and A. De-Groot, 107–56. Jerusalem: Israeli Antiquities Authority, 2004.

Person, Raymond F., Jr. *The Deuteronomic History and the Book of Chronicles: Scribal Works in an Oral World*. Atlanta: Society of Biblical Literature, 2010.

———. *The Deuteronomic School: History, Social Setting, and Literature*. Studies in Biblical Literature 2. Atlanta: Society of Biblical Literature, 2002.

Pitard, Wayne T. "A New Edition of the 'Rāpi'ūma' Texts: KTU 1.20–22." *Bulletin of the American Schools of Oriental Research* 285 (1992): 33–77.

———. "The Ugaritic Funerary Text RS 34.126." *Bulletin of the American Schools of Oriental Research* 232 (1978): 65–75.

Polzin, R. *Moses and the Deuteronomist: A Literary Study of the Deuteronomic History*. New York: Seabury, 1980.

Pope, Marvin. "A Divine Banquet at Ugarit." In *The Use of the Old Testament in the New and Other Essays: Studies in Honor of William Franklin*

Stinespring, edited by J. M. Efird, 170–203. Durham: Duke University Press, 1972.

———. *Job: Introduction, Translation, and Notes.* Anchor Bible 15. Garden City: Doubleday & Company, 1973.

Pritchard, James B., ed. *Ancient Near Eastern Texts Relating to the Old Testament.* 3rd ed. Princeton: Princeton University Press, 1969.

Propp, William H. C. "Milk and Honey: Biblical Comfort Food." *Biblical Research* 15 (1999): 16, 54.

Pury, Albert de, Thomas Römer, and Jean-Daniel Maachi, eds. *Israel Constructs Its History: Deuteronomistic Historiography in Recent Research.* Sheffield: Sheffield Academic Press, 2000.

Rainey, A. F. "The Ugaritic Texts in Ugaritica 5." *Journal of the American Oriental Society* 94 (1974): 184–94.

Ray, Benjamin. "Sacred Space and Royal Shrines in Buganda." *History of Religions* 16 (1977): 363–73.

Redford, Donald B. *A Study of the Biblical Story of Joseph (Genesis 37–50).* Leiden: Brill, 1970.

Rendtorff, Rolf. *Das Alte Testament: Eine Einführung.* Neukirchen-Vluyn: Neukirchener, 1993.

Renfrew, Colin, and Paul Bahn. *Archaeology: Theories, Methods, and Practice.* 2nd ed. London: Thames and Hudson Ltd, 1996.

Richter, Sandra L. *The Deuteronomistic History and the Name Theology: Lĕšakkēn Šĕmô Šām in the Bible and the Ancient Near East.* Berlin: Walter de Gruyter, 2002.

Rochberg, Francesca. *The Heavenly Writing: Divination, Horoscopy, and Astronomy in Mesopotamian Culture.* Cambridge: Cambridge University Press, 2004.

Rofé, Alexander. *The Prophetical Stories: The Narratives about the Prophets in the Hebrew Bible, Their Literary Types and History.* Jerusalem: Magnes Press, 1988.

Römer, Thomas. *The So-Called Deuteronomistic History: A Sociological, Historical, and Literary Introduction.* London: T&T Clark, 2005.

Rooke, Deborah W. "Kingship as Priesthood: The Relationship between the High Priesthood and the Monarchy." In *King and Messiah in Israel and the Ancient Near East: Proceedings of the Oxford Old Testament Seminar*, edited by J. Day, 187–208. Journal for the Study of the Old Testament: Supplement Series 270. Sheffield: Sheffield Academic Press, 1998.

Rudolph, Wilhelm. *Micha, Nahum, Habakuk, Zephanja.* Gütersloh: Gerd Mohn, 1975.

Sanders, J. A. "Census." In *The Interpreter's Dictionary of the Bible*, ed. G. A. Buttrick, 1:547. Nashville: Abingdon Press, 1962.

Sanders, Seth. *The Invention of Hebrew.* Urbana: University of Illinois Press, 2009.

Sarna, Nahum M. *Genesis = Be-Reshit: The Traditional Hebrew Text with New JPS Translation.* JPS Torah Commentary. Philadelphia: Jewish Publication Society, 1989.

Sasson, Jack M. *Ruth: A New Translation with a Philological Commentary and a Formalist-Folklorist Interpretation.* Baltimore: The Johns Hopkins University Press, 1979.

Schäfer-Lichtenberger, Christa. "Bedeutung und Funktion von Herem in biblische-hebräische Texten." *Biblische Zeitschrift* 38 (1994): 270–75.

Schearing, Linda S., and Steven L. McKenzie, eds. *Those Elusive Deuteronomists: The Phenomenon of Pan-Deuteronomism.* Sheffield: Sheffield Academic Press, 1999.

Scherer, Andreas. "Das Ephod im alten Israel." *Ugarit-Forschungen* 35 (2003): 589–604.

———. "Gideon–ein Anti-Held? Ein Beitrag zur Auseinandersetzung mit dem sog. 'Flawed-Hero Approach' am Beispiel von Jdc. vi 36–40." *Vetus Testamentum* 55 (2005): 269–73.

Schlenke, Barbara, and Peter Weimar. "'Und JHWH eiferte für sein Land und erbarmte sich seines Volkes' (Joel 2,18): Zu Struktur und Komposition von Joel (II)." *Biblische Zeitschrift* 53 (2009): 212–37.

Schmid, Konrad, and Raymond F. Person Jr., eds. *Deuteronomy in the Pentateuch, Hexateuch, and the Deuteronomistic History*. FAT 2/56. Tübingen: Mohr Siebeck, 2012.

Schmidt, Ludwig. *Studien zur Priesterschrift*. Berlin: de Gruyter, 1993.

Schniedewind, William M. "Tel Dan Stela: New Light on Aramaic and Jehu's Revolt." *Bulletin of the American Schools of Oriental Research* 302 (1996): 75–90.

Schweitzer, Steven James. "Exploring the Utopian Space of Chronicles: Some Spatial Anomalies." In *Constructions of Space I: Theory, Geography, and Narrative*, edited by Jon L. Berquist and Claudia V. Camp, 141–56. New York: T&T Clark, 2007.

Scott, R. B. Y. "Isaiah XXI 1–10: The Inside of a Prophet's Mind." *Vetus Testamentum* 2 (1952): 278–82.

Scurlock, Jo Ann. "Prophecy as a Form of Divination; Divination as a Form of Prophecy." In *Divination and Interpretation of Signs in the Ancient World*, edited by Amar Annus, 277–316. Chicago: Oriental Institute of the University of Chicago, 2010.

Segal, Moses Hirsch. "The Composition of the Books of Samuel." *Jewish Quarterly Review* 55 (1964): 318–39.

Selman, Martin J. *2 Chronicles: A Commentary*. Leicester: InterVarsity Press, 1994.

Seow, C. L. "Ark of the Covenant." In *The Anchor Bible Dictionary*, edited by D. N. Freedman, 1:386–93. New York: Doubleday, 1992.

———. "Hosea." In *The Anchor Bible Dictionary*, edited by D. N. Freedman, 3:291–97. New York: Doubleday, 1992.

Shahack-Gross, Ruth, Mor Gafri, and Israel Finkelstein. "Identifying Threshing Floors in the Archaeological Record: A Test Case at Iron Age Tel Megiddo, Israel." *Journal of Field Archaeology* 34 (2009): 171–84.

Shanks, Hershel, ed. *Ancient Israel: A Short History from Abraham to the Roman Destruction of the Temple*. Washington, DC: Biblical Archaeology Society, 1988.

Shectman, Sarah, and Joel S. Baden, eds. *The Strata of the Priestly Writings: Contemporary Debate and Future Directions*. ATANT 95. Zurich: Theologischer Verlag, 2009.

Ska, Jean-Louis. *The Exegesis of the Pentateuch: Exegetical Studies and Basic Questions*. Tübingen: Mohr Siebeck, 2009.

———. *Introduction to Reading the Pentateuch*. Winona Lake: Eisenbrauns, 2006.

Skinner, John. *A Critical and Exegetical Commentary on Genesis*. The International Critical Commentary on the Holy Scriptures of the Old and New Testaments 1a. Edinburgh: C. Scribner's Sons, 1969.

Skinner, Matthew. *Locating Paul: Places of Custody as Narrative Settings in Acts 21–28*. Academia Biblica. Atlanta: Society of Biblical Literature, 2003.

Smend, Rudolph. "Das Gesetz und die Völker: Ein Beitrag zur deuteronomistischen Redaktionsgeschichte." In *Probleme biblischer Theologie: G. von Rad zum 70. Geburtstag*, edited by H. W. Wolff, 494–509. Munich: Kaiser, 1971.

Smith, Jonathan Z. *To Take Place: Toward Theory in Ritual*. Chicago: University of Chicago Press, 1987.

Smith, Mark S. *The Early History of God: Yahweh and the Other Deities in Ancient Israel*. 2nd ed. Grand Rapids: Wm. B. Eerdmans, 2002.

Smith, Sidney. "The Threshing Floor and the City Gate." *Palestine Exploration Quarterly* 78 (1946): 5–15.

———. "On the Meaning of *Goren*." *Palestine Exploration Quarterly* 85 (1953): 42–45.

Soggin, J. Alberto. *Introduction to the Old Testament: From Its Origins to the Closing of the Alexandrian Canon*. Revised ed. Translated by J. Bowden. Old Testament Library. Philadelphia: Westminster, 1977.

———. *Judges: A Commentary*. Old Testament Library. Philadelphia: Westminster Press, 1981.

Soja, Edward. "Afterword." In *Postmodern Geography: Theory and Praxis*, edited by Claudio Minca, 282–94. Oxford: Blackwell, 2010.

———. *Postmodern Geographies: The Reassertion of Space in Critical Social Theory*. London: Verso, 1989.

———. *Thirdspace: Journeys to Los Angeles and Other Real-and-Imagined Places*. Cambridge: Blackwell, 1996.

Speiser, E. A. "Census and Ritual Expiation in Mari and Israel." *Bulletin of the American Schools of Oriental Research* 149 (1958): 17–25.

———. *Genesis: A New Translation with Introduction and Commentary*. Anchor Bible 1. Garden City: Doubleday, 1964.

Stackert, Jeffrey. "Rewriting the Torah: Literary Revision in Deuteronomy and the Holiness Legislation." PhD diss., Brandeis University, 2006.

Stavrakopoulou, Francesca. *King Manasseh and Child Sacrifice: Biblical Distortions of Historical Realities*. Berlin: Walter de Gruyter, 2004.

Stern, Philip D. *The Biblical Herem: A Window on Israel's Religious Experience*. Providence: Brown Judaic Studies, 1991.

Stökl, Jonathan. "Magic and Divination in the Old Testament." *Journal of Theological Studies* 61 (2010): 264–65.

Sweeney, Marvin A. *I & II Kings: A Commentary*. Louisville: Westminster John Knox Press, 2007.

Tanner, J. P. "The Gideon Narrative as the Focal Point of Judges." *Bibliotheca Sacra* 149 (1992): 146–61.

Tappy, Ron E. *The Archaeology of Israelite Samaria*. Vol. 1, *Early Iron Age through the Ninth Century BCE*. Atlanta: Scholars Press, 1992.

———. *The Archaeology of Israelite Samaria.* Vol. 2, *The Eighth Century* BCE. Winona Lake: Eisenbrauns, 2001.

Thelle, Rannfrid I. *Approaches to the "Chosen Place": Accessing a Biblical Concept.* New York: T&T Clark, 2012.

Thompson, Thomas L. *The Early History of the Israelite People: From the Written and Archaeological Sources.* Leiden: Brill, 1992.

Tomback, Richard S. *A Comparative Semitic Lexicon of the Phoenician and Punic Languages.* SBL Dissertation Series 32. Ann Arbor: Edwards Brothers, Inc., 1978.

Tremblay, Hervé. "Yahvé contre Baal? Ou plutot Yahvé a la place de Baal? Jalons pour la naissance d'un monothéisme." *Science et Esprit* 61 (2009): 51–71.

Trible, Phyllis. *God and the Rhetoric of Sexuality.* Overtures to Biblical Theology. Philadelphia: Fortress, 1978.

Tropper, Josef. *Kleines Wörterbuch des Ugaritischen.* Elementa Linguarum Orientis 4. Wiesbaden: Harrassowitz Verlag, 2008.

Tsartsidou, Georgia, Simcha Lev-Yadun, Nikos Efstratiou, and Steve Weiner. "Ethnoarchaeological Study of Phytolith Assemblages from an Agro-Pastoral Village in Northern Greece (Sarakini): Development and Application of a Phytolith Difference Index." *Journal of Archaeological Science* 35 (2008): 600–613.

Tuan, Yi-Fu. *Space and Place: The Perspective of Experience.* Minneapolis: University of Minnesota Press, 1977.

Tur-Sinai, N. H. "The Ark of God at Beit Shemesh (1 Sam. VI) and Pereṣ 'Uzza (2 Sam. VI; 1 Chron. XIII)." *Vetus Testamentum* 1 (1951): 275–86.

Turner, Harold W. *From Temple to Meeting House: The Phenomenology and Theology of Places of Worship.* The Hague: Mouton Publishers, 1979.

Turner, Victor. *The Forest of Symbols: Aspects of Ndembu Ritual.* Ithaca: Cornell University Press, 1967.

———. *The Ritual Process: Structure and Anti-Structure.* Chicago: Aldine Publishing Co., 1969.

Ulrich, Eugene Charles. *The Qumran Text of Samuel and Josephus.* Harvard Semitic Monographs 19. Missoula: Scholars Press, 1978.

Van Dam, Cornelis. *The Urim and Thummim: A Means of Revelation in Ancient Israel.* Winona Lake: Eisenbrauns, 1997.

Van de Mieroop, Marc. *The Ancient Mesopotamian City.* Oxford: Clarendon Press, 1997.

Van Seters, John. "Creative Imitation in the Hebrew Bible." *Studies in Religion* 29 (2000): 395–409.

———. *The Edited Bible: The Curious History of the "Editor" in Biblical Criticism.* Winona Lake: Eisenbrauns, 2006.

———. *In Search of History: Historiography in the Ancient World and the Origins of Biblical History.* New Haven: Yale University Press, 1983.

———. "Solomon's Temple: Fact and Ideology in Biblical and Near Eastern Historiography." *Catholic Biblical Quarterly* 59 (1997): 45–57.

———. "Review of S. Richter, The Deuteronomistic History and the Name Theology: *Lĕšakkēn Šĕmô Šām* in the Bible and the Ancient Near East." *Journal of the American Oriental Society* 123 (2003): 871–72.

Veijola, Timo. *Die ewige Dynastie: David und die Entstehung seiner Dynastie nach der deuteronomistischen Darstellung.* Annales Academiae Scientiarum Fennicae B 193. Helsinki: Suomalainen Tiedeakatemia, 1975.

Vielhauer, Roman. "Hosea in the Book of the Twelve." In *Perspectives on the Formation of the Book of the Twelve*, edited by R. Albertz, J. Nogalski, and J. Wöhrle, 55–75. Berlin: de Gruyter, 2012.

Virolleaud, Charles. "Les Rephaïm." *Répertoire d'épigraphie sémitiques* 7 (1940): 77–83.

———. "Les Rephaïm: Fragments de poèmes de Ras-Shamra." *Syria* 22 (1941): 1–30.

von Rad, Gerhard. "Deuteronomy's 'Name' Theology and the Priestly Document's 'Kabod' Theology." In *Studies in Deuteronomy*, 37–44. London: SCM Press, 1953.

———. *Genesis: A Commentary*. Old Testament Library. Philadelphia: Westminster Press, 1961.

Waltke, Bruce K., and M. O'Connor. *An Introduction to Biblical Hebrew Syntax*. Winona Lake: Eisenbrauns, 1990.

Weinfeld, Moshe. *Deuteronomy and the Deuteronomic School*. Oxford: Clarendon Press, 1972.

Weippert, H. "Das deuteronomistische Geschichtswerk: Sein Ziel und Ende in der neueren Forschung." *Theologische Rundschau* 50 (1985): 213–49.

Weisman, Zeev. "Reflections on the Transition to Agriculture in Israelite Religion and Cult." In *Studies in Historical Geography and Biblical Historiography*, edited by G. Galil and M. Weinfeld, 251–61. Leiden: Brill, 2000.

Wenham, Gordon. *Genesis 16–50*. Word Biblical Commentary 2. Nashville: Thomas Nelson Publishers, 1994.

———. "Pondering the Pentateuch: The Search for a New Paradigm." In *The Face of Old Testament Studies: A Survey of Contemporary Approaches*, edited by D. Baker and B. Arnold, 116–44. Grand Rapids: Baker Books, 1999.

Westbrook, Raymond. "What Is the Covenant Code?" In *Theory and Method in Biblical and Cuneiform Law*, edited by B. Levinson, 13–34. Journal for the Study of the Old Testament: Supplement Series 181. Sheffield: Sheffield Academic Press, 1994.

Westermann, Claus. *Genesis 37–50*. Translated by John J. Scullion. Continental Commentary. Minneapolis: Fortress Press, 2002.

Wheatley, Paul. *The Pivot of the Four Quarters: A Preliminary Enquiry into the Origins and Character of the Ancient Chinese City*. Chicago: Aldine Publishing Company, 1971.

Whittaker, John C. "The Ethnoarchaeology of Threshing in Cyprus." *Near Eastern Archaeology* 63 (2000): 62–69.

Wildberger, Hans. *Isaiah 13–27*. Translated by Thomas H. Trapp. Continental Commentary. Minneapolis: Fortress Press, 1997.

Wiseman, Donald J. *1 & 2 Kings: An Introduction & Commentary*. Leicester: Inter-Varsity Press, 1993.

Wolff, Hans Walter. *Joel and Amos: A Commentary on the Books of the Prophets Joel and Amos*. Edited by S. Dean McBride. Hermeneia. Philadelphia: Fortress Press, 1977.

———. *Micah: A Commentary*. Translated by Gary Stansell. Minneapolis: Augsburg, 1990.

Würthwein, Ernst. *Die Erzählung von der Thronfolge Davids—theologische oder politische Geschichtsschreibung?* Theologische Studien 115. Zürich: Theologischer Verlag, 1974.

Wyatt, Nick. "On Calves and Kings." In *The Mythic Mind: Essays on Cosmology and Religion in Ugaritic and Old Testament Literature*, 72–91. London: Equinox, 2005.

———. *Religious Texts from Ugarit*. The Biblical Seminar 53. London: Continuum, 2002.

Xella, Paolo. "L'episode de Dnil et Kothar (KTU 1.17 [= CTA 17] V 1–31) et Gen. XVIII 1–16." *Vetus Testamentum* 28 (1978): 483–88.

Yeivin, Sh. "The Threshing Floor of Araunah." *Journal of Educational Sociology* 36 (1963): 396–400.

Zevit, Ziony. "Israel's Royal Cult in the Ancient Near Eastern Kulturkreis." In *Text, Artifact, and Image: Revealing Ancient Israelite Religion*, edited by G. Beckman and T. Lewis, 189–200. Providence: Brown Judaic Studies, 2006.

———. *The Religions of Ancient Israel: A Synthesis of Parallactic Approaches*. New York: Continuum, 2001.

Ziegler, Yael. *Promises to Keep: The Oath in Biblical Narrative*. Leiden: Brill, 2008.

Index of Names

Amit, Yairah, 22, 41, 83
Claassens, L. Juliana M., 73, 145
Cross, Frank Moore, 42, 60, 152
Day, John, 32, 35, 136, 152
Eliade, Mircea, 16–20
Japhet, Sara, 16, 19–20, 65, 83, 139–40
Kalimi, Isaac, 83–85, 127
Knoppers, Gary N., 41–42, 83–84, 107, 114, 125, 127
Lefebvre, Henri, 16, 22–24, 45, 49, 82, 89–90, 139, 143
Levinson, Bernard, 65, 67–68, 136
Lewis, Theodore J., 127, 155, 157
McCarter, P. Kyle, Jr., 41, 96–100, 102–4, 108

McKenzie, Steven, 41–42, 83–85
Noth, Martin, 41–42
Pardee, Dennis, 152–53, 158–59, 161–62
Person, Raymond F., Jr., 41, 64, 83–84
Seow, C. L., 30, 44, 95
Smith, Jonathan Z., 16, 18–19, 36, 83
Soja, Edward, 16, 22–24, 36, 100
Turner, Victor, 122–23
Van Seters, John, 41–42, 84, 91, 127, 134
von Rad, Gerhard, 41, 91, 134
Whittaker, John C., 2, 7–9
Wolff, Hans Walter, 37–38, 41, 55

Index of Bible and Ancient Literature

BIBLICAL TEXTS

1 Chronicles
1–8......84
5:20......94
13......26, 95–96, 115
13:1-2......113
13:2......113–14, 130
13:7......96
13:8......96
13:9-10......20, 24, 27, 81, 97, 99, 100–101, 123, 148
13:9......11
13:10-11......13, 15, 18
13:12-14......99
15:2......114
21......26, 125
21:1-14......101
21:14-27......13, 18, 20, 27, 101–2, 115, 148
21:14-16......81
21:14-15......123
21:15......11
21:15a......102
21:15b-16a......102–3
21:16-27......15
21:16......123
21:18-20......17
21:18......105, 116
21:20......4, 71
21:20b......105
21:21b......106
21:22......106
21:23......4, 105, 106, 140
21:26-27......106
21:26......148
21:29-30......125
22:1......126, 141

1 Kings
1:25......141
2:35......141
3:4-5......107
4:1-6......135

6......128, 130–33
6:2-20......141
6:5, 16, 19......139
6:7-10, 15-18, 20-22......141
6:23-26......141
8:1—9:10......141
8:6-10......139
8:64......108
12:25-33......142
12:26—13:1......136
15:18-20......46
16:30-34......89
16:31-34......142
16:33......110
18:24-38......107
19:18......34
22......111
22:1-3......86
22:5......86
22:6......86
22:7-8......86
22:10......11–13, 15, 18, 20, 24, 27, 83–85, 86, 87, 89–90, 110, 123, 129, 148, 159
22:11......111
22:20-23......111
22:20......89
22:21-23......89
22:29-38......89
22:41-50......111

1 Samuel
5:1-8......99
5:9-12......99
7:1......114
18:28a......104
22:3-5......116
23:1-5......15, 27, 40–43, 45, 85, 147
23:1......11, 29, 40, 43–45, 129
23:1b......43
23:2-5......44, 50, 86
23:2-4......43
23:4b......43
23:5......43
23:6-12......44

2 Chronicles
3:1......20, 28, 104, 120, 126–28, 148
7:7......108
17:1-19......111
18......111
18:5......86
18:6-7......86
18:9......11–13, 15, 18, 20, 24, 27, 78, 83, 85–90, 110, 123, 129, 148, 159
18:10......111
18:19-22......111
18:19......89
18:21-22......89

INDEX OF BIBLE AND ANCIENT LITERATURE

19:1—20:37......111
21:27—22:1......132

2 Kings
6–7......48
6:24-27......40–43
6:24-25......40, 46
6:24......29
6:26......47
6:27......15, 27, 47, 48–49, 85, 87, 129, 147
6:28b-29......47
7:1-2, 16......46, 48
7:1......87
7:2, 19......48
7:6-7......48
16:10-14......136
16:12-15......136
18:1-4......136
21:1—23:24......136
21:3, 13......110
23......142, 152

2 Samuel
6......26, 95–96
6:1-2......113
6:1......96
6:3......96
6:5......96
6:6-7......13, 15, 20, 24, 27, 81, 95–101, 120, 123, 148

6:6......11, 119
6:9-11......99
7:12-17......134
14:2......47
15:1-6......87
24......26, 125
24:1-14......101
24:15-26......15
24:15-25......13, 18, 20, 27, 101–9, 115, 120, 148
24:15......123
24:16......11, 102
24:18-24......119
24:18......105
24:20b......106
24:22......4, 106, 140
24:25......107–8, 128

Amos
1:3......4–5
5:16......93

Daniel
2:1-3......5
2:35......5, 12

Deuteronomy
4:16......34
8:5......104
10:8......114
12......67, 143

203

12:2-3......67
12:11......133
14:23......133
15:12-15......27, 64–65, 147
15:12-13......64
15:14-15......64, 65
16:2-11......133
16:13-15......27, 66–68, 119, 147
16:13b-14a......66
16:14b......66
16:21-22......152
18:4......80
21:19......87
22:15......87
25:4......4
26:2......134
27:1-8......107
33:13......80

Genesis
1–2......145
1:29, 9:3-5......145
6......81
19......81
32:22-32......93
50......26, 91
50:1-4, 10-11......47
50:7-11......112
50:7-9......92
50:10-11......13, 15, 18, 20, 24, 27, 40, 91–95, 97, 148

Ezekiel
1:1-28......133
7:31-32......93
8:16......152
10:18-19......133
16:8-9......72
16:8......72
27:30......93
27:31......93
40:34-35......133
43:1-12......133
44:1-21......118
44:30......62

Hosea
2:8-9......33
2:10......36
2:13......32
4:12-13......32
9:1-2......15, 27, 30–34, 49, 68, 146
9:1......34
9:4, 10......33
13:1......34, 36
13:2......34
13:3......30, 34–36

Isaiah
1–39......52
1:1......52

21:1-10......53
21:10......52–54, 147
21:10a......53
28:27-28......5, 54
41:15-16......5, 54
41:15......4
42:10-13......81

Jeremiah
6:26......93
14:2......47
31:25......94
51:33......24, 56–58, 147
51:33a......57
51:33b......58

Job
26:5......156
31:20......80
39:12......5, 24

Joel
1:1—2:20......38
1:11-12......39
1:17......39
2:12......93
2:21-22......38
2:23-24......15, 37–40, 94, 146
2:24......27, 39
2:26......40

Judges
1:21......103
6......35
6:1-16......15, 40–43, 49–50
6:1-11......29
6:1-5......40
6:1-2......49
6:1......49
6:2-14......27, 147
6:3-6......49
6:8-10......50
6:11-15......50
6:14-16......50
6:15-21......81
6:15-21, 37-40......86
6:24......105
6:25-27......152
6:36-40......78–82
6:37-40......13, 15, 18, 20, 27, 120, 148
6:37......79
6:38-40......123
6:38b......79
6:39......79, 100
6:40......80
7......81
19:10-13......103
21......31–32

Micah
1:1......54

1:8......93
4:12-13......27, 54–56, 147
4:12......57
4:12b......55
4:13a......55
4:13b......56

Numbers
1......102
11......146
11:1-3......81
13:27......146
13:29......103
14:8......146
14:24......104
15:17-21......60, 62, 63, 65, 66
15:17-20......27, 60, 147
15:19-20......61
15:19......61
15:20......60, 62
15:21......61
16:13-14......146
18:25-32......63
18:25-29......27, 147
18:27-32......63
18:27......63
18:30b......63
21:1-3......81
25:9......81
27:21......79
28–29......62

31:17......74

Psalms
3:4......94
18......81
24:8......81
30:11......93
34:4-17......94
35:13......93
40:1-2......94
58:10......92
68:16-17......107
78:24-25......146
84:7......38
88:10......156
98:1-3......81
119:28......94
149:6-9......81

Ruth
1:1......69
1:8-19......70
2:1-23......70
3......27, 31–32, 60, 73
3:2......71
3:3......72
3:7......4, 105
3:9b......71
3:10-11......72
3:12......72
3:13......73, 74

3:14b......74
4......73
4:1-11......87

UGARITIC TEXTS

Aqhatu (KTU 1.17-1.19), 80, 154–55, 157–60, 162

Bilingual Ritual Text (KTU 1.116), 161–62

Kirta (KTU 1.14-1.16), 152–54, 159, 162

Rapiuma (KTU 1.20–1.22), 154–57

www.ingramcontent.com/pod-product-compliance
Lightning Source LLC
Chambersburg PA
CBHW071158070526
44584CB00019B/2841